"A witty, concise and delightfully logical guide for the high-tech entrepreneur. Everything you need to know, but not a line more. I'm already recommending it to the faculty, students and business colleagues who are starting companies."

Lita Nelsen
Director, Technology Licensing Office
Massachusetts Institute of Technology
Cambridge, Massachusetts

"I wish this book were around when I started my first company. The entrepreneur can learn in one evening's reading what it took me two years of learning-by-doing! I plan on giving a copy to every CEO in our venture fund's portfolio."

Gordon B. Baty
Partner, Zero Stage Capital
Cambridge, Massachusetts

~

★★★★★ *5 Star Reviews from Amazon.com Readers*

The Best Book on Financial Statements, Period! *Wow, what a great book!* I'm a technical professional and now no longer in the financially confused majority.

—Robert I. Hedges (Burnsville, MN)

Simply the Best! Clearly the first introductory book one should read. This book—a must on every managers shelf—adds value by providing clear and concise definitions and relates them visually to the changing financial statements. A tremendous bang for buck. *Simply go get it and read it.*

—ClimbHigh

The author has a gift that few experts have. He anticipates all my newbie/beginner stupid questions... As soon as the little voice in my head asks, "But why did they do it this way?" the author gives me the answer. *This book has been of enormous value to me. It is an essential reference for anyone who needs to understand what business finances are about.*

—M. Kramer (United States)

A Masterpiece. Every single financial term is clarified with a layman's language. Moreover, for every single term, there is a very understandable example. Likewise, in every page there is a sheet explaining all the transactions. *I strongly believe that this book is a masterpiece for non-financial managers.*

—a reader

Excellent! I purchased this book for an MBA course and ended up using it more than the assigned text. *The author makes a complicated subject seem like child's play!*

—Bill Holcomb (Cleveland, OH)

Perfect book when first learning... This is a wonderfully clear and concise introduction to the interpretation of financial statements... Read this if you are not a CPA or MBA, but must "get a handle" on Balance Sheets, Income Statements and Cash Flow Statements. *This should be the first book you buy.*

—Jack Fossen (Dallas, TX)

Outstanding!! Looking to understand how financial statements work?...then purchase this book—*there's none better.* I am a graduate student nearing the completion of my MBA degree. The author speaks in basic terms about what financial statements mean and how they work. This book puts it all together for the reader.

—Joseph P. Gallagher (Bellinghan, WA)

A very useful book. While the book gets only skin deep on accounting concepts, it does an excellent job in deconstructing how the Income Statement, Statement of Cash Flows, and Balance Sheet are changed. Very few accounting related books make explicit what happens the way this book does.

—R. Chonchol (Florida)

Want to understand financial statements? I took an accounting class...and I had difficulty interpreting financial statements. So I gambled and bought this book with a hope to unravel the mystery on financial statements. It really worked! *Overall, the knowledge gained exceeds multiple folds of the time and money invested on this book!*

—Tuan minh Tran

Excellent, buy it!! If you are in the finance business, of any kind, and you are not an accountant, *this book is for you.*

—Richard Gomez (San Diego, CA)

WOW, Incredible. I took an accounting course at University, I now wish that my professor used this book in the course. So easy to understand and with great examples. *Suitable for anyone who wants to learn accounting the fast and easy way.*

—Kavkazy (Toronto, Canada)

Revised and Expanded Edition

Financial Statements

A Step-by-Step Guide to Understanding and Creating Financial Reports

CAREER PRESS

Pompton Plains NJ

Revised and Expanded Edition

Financial Statements

A Step-by-Step Guide to Understanding and Creating Financial Reports

by Thomas R. Ittelson

FINANCIAL STATEMENTS, REVISED AND EXPANDED EDITION
Cover design by Jeff Piasky
Printed in the U.S.A.

To order this title, please call toll-free 1-800-CAREER-1 (NJ and Canada: 201-848-0310) to order using VISA or MasterCard, or for further information on books from Career Press.

CAREER
PRESS

The Career Press, Inc., 220 West Parkway, Unit 12
Pompton Plains, NJ 07444
www.careerpress.com

Library of Congress Cataloging-in-Publication Data

Available upon request.

I dedicate this book to Alesdair, who has had the good sense to become a lawyer and not an accountant.

Acknowledgments

Many people helped make this book possible. My special thanks go to Isay Stemp, who first showed me that knowing a little finance and accounting could be fun; to my agent, Michael Snell, who taught me how to write a book proposal; and to Lisa Berkman, whose encouragement was invaluable as I drafted this revised and expanded edition.

Many thanks to my publisher, Ronald Fry of Career Press, for seeing promise in a preliminary version of this book and to Kristen Parkes, editorial director for Career Press, for her guiding of this book through to publication.

Again with this second edition, as was the case with the first, I am indebted to my colleague Jack Turner for his thoughtful review of the words and numbers in this book. Also a special thanks to Graham Eacott for his careful reading and correction of the first edition.

These clients, colleagues and friends at one time or another helped me to develop (whether they realized it or not) the concepts presented in this book. My thanks to Gwen Acton, Marci Anderson, Molly Downer, Tim Duncan, Cavas Gobhai, Jack Haley, Katherine Leahey, Paul McDonough, Lita Nelsen, Paul O'Brien, Mel Platte, and Iruna and Chris Simmons.

Contents

Section A. Financial Statements: Structure & Vocabulary

Much of what passes for complexity in accounting and financial reporting is just specialized vocabulary and simple numeric structures. This section will introduce the words, the basic accounting principles and the structure of the main financial statements.

Accountants have some basic rules upon which all their work in preparing financial statements is based. Who makes these rules? The simple answer is that the "FASB" makes the rules and they are called "GAAP." Got that?

The Balance Sheet is one of the two main business financial statements... the other is the Income Statement. The Balance Sheet states the basic equation of accounting at an instant in time: *What you have minus what you owe is what you're worth.*

One of the two main financial statements of a business...the other is the Balance Sheet. The Income Statement gives a significant perspective on the health of the enterprise by showing its profitability.

Where the company gets cash, and where that cash goes. The Cash Flow Statement tracks the movement of cash through the business over a defined period of time.

The financial statements are connected; an entry in one may well affect each of the others. This interlocking flow of numbers allows the three statements together to form a cohesive picture of the company's financial position.

Section B. Transactions:
Exploits of AppleSeed Enterprises, Inc.

With our knowledge of the three main financial statements, we will now draft the books of a hypothetical company, AppleSeed Enterprises, Inc. We will report the common and everyday actions that AppleSeed takes as it goes about its business of making and selling applesauce. Accounting for these "transactions" (T1 through T33 below) is the subject of much of this book. We will describe the Balance Sheet, Income Statement and Cash Flow Statement entries for common and ordinary business actions from selling stock, to shipping product, to paying the owners a dividend.

Welcome to our little business, AppleSeed Enterprises, Inc. Imagine that you are AppleSeed's entrepreneurial chief executive officer (CEO). You also double as treasurer and chief financial officer (CFO).

T1. Sell 150,000 shares of AppleSeed's common stock ($1 par value) for $10 per share.

T2. Pay yourself your first month's salary. Book all payroll-associated fringe benefits and taxes.

T3. Borrow $1 million to buy a building. Terms of this 10 year mortgage are 10% per annum.

T4. Pay $1.5 million for a building to be used for office, manufacturing and warehouse space. Set up a depreciation schedule.

T5. Hire administrative and sales staff. Pay first month's salaries and book fringe benefits and taxes.

T6. Pay employee health, life and disability insurance premiums plus FICA, unemployment and withholding taxes.

Now begins the fun stuff. In a few short weeks we will be producing thousands of cases of the best applesauce the world has ever tasted.

T7. Order $250,000 worth of manufacturing machinery. Pay one-half down.

T8. Receive and install manufacturing machinery. Pay the remaining $125,000 due.

T9. Hire production workers; expense first month's salary and wages.

- Prepare bill of materials and establish labor requirements.

- Set up plant and machinery depreciation schedules.

- Plan monthly production schedule and set standard costs.

T10. Place standing orders for raw materials with suppliers; receive 1 million jar labels.

Section C. Financial Statements: Construction & Analysis

"Cooking the books" means intentionally hiding or distorting the real financial performance or financial condition of a company. Cooking is most often accomplished by incorrectly and fraudulently moving Balance Sheet items onto the Income Statements and vise versa. Outright lying is also a favorite technique.

Section D. Business Expansion: Strategy, Risk & Capital

"The numbers" are just a single tool—albeit a very useful one—to use with other management tools (and common sense) in deciding how to invest capital for expansion. But remember: A strategically unsound business expansion is very seldom financially sound...regardless of what the numbers say. *Think strategy first.* This section is all about planning the future and raising capital.

How to expand? Why expand? Why stick our necks out? What strategies should we employ to help us meet our goals? What are our goals anyway? Think through AppleSeed's mission, vision, goals, strategies, actions and tactics. The Board of Directors want to see our strategic plan!

- Mission, Vision & Goals...*a hierarchy of destinations*
- Strategies, Actions & Tactics...*a hierarchy of ways to get there*

Every action (or even inaction) carries a risk of failure and an uncertainty of outcome. Understanding risk and uncertainty help minimize the chance of "negative surprises" coming from important business decisions. This chapter describes ways to minimize risk and uncertainty.

- Risk, Uncertainty, Threats and Avoiding a "Bet-Your-Company Risk."

AppleSeed's Board of Directors thinks that we can successfully expand and that now is a good time to do it. What are our business expansion alternatives and how should we decide between them?

- Decision Tree Analysis
- Strategic Alternatives
- AppleSeed's "Make vs. Buy" Decision

Taking on debt (borrowing money) and/or selling equity (exchanging an ownership portion of the company for money) are the two ways of raising capital for expansion. More debt adds risk; but selling stock means our little portion of the pie gets even smaller. Sigh. AppleSeed will need more capital to expand. Our venture investor understands the mathematics of buying and selling stock, and can do the manipulations in her head. We had better understand as well. Otherwise, this friendly venture investor will eat our applesauce.

- Business Valuation: "Pre-Money" & "Post-Money" Values
- Selling Stock & Ownership Dilution.
- Cost of Equity Capital & Weighted Average Cost of Capital

T32. Financial expansion! Sell more stock and negotiate a line of credit.

Section E. Making Good Capital Investment Decisions

Capital investment decisions are among the most important that a company's management can make. Often capital is a company's scarcest resource and using capital well is essential for success. The chief determinant of what a company will become is the investments it makes today. Capital budgeting decisions require analyzing business cash flows spanning years. Accounting for the "time value of money" is essential in these analyses.

Would you rather I give you $1,000 today or in five years? Most everyone intuitively knows that a "bird in the hand is worth two in the bush." Now you understand the "time value of money." The rest is details.

- Present Value (PV)
- Future Value (FV)
- Interest and Interest Rates
- Discounting and Discount Rates
- Computing Discounted Values
- Present Value Table

We are going to invest cash now with high hopes of a large future return. But will the anticipated payback be enough to cover our initial investment? Further, would any of our alternative projects provide us with a better financial return? Net Present Value (NPV) computations are the "gold standard" for capital budgeting. NPV and Internal Rate of Return (IRR) are the two mainstays of investment valuation.

- Net Present Value (NPV)
- Internal Rate of Return (IRR)
- Cash Flow Forecasting for NPV and IRR Analysis
- Other Capital Budgeting Techniques: ROI, Payback Period, Real Options and Monte Carlo Analysis

Let's apply all that we have learned about capital budgeting and select the best business expansion course for AppleSeed. After all, the kids are getting older and will graduate soon; maybe one will want to join the business?

- Make vs. Buy Decision for AppleSeed's Business Expansion
- Forecasting Cash Flows
- NPV & IRR Analysis of AppleSeed's Expansion Alternatives
- Business Combination Accounting

T33. Chips-R-Us joins the AppleSeed happy family of companies!

Crooked investment promoters, speculative investment bubbles waiting to pop and even outright business fraud in high places have been with us for centuries. There are many ways to lose money. Some of the most infamous are discussed in this chapter. Congress recently passed far-reaching legislation to stop these shenanigans—the Sarbanes-Oxley Act—requiring that business bosses certify their company's financial statements are correct under penalty of going to jail and paying a big fines. *Don't you feel much safer?*

- Ponzi Schemes and Pyramids
- Bubbles: Tulips, Technology Stocks and U.S. Houses
- Garden-Variety Frauds

In financial calculations spanning time, currency value can be looked at from two different perspectives. It's important when doing historical analysis or making financial projections to understand these two views of value. In "nominal dollars" a McDonald's Big Mac only cost 50¢ 20 years ago, and it costs $3.75 today. Prices tend to increase over time primarily due to inflation. Sometimes it is useful to look at values (i.e., "real dollars") of goods in the past (or expected values in the future) rather than what they actually cost way back when in nominal dollars.

Preface

If the first edition of this book was an entrepreneurial business, it would be a huge success. Now over 100,000 copies of *Financial Statements: A Step-by-Step Guide to Understanding and Creating Financial Reports* are in-press and helping non-financial managers and students of accounting and finance cope with the "numbers of business."

With this new revised second edition, we have expanded the book into five sections from the original three. Many readers of the first edition wanted to better understand capital investment decision-making, which is the focus of our two new sections.

Capital is often a company's scarcest resource, and using capital wisely is essential for success. The chief determinant of what a company will become is the capital investments it makes today. So in this new edition, we will use the financial analysis techniques of net present value (NPV) and internal rate of return (IRR) as capital investment decision-making tools

Preface to the First Edition:

We needed to hire an accountant to keep the books at a venture-capital backed, high-technology startup of which I was a founder and CEO. I interviewed a young woman—just out of school—for the job and asked her why she wanted to become an accountant. Her answer was a surprise to all of us,

"Because accounting is so symmetrical, so logical, so beautiful and it always comes out right," she said.

We hired her on the spot, thinking it would be fun to have almost-a-poet keeping our books. She worked out fine.

I hope you take away from this book a part of what my young accountant saw.

Knowing a little accounting and financial reporting can be very, very satisfying. Yes, it does all come out right at the end, and there is real beauty and poetry in its structure.

~

But let's discuss perhaps the real reason you've bought and are now reading this book. My bet is that it has to do with power. You want the power you see associated with knowing how numbers flow in business.

Be it poetry or power, this accounting and financial reporting stuff is not rocket science. You've learned all the math required to master accounting by the end of the fourth grade—mostly addition and subtraction with a bit of multiplication and division thrown in to keep it lively.

The specialized vocabulary, on the other hand, can be confusing. You will need to learn the accounting definitions of revenue, income, cost and expense. You'll also need to understand the structure and appreciate the purpose of the three major numeric statements that describe a company's financial condition.

Here's a hint: Watch where the money flows; watch where goods and services flow. Documenting these movements of cash and product is all that financial statements do. It is no more complicated than that. Everything else is details.

But why is it all so boring, you ask? Well, it's only boring if you do not understand it. Yes, the day-to-day repetitive accounting tasks are boring. However, how to finance and extract cash from the actions of the enterprise is not boring at all. It is the essence of business and the generation of wealth.

Not boring at all.

Introduction

Many non-financial managers have an accounting phobia ...a financial vertigo that limits their effectiveness. If you think "inventory turn" means rotating stock on the shelf, and that "accrual" has something to do with the Wicked Witch of the West, then this book's for you.

Financial Statements: A Step-by-Step Guide to Understanding and Creating Financial Reports is designed for those business professionals (1) who know very little about accounting and financial statements, but feel they should, and those (2) who need to know a little more, but for whom the normal accounting and financial reporting texts are mysterious and unenlightening. In fact, the above two categories make up the majority of all people in business. You are not alone.

Financial Statements: A Step-by-Step Guide to Understanding and Creating Financial Reports is a transaction-based, business training tool with clarifying, straightforward, real-life examples of how financial statements are built and how they interact to present a true financial picture of the enterprise.

We will not get bogged down in details that get in the way of conceptual understanding. Just as it is not necessary to know how the microchips in your computer work to multiply a few numbers, it's not necessary to be a Certified Public Accountant (CPA) to have a working knowledge of the "accounting model of the enterprise."

~

Transactions. This book describes a sequence of "transactions" of our sample company, AppleSeed Enterprises, Inc., as it goes about making and selling delicious applesauce. We will sell stock to raise money, buy machinery to make our product, and then satisfy our customers by shipping wholesome applesauce. We'll get paid and we will hope to make a profit. Then we will expand the business.

Each step along the way will generate account "postings" on AppleSeed's books. We'll discuss each transaction to get a hands-on feel for how a company's financial statements are constructed. We'll learn how to report using the three main financial statements of a business—the

---

"Accounting is a language, a means of communicating among all the segments of the business community. It assumes a reference base called the accounting model of the enterprise. While other models of the enterprise are possible, this accounting model is the accepted form, and is likely to be for some time.

"If you don't speak the language of accounting or feel intuitively comfortable with the accounting model, you will be at a severe disadvantage in the business world. Accounting is a fundamental tool of the trade."

Gordon B. Baty
Entrepreneurship
Prentice Hall, Englewood Cliffs, NJ, 1990

Financial Statements

Balance Sheet, Income Statement and Cash Flow Statement—for these common business dealings:

1. selling stock
2. borrowing money
3. receiving orders
4. shipping goods
5. invoicing customers
6. receiving payments
7. paying sales commissions
8. writing off bad debts
9. prepaying expenses
10. ordering equipment
11. paying deposits
12. receiving raw materials
13. scrapping damaged product
14. paying suppliers
15. booking manufacturing variances
16. depreciating fixed assets
17. valuing inventory
18. hiring staff and paying salary, wages and payroll taxes
19. computing profit
20. paying income taxes
21. issuing dividends
22. acquiring a business
23. and more

By the end of this book, you'll know your way around the finances of our applesauce-making company, AppleSeed Enterprises, Inc.

Goals. My goal in writing this book is to help people in business master the basics of accounting and financial reporting. This book is especially directed at those managers, scientists and salespeople who should know how a Balance Sheet, Income Statement and Cash Flow Statement work…but don't.

Your goal is to gain knowledge of accounting and finance to assist you in your business dealings. You want the power that comes from understanding financial manipulations. You must know how the score is kept in business. You recognize, as Gordon Baty says, you must "feel intuitively comfortable with the accounting model" to succeed in business.

~

This book is divided into five main sections, each with a specific teaching objective:

Section A. Financial Statements: Structure & Vocabulary will introduce the three main financial statements of the enterprise and define the special vocabulary that is necessary to understand the books and to converse with accountants.

Section B. Transactions: Exploits of AppleSeed Enterprises, Inc. will take us through 31 business transactions, showing how to report financial impact of each on the Balance Sheet, Income Statement and Cash Flow Statement of AppleSeed Enterprises.

Section C. Financial Statements: Construction & Analysis will subject the financial statement of our sample company to a rigorous analysis using common ratio analysis techniques. Then finally we will touch on how to "cook the books," why someone would want to, and how to detect financial fraud.

"…even if it's boring and dull and soon to be forgotten, continue to learn double-entry bookkeeping. People think I'm joking, but I'm not. You should love the mathematics of business."

Kenneth H. Olsen
entrepreneurial founder of Digital Equipment Corporation

Section D. Business Expansion: Strategy, Risk & Capital will describe the strategic decisions that a fledgling company must make when it expands. We will answer the questions, "Where will we get the money?" and "How much will it cost?"

Then in ***Section E. Making Good Capital Investment Decisions*** we will analyze business expansion alternatives and select the best using sophisticated net present value (NPV) techniques.

~

With your newly acquired understanding of the structure and flow of money in business, you will appreciate these important business quandaries:

- How an enterprise can be rapidly growing, highly profitable and out of money all at the same time...and why this state of affairs is fairly common.
- Why working capital is so very important and which management actions lead to more, which lead to less.
- The difference between cash in the bank and profit on the bottom line, and how the two are interrelated.
- When in the course of business affairs a negative cash flow is a sign of good things happening... and when it's a sign of impending catastrophe.

- Limits of common product costing systems and when to apply (and, more importantly, when to ignore) the accountant's definition of cost.
- Why a development investment made today must return a much greater sum to the coffers of the company in later years.
- How discounts drop right to the bottom line as lost profits and why they are so very dangerous to a company's financial health.
- How risk is different than uncertainty, and which is worse.
- Why a dollar in your pocket today can be worth a lot more than a dollar received tomorrow.
- The necessity (and limitation) of forecasting cash flows over time when making capital investment decisions.
- When to use NPV analysis and when to use IRR, and why it is important in capital investment decision-making.

To be effective in business, you must understand accounting and financial reporting. Don't become an accountant, but do "speak the language" and become intuitively comfortable with the accounting model of the enterprise.

Read on.

Section A. Financial Statements: Structure & Vocabulary

About This Section

This book is written for people who need to use financial statements in their work but have no formal training in accounting and financial reporting. Don't feel bad if you fall into this category. My guess is that 95 percent of all non-financial managers are financially illiterate when it comes to understanding the company's books. Let's proceed toward some enlightenment.

～

This section is about financial statement structure and about the specialized vocabulary of financial reporting. We will learn both together. It's easier that way. Much of what passes as complexity in accounting and financial reporting is just specialized (and sometimes counterintuitive) vocabulary and basically simple reporting structure that gets confusing only in the details.

Vocabulary. In accounting, some important words may have meanings that are different from what you would think.

The box below shows some of this confusing vocabulary. It is absolutely essential to use these words correctly when discussing financial statements. You'll just have to learn them. It's really not that much, but it is important. Look at these examples:

1. *Sales* and *revenue* are synonymous and mean the "top line" of the Income Statement, the money that comes in from customers.

2. *Profits, earnings* and *income* are all synonymous and mean the "bottom line," or what is left over from revenue after all the costs and expenses spent in generating that revenue are subtracted.

Note that *revenue* and *income* have different meanings. *Revenue* is the "top line" and *income* is the "bottom line" of the Income Statement. Got that?

3. *Costs* are money (mostly for materials and labor) spent making a product. *Expenses* are money spent to develop it, sell it, account for it and manage this whole making and selling process.

Sales and **revenue** mean the same thing.
Profit, earnings and **income** mean the same thing.
Now, **revenue** and **income** *do not* mean the same thing.

Costs are different from **expenses.**
Expenses are different from **expenditures.**

Sales are different from **orders** but are the same
as **shipments.**

Profits are different from **cash.**
Solvency is different from **profitability.**

---

4. Both costs and expenses become *expenditures* when money is actually sent to vendors to pay for them.

5. *Orders* are placed by customers and signify a request for the future delivery of products. *Orders* do not have an impact on any of the financial statements in any way until the products are actually shipped. At this point these *shipments* become *sales.* *Shipments* and *sales* are synonymous.

6. *Solvency* means having enough money in the bank to pay your bills. Profitability means that your sales are greater than your costs and expenses. You can be profitable and insolvent at the same time. You are making money but still do not have enough cash to pay your bills.

Financial Statements. Once you understand the specialized accounting vocabulary, you can appreciate financial statement structure. For example, there will be no confusion when we say that *revenue* is at the top of an Income Statement and *income* is at the bottom.

In this section, we will learn vocabulary and financial statement structure simultaneously. Then follows a chapter on each one of the three main financial statements: the Balance Sheet, the Income Statement and the Cash Flow Statement. To end the section, we will discuss how these three statements interact and when changing a number in one necessitates changing a number in another.

~

Chapter 1 will lay some ground rules for financial reporting—starting points and assumptions that accounting professionals require to let them make sense of a company's books. In **Chapter 2,** we will discuss the Balance Sheet—what you own and what you owe. Then in **Chapter 3** comes the Income Statement reporting on the enterprise's product selling activities and whether there is any money left over after all these operations are done and accounted for.

The last statement, but often the most important in the short term, is the Cash Flow Statement discussed in **Chapter 4.** Look at this statement as a simple check register with deposits being cash in and any payments cash out.

Chapter 5 puts all three financial statements together and shows how they work in concert to give a true picture of the enterprise's financial health.

Chapter 1. Twelve Basic Principles

Accountants have some basic rules and assumptions upon which rest all their work in preparing financial statements. These accounting rules and assumptions dictate *what* financial items to measure and *when* and *how* to measure them. By the end of this discussion, you will see how necessary these rules and assumptions are to accounting and financial reporting.

So, here are the 12 very important accounting principles:

1. accounting entity
2. going concern
3. measurement
4. units of measure
5. historical cost
6. materiality
7. estimates and judgments
8. consistency
9. conservatism
10. periodicity
11. substance over form
12. accrual basis of presentation

These rules and assumptions define and qualify all that accountants do and all that financial reporting reports. We will deal with each in turn.

1. Accounting Entity. The *accounting entity* is the business unit (regardless of the legal business form) for which the financial statements are being prepared. The accounting entity principle states that there is a "business entity" separate from its owners...a fictional "person" called a company for which the books are written.

2. Going Concern. Unless there is evidence to the contrary, accountants assume that the life of the business entity is infinitely long. Obviously this assumption can not be verified and is hardly ever true. But this assumption does greatly simplify the presentation of the financial position of the firm and aids in the preparation of financial statements.

If during the review of a corporation's books, the accountant has reason to believe that the company may go bankrupt, he must issue a "qualified opinion" stating the potential of the company's demise. More on this concept later.

3. Measurement. Accounting deals with things that can be *quantified*— resources and obligations upon which there is an agreed-upon value. Accounting only deals with things that can be measured.

This assumption leaves out many very valuable company "assets." For example, loyal customers, while necessary for company success, still cannot be quantified and assigned a value and thus are not stated in the books.

Financial statements contain only the quantifiable estimates of assets (what the business owns) and liabilities (what the business owes). The difference between the two equals owner's equity.

4. Units of Measure. U.S. dollars are the units of value reported in the financial statements of U.S. companies. Results of any foreign subsidiaries are translated into dollars for consolidated reporting of results. As exchange rates vary, so do the values of any foreign currency denominated assets and liabilities.

5. Historical Cost. What a company owns and what it owes are recorded at their original (historical) cost with no adjustment for inflation.

A company can own a building valued at $50 million yet carry it on the books at its $5 million original purchase price (less accumulated depreciation), a gross understatement of value.

This assumption can greatly understate the value of some assets purchased in the past and depreciated to a very low amount on the books. Why, you ask, do accountants demand that we obviously understate assets? Basically, it is the easiest thing to do. You do not have to appraise and reappraise all the time.

6. Materiality. Materiality refers to the relative importance of different financial information. Accountants don't sweat the small stuff. But all transactions must be reported if they would materially affect the financial condition of the company.

Remember, what is material for a corner drug store is not material for IBM (lost in the rounding errors). Materiality is a straightforward judgment call.

7. Estimates and Judgments. Complexity and uncertainty make any measurement less than exact. Estimates and judgments must often be made for financial reporting. It is okay to guess if: (1) that is the best you can do and (2) the expected error would not matter much anyway. But accountants should use the same guessing method for each period. Be consistent in your guesses and do the best you can.

8. Consistency. Sometimes identical transactions can be accounted for differently. You could do it this way or that way, depending upon some preference. The principle of consistency states that each individual enterprise must choose a single method of reporting and use it consistently over time. You cannot switch back and forth. Measurement techniques must be consistent from any one fiscal period to another.

9. Conservatism. Accountants have a downward measurement bias, preferring understatement to overvaluation. For example, losses are recorded when you feel that they have a great probability of occurring, not later, when they actually do occur. Conversely, the recording of a gain is postponed until it *actually* occurs, not when it is only anticipated.

10. Periodicity. Accountants assume that the life of a corporation can be divided into periods of time for which profits and losses can be reported, usually a month, quarter or year.

What is so special about a month, quarter or year? They are just convenient periods; short enough so that management can remember what has happened, long enough to have meaning and not just be random fluctuations. These periods are called "fiscal" periods. For example, a "fiscal year" could extend from October 1 in one year till September 30 in the next year. Or a company's fiscal year could be the same as the calendar year starting on January 1 and ending on December 31.

11. Substance Over Form. Accountants report the economic "substance" of a transaction rather than just its form. For

---

"Lines" are perhaps not as important as principles, but they can be confusing if you don't know how accountants use them in financial statements. Financial statements often have two types of lines to indicate types of numeric computations.

Single lines on a financial statement indicate that a calculation (addition or subtraction) has been made on the numbers just preceding in the column.

The double underline is saved for the last. That is, use of a double underline signifies the very last amount in the statement.

Note that while all the numbers in the statement represent currency, only the top line and the bottom line normally show a dollar sign.

a	**SALES [$]**
b	**COST OF GOODS SOLD**
$a-b=c$	**GROSS MARGIN**
d	**SALES & MARKETING**
e	**R&D**
f	**G&A**
$d+e+f=g$	**TOTAL EXPENSES**
h	**INTEREST INCOME**
i	**INCOME TAXES**
$c-g+h-i=j$	**NET INCOME [$]**

FASB[1] makes the rules and they are called GAAP.[2]

[1]Financial Accounting Standards Board; [2]Generally Accepted Accounting Principles

---

example, an equipment lease that is really a purchase dressed in a costume, is booked as a purchase and not as a lease on financial statements. This substance over form rule states that if it's a duck...then you must report it as a duck.

12. Accrual Basis of Presentation. This concept is very important to understand. Accountants translate into dollars of profit or loss all the money-making (or losing) activities that take place during a fiscal period. In accrual accounting, if a business action in a period makes money, then all its product costs and its business expenses should be reported in that period. Otherwise, profits and losses could flop around depending on which period entries were made.

In accrual accounting, this documentation is accomplished by matching for presentation: (1) the revenue received in selling product and (2) the costs to make that specific product sold. Fiscal period expenses such as selling, legal, administrative and so forth are then subtracted.

Key to accrual accounting is determining: (1) when you may report a sale on the financial statements, (2) matching and then reporting the appropriate costs of products sold and (3) using a systematic and rational method allocating all the other costs of being in business for the period. We will deal with each point separately:

Revenue recognition. In accrual accounting, a sale is recorded when all the necessary activities to provide the good or service have been completed regardless of when cash changes hands. A customer just ordering a product has not yet generated any revenue. Revenue is recorded when the product is shipped.

Matching principle. In accrual accounting, the costs associated with making products (Cost of Goods Sold) are recorded at the same time the matching revenue is recorded.

Allocation. Many costs are not specifically associated with a product. These costs must be allocated to fiscal periods in a reasonable fashion. For example, each month can be charged with one-twelfth of the general business insurance policy even though the policy was paid in full at the beginning of the year. Other expenses are recorded when they arise (period expenses).

Note that all businesses with inventory must use the accrual basis of accounting. Other businesses may use a "cash basis" if they desire. Cash basis financial statements are just like the Cash Flow Statement or a simple checkbook. We'll describe features of accrual accounting in the chapters that follow.

~

Who makes all these rules? The simple answer is that "FASB" makes the rules and they are called "GAAP." Note also that FASB is made up of "CPAs." Got that?

Financial statements in the United States must be prepared according to the accounting profession's set of rules and guiding principles called the *Generally Accepted Accounting Principles,* GAAP for short. Other countries use different rules.

GAAP is a series of conventions, rules and procedures for preparing and reporting financial statements. The *Financial Accounting Standards Board,* FASB for short, lays out the GAAP conventions, rules and procedures.

The FASB's mission is "to establish and improve standards of financial accounting and reporting for guidance and education of the public, including issuers, auditors, and users of financial information." The

Securities and Exchange Commission (SEC) designates FASB as the organization responsible for setting accounting standards for all U.S. public companies.

CPAs CPAs are, of course, Certified Public Accountants. These very exalted individuals are specially trained in college, and have practiced auditing companies for a number of years. In addition, they have passed a series of exams testing their clear understanding of both accounting principles and auditing procedures. Note that FASB is made up mostly of CPAs and that CPAs both develop, interpret and apply GAAP when they audit a company. All this is fairly incestuous.

Chapter 2. The Balance Sheet

One of the two main financial statements of a business...

the other is the *Income Statement.*

The Basic Equation of Accounting

- The basic equation of accounting states: "What you have minus what you owe is what you're worth."

Assets – Liabilities = Worth
"have"   *"owe"*   *"value to owners"*

- Worth, net worth, equity, owners' equity and shareholders' equity all mean the same thing—the value of the enterprise belonging to its owners.

The Balance Sheet

- The Balance Sheet presents the basic equation of accounting in a slightly rearranged form:

Assets = Liabilities + Worth
"have"   *"owe"*   *"value to owners"*

- By definition, this equation must always be "in balance" with assets equaling the sum of liabilities and worth.

- So, if you add an asset to the left side of the equation, you must also increase the right side by adding a liability or increasing worth. Two entries are required to keep the equation in balance.

Balance Sheet Format
as of a specific date

ASSETS	LIABILITIES & EQUITY
CASH	ACCOUNTS PAYABLE
ACCOUNTS RECEIVABLE	ACCRUED EXPENSES
INVENTORY	CURRENT PORTION OF DEBT
PREPAID EXPENSES	INCOME TAXES PAYABLE
CURRENT ASSETS	CURRENT LIABILITIES
OTHER ASSETS	LONG-TERM DEBT
FIXED ASSETS AT COST	CAPITAL STOCK
ACCUMULATED DEPRECIATION	RETAINED EARNINGS
NET FIXED ASSETS	SHAREHOLDER'S EQUITY
TOTAL ASSETS	TOTAL LIABILITIES & EQUITY

The Balance Sheet—a snapshot in time.

- The Balance Sheet presents the financial picture of the enterprise on one particular day, an instant in time, the date it was written.

- The Balance Sheet presents:

  > what the enterprise *has* today: **assets**
  > how much the enterprise *owes* today: **liabilities**
  > what the enterprise is *worth* today: **equity**

- The Balance Sheet reports:

  > **Has today = Owes today + Worth today**
  > *"assets"*   *" liabilities"*   *"shareholders' equity"*

Balance Sheet Format
as of a specific date

ASSETS

CASH	A
ACCOUNTS RECEIVABLE	B
INVENTORY	C
PREPAID EXPENSES	D
CURRENT ASSETS	$A + B + C + D = E$
OTHER ASSETS	F
FIXED ASSETS AT COST	G
ACCUMULATED DEPRECIATION	H
NET FIXED ASSETS	$G - H = I$
TOTAL ASSETS	$E + F + I = J$

What are Assets?

- **Assets** are everything you've got—cash in the bank, inventory, machines, buildings—all of it.

- **Assets** are also certain "rights" you own that have a monetary value...like the right to collect cash from customers who owe you money.

- **Assets** are *valuable* and this value must be *quantifiable* for an asset to be listed on the Balance Sheet. Everything in a company's financial statements must be translated into dollars and cents.

Balance Sheet Format
as of a specific date

ASSETS

CASH	A	*most liquid*
ACCOUNTS RECEIVABLE	B	
INVENTORY	C	
PREPAID EXPENSES	D	
CURRENT ASSETS	$A + B + C + D = E$	
OTHER ASSETS	F	
FIXED ASSETS AT COST	G	
ACCUMULATED DEPRECIATION	H	
NET FIXED ASSETS	$G - H = I$	
TOTAL ASSETS	$E + F + I = J$	*least liquid*

Grouping Assets for Presentation

- Assets are grouped for presentation on the Balance Sheet according to their characteristics:

  very liquid assets ..... cash and securities
  productive assets ..... plant and machinery
  assets for sale .... inventory

- **Accounts receivable** are a special type of asset group —the obligations of customers of a company to pay the company for goods shipped to them on credit.

- **Assets** are displayed in the asset section of the Balance Sheet in the *descending order of liquidity (the ease of convertibility into cash)*. Cash itself is the most liquid of all assets; fixed assets are normally the least liquid.

Balance Sheet Format
as of a specific date

ASSETS

CASH	A
ACCOUNTS RECEIVABLE	B
INVENTORY	C
PREPAID EXPENSES	D
CURRENT ASSETS	A + B + C + D = E
OTHER ASSETS	F
FIXED ASSETS AT COST	G
ACCUMULATED DEPRECIATION	H
NET FIXED ASSETS	G − H = I
TOTAL ASSETS	E + F + I = J

Current Assets

By definition, **current assets** are those assets that are expected to be converted into cash in less than 12 months.

- **Current asset** groupings are listed in order of liquidity with the most easy to convert into cash listed first:

    1. Cash
    2. Accounts receivable
    3. Inventory

- The money the company will use to pay its bills in the near term (within the year) will come when its **current assets** are converted into cash (that is, inventory is sold and accounts receivable are then paid to the company by customers).

Balance Sheet Format
as of a specific date

ASSETS

CASH	A
ACCOUNTS RECEIVABLE	B
INVENTORY	C
PREPAID EXPENSES	D
CURRENT ASSETS	A + B + C + D = E
OTHER ASSETS	F
FIXED ASSETS AT COST	G
ACCUMULATED DEPRECIATION	H
NET FIXED ASSETS	G − H = I
TOTAL ASSETS	E + F + I = J

Current Assets: Cash

- **Cash** is the ultimate liquid asset: on-demand deposits in a bank as well as the dollars and cents in the petty cash drawer.

- When you write a check to pay a bill, you are taking money out of **cash** assets.

- Like all the rest of the Balance Sheet, **cash** is denominated in U.S. dollars for corporations in the United States. A U.S. company with foreign subsidiaries would convert the value of any foreign currency it holds (and also other foreign assets) into dollars for financial reporting.

Balance Sheet Format
as of a specific date

ASSETS

CASH	A
ACCOUNTS RECEIVABLE	**B**
INVENTORY	C
PREPAID EXPENSES	D
CURRENT ASSETS	A + B + C + D = E
OTHER ASSETS	F
FIXED ASSETS AT COST	G
ACCUMULATED DEPRECIATION	H
NET FIXED ASSETS	G − H = I
TOTAL ASSETS	E + F + I = J

Current Assets: Accounts Receivable

- When the enterprise ships a product to a customer on credit, the enterprise acquires a *right* to collect money from that customer at a specified time in the future.

- These collection rights are totaled and reported on the Balance Sheet as **accounts receivable.**

- **Accounts receivable** are owed to the enterprise from customers (called "accounts") who were shipped goods but have not yet paid for them. Credit customers—most business between companies is done on credit—are commonly given payment terms that allow 30 or 60 days to pay.

Balance Sheet Format
as of a specific date

ASSETS

CASH	A
ACCOUNTS RECEIVABLE	B
INVENTORY	**C**
PREPAID EXPENSES	D
CURRENT ASSETS	A + B + C + D = E
OTHER ASSETS	F
FIXED ASSETS AT COST	G
ACCUMULATED DEPRECIATION	H
NET FIXED ASSETS	G − H = I
TOTAL ASSETS	E + F + I = J

Current Assets: Inventory

- **Inventory** is both finished products for ready sale to customers and also materials to be made into products. A manufacturer's **inventory** includes three groupings:

    1. **Raw material inventory** is unprocessed materials that will be used in manufacturing products.
    2. **Work-in-process inventory** is partially finished products in the process of being manufactured.
    3. **Finished goods inventory** is completed products ready for shipment to customers when they place orders.

- As *finished goods inventory* is sold it becomes an *accounts receivable* and then *cash* when the customer pays.

Balance Sheet Format
as of a specific date

ASSETS

CASH	A
ACCOUNTS RECEIVABLE	B
INVENTORY	C
PREPAID EXPENSES	**D**
CURRENT ASSETS	A + B + C + D = E
OTHER ASSETS	F
FIXED ASSETS AT COST	G
ACCUMULATED DEPRECIATION	H
NET FIXED ASSETS	G − H = I
TOTAL ASSETS	E + F + I = J

Current Assets: Prepaid Expenses

- **Prepaid expenses** are bills the company has already paid...but for services not yet received.

- **Prepaid expenses** are things like prepaid insurance premiums, prepayment of rent, deposits paid to the telephone company, salary advances, etc.

- **Prepaid expenses** are current assets not because they can be turned into cash, but because the enterprise will not have to use cash to pay them in the near future. They have been paid already.

Current Asset Cycle

- **Current assets** are said to be "working assets" because they are in a constant cycle of being converted into cash. The repeating **current asset cycle** of a business is shown below:

cash buys *inventory*

inventory when sold becomes *accounts receivable*

accounts receivable upon collection becomes *cash*

More asset types

- In addition to a company's current assets, there are two other major asset groups listed on the Balance Sheet: **Other assets** and **fixed assets**. These so-called *"non-current assets"* are not converted into cash during the normal course of business.

- **Other assets** is a catchall category that includes intangible assets such as the value of patents, trade names and so forth.

- The company's **fixed assets** (so-called *property, plant and equipment, or PP&E*) is generally the largest and most important non-current asset grouping.

Balance Sheet Format
as of a specific date

ASSETS

CASH	A
ACCOUNTS RECEIVABLE	B
INVENTORY	C
PREPAID EXPENSES	D
CURRENT ASSETS	$A + B + C + D = E$
OTHER ASSETS	F
FIXED ASSETS AT COST	G
ACCUMULATED DEPRECIATION	H
NET FIXED ASSETS	$G - H = I$
TOTAL ASSETS	$E + F + I = J$

Fixed Assets at Cost

- Fixed assets are productive assets not intended for sale. They will be used over and over again to manufacture the product, display it, warehouse it, transport it and so forth.

- Fixed assets commonly include land, buildings, machinery, equipment, furniture, automobiles, trucks, etc.

- **Fixed assets at cost** are reported on the Balance Sheet at original purchased price. Fixed assets are also show as *net fixed assets*—valued at original cost minus an allowance for depreciation. See the *depreciation* discussion following.

Balance Sheet Format
as of a specific date

ASSETS

CASH	A
ACCOUNTS RECEIVABLE	B
INVENTORY	C
PREPAID EXPENSES	D
CURRENT ASSETS	A + B + C + D = E
OTHER ASSETS	F
FIXED ASSETS AT COST	G
ACCUMULATED DEPRECIATION H	
NET FIXED ASSETS	G − H = I
TOTAL ASSETS	E + F + I = J

Depreciation

- Depreciation is an *accounting convention* reporting (on the Income Statement) the decline in useful value of a fixed asset due to wear and tear from use and the passage of time.

- "Depreciating" an asset means spreading the cost to acquire the asset over the asset's whole useful life. **Accumulated depreciation** (on the Balance Sheet) is the sum of all the depreciation charges taken since the asset was first acquired.

- Depreciation charges taken in a period do lower *profits* for the period, but do not lower *cash*. Cash was required to purchase the fixed asset originally.

Balance Sheet Format
as of a specific date

ASSETS

CASH	A
ACCOUNTS RECEIVABLE	B
INVENTORY	C
PREPAID EXPENSES	D
CURRENT ASSETS	A + B + C + D = E
OTHER ASSETS	F
FIXED ASSETS AT COST	G
ACCUMULATED DEPRECIATION	H
NET FIXED ASSETS	**G − H = I**
TOTAL ASSETS	E + F + I = J

Net Fixed Assets

- The **net fixed assets** of a company are the sum of its fixed assets' purchase prices *("fixed assets @ cost")* minus the depreciation charges taken on the Income Statement over the years *("accumulated depreciation")*.

- The so-called *book value* of an asset—its value as reported on the books of the company—is the asset's purchase price minus its accumulated depreciation.

- Note that depreciation does not necessarily relate to an actual decrease in value. In fact, some assets appreciate in value over time. However, such appreciated assets are by convention still reported on the Balance Sheet at their lower book value.

Balance Sheet Format
as of a specific date

ASSETS

CASH	A
ACCOUNTS RECEIVABLE	B
INVENTORY	C
PREPAID EXPENSES	D
CURRENT ASSETS	$A + B + C + D = E$
OTHER ASSETS	**F**
FIXED ASSETS AT COST	G
ACCUMULATED DEPRECIATION	H
NET FIXED ASSETS	$G - H = I$
TOTAL ASSETS	$E + F + I = J$

Other Assets

- The **other asset** category on the Balance Sheet includes assets of the enterprise that cannot be properly classified into *current asset* or *fixed asset* categories.

- *Intangible assets* (a major type of other assets) are things owned by the company that have value but are not tangible (that is, not physical property) in nature.

- For example, a patent, a copyright, or a brand name can have considerable value to the enterprise, yet these are not *tangible* like a machine or inventory is.

- *Intangible assets* are valued by management according to various accounting conventions too complex, arbitrary and confusing to be of interest here.

Balance Sheet Format
as of a specific date

	LIABILITIES & EQUITY
K	ACCOUNTS PAYABLE
L	ACCRUED EXPENSES
M	CURRENT PORTION OF DEBT
N	INCOME TAXES PAYABLE
K + L + M + N = O	CURRENT LIABILITIES
P	LONG-TERM DEBT
Q	CAPITAL STOCK
R	RETAINED EARNINGS
Q + R = S	SHAREHOLDER'S EQUITY
O + P + S = T	TOTAL LIABILITIES & EQUITY

What are Liabilities?

- **Liabilities** are economic obligations of the enterprise, such as money that the corporation owes to lenders, suppliers, employees, etc.

- **Liabilities** are categorized and grouped for presentation on the balance sheet by: (1) to whom the debt is owed and (2) whether the debt is payable within the year (*current liabilities*) or is a long-term obligation.

- *Shareholders' equity* is a very special kind of **liability.** It represents the value of the corporation that belongs to its owners. However, this "debt" will never be repaid in the normal course of business.

Balance Sheet Format
as of a specific date

	LIABILITIES & EQUITY
K	**ACCOUNTS PAYABLE**
L	**ACCRUED EXPENSES**
M	**CURRENT PORTION OF DEBT**
N	**INCOME TAXES PAYABLE**
K + L + M + N = O	**CURRENT LIABILITIES**
P	LONG-TERM DEBT
Q	CAPITAL STOCK
R	RETAINED EARNINGS
Q + R = S	SHAREHOLDER'S EQUITY
O + P + S = T	TOTAL LIABILITIES & EQUITY

Current Liabilities

- **Current liabilities** are bills that must be paid within one year of the date of the Balance Sheet. **Current liabilities** are the reverse of current assets:

    current assets...provide cash within 12 months.
    current liabilities...take cash within 12 months.

- The cash generated from current assets is used to pay **current liabilities** as they become due.

- **Current liabilities** are grouped depending on to whom the debt is owed: (1) *accounts payable* owed to suppliers, (2) *accrued expenses* owed to employees and others for services, (3) *current debt* owed to lenders and (4) *taxes* owed to the government.

Balance Sheet Format
as of a specific date

	LIABILITIES & EQUITY
K	**ACCOUNTS PAYABLE**
L	ACCRUED EXPENSES
M	CURRENT PORTION OF DEBT
N	INCOME TAXES PAYABLE
K + L + M + N = O	CURRENT LIABILITIES
P	LONG-TERM DEBT
Q	CAPITAL STOCK
R	RETAINED EARNINGS
Q + R = S	SHAREHOLDER'S EQUITY
O + P + S = T	TOTAL LIABILITIES & EQUITY

Current Liabilities: Accounts Payable

- **Accounts payable** are bills, generally to other companies for materials and equipment bought on credit, that the corporation must pay soon.

- When it receives materials, the corporation can either pay for them immediately with cash or wait and let what is owed become an **account payable.**

- Business-to-business transactions are most often done on credit. Common trade payment terms are usually 30 or 60 days with a discount for early payment, such as 2% off if paid within 10 days, or the total due in 30 days (*"2% 10; net 30"*).

Balance Sheet Format
as of a specific date

	LIABILITIES & EQUITY
K	ACCOUNTS PAYABLE
L	**ACCRUED EXPENSES**
M	CURRENT PORTION OF DEBT
N	INCOME TAXES PAYABLE
K + L + M + N = O	CURRENT LIABILITIES
P	LONG-TERM DEBT
Q	CAPITAL STOCK
R	RETAINED EARNINGS
Q + R = S	SHAREHOLDER'S EQUITY
O + P + S = T	TOTAL LIABILITIES & EQUITY

Current Liabilities: Accrued Expenses

- **Accrued expenses** are monetary obligations similar to accounts payable. The business uses one or the other classification depending on to whom the debt is owed.

- *Accounts payable* is used for debts to regular suppliers of merchandise or services bought on credit.

- Examples of **accrued expenses** are salaries earned by employees but not yet paid to them, lawyers' bills not yet paid, interest due but not yet paid on bank debt and so forth.

Balance Sheet Format
as of a specific date

	LIABILITIES & EQUITY
K	ACCOUNTS PAYABLE
L	ACCRUED EXPENSES
M	**CURRENT PORTION OF DEBT**
N	INCOME TAXES PAYABLE
K + L + M + N = O	CURRENT LIABILITIES
P	**LONG-TERM DEBT**
Q	CAPITAL STOCK
R	RETAINED EARNINGS
Q + R = S	SHAREHOLDER'S EQUITY
O + P + S = T	TOTAL LIABILITIES & EQUITY

Current Debt and Long-Term Debt

- Any *notes payable* and the *current portion of long-term debt* are both components of current liabilities and are listed on the Balance Sheet under **current portion of debt.**

- If the enterprise owes money to a bank and the terms of the loan say it must be repaid in less than 12 months, then the debt is called a *note payable* and is a current liability.

- A loan with an overall term of more than 12 months from the date of the Balance Sheet is called **long-term debt.** A mortgage on a building is a common example.

  The so-called *current portion of long-term debt* is that amount due for payment within 12 months and is a current liability listed under **current portion of debt.**

Balance Sheet Format
as of a specific date

	LIABILITIES & EQUITY
K	ACCOUNTS PAYABLE
L	ACCRUED EXPENSES
M	CURRENT PORTION OF DEBT
N	**INCOME TAXES PAYABLE**
K + L + M + N = O	CURRENT LIABILITIES
P	LONG-TERM DEBT
Q	CAPITAL STOCK
R	RETAINED EARNINGS
Q + R = S	SHAREHOLDER'S EQUITY
O + P + S = T	TOTAL LIABILITIES & EQUITY

Current Liabilities: Income Taxes Payable

- Every time the company sells something and makes a profit on the sale, a percentage of the profit will be owed the government as *income taxes.*

- **Income taxes payable** are income taxes that the company owes the government but that the company has not yet paid.

- Every three months or so the company will send the government a check for the income taxes owed. For the time between when the profit was made and the time when the taxes are actually paid, the company will show the amount to be paid as **income taxes payable** on the Balance Sheet.

Working Capital

- The company's **working capital** is the amount of money left over after you subtract current liabilities from current assets.

"the good stuff"	*"the less good stuff"*	*"the great stuff"*
Current Assets –	**Current Liabilities** =	**Working Capital**
Cash	Accounts Payable	
Accounts Receivable	Accrued Expenses	
Inventory	Current Portion of Debt	
Prepaid Expenses	Income Taxes Payable	

- **Working capital** is the amount of money the enterprise has to "work with" in the short-term. **Working capital** feeds the operations of the enterprise with dollar bills. **Working capital** is also called *"net current assets"* or simply *"funds."*

Sources and Uses of Working Capital

- **Sources** of working capital are ways working capital *increases* in the normal course of business. This increase in working capital happens when:

    1. current liabilities decrease and/or
    2. current assets increase

- **Uses** of working capital (also called *applications*) are ways working capital *decreases* during the normal course of business. For example, when:

    1. current assets decrease and/or
    2. current liabilities increase

- With lots of working capital it will be easy to pay your "current" financial obligations…bills that come due in the next 12 months.

Balance Sheet Format
as of a specific date

	LIABILITIES & EQUITY
K	ACCOUNTS PAYABLE
L	ACCRUED EXPENSES
M	CURRENT PORTION OF DEBT
N	INCOME TAXES PAYABLE
K + L + M + N = O	CURRENT LIABILITIES
P	LONG-TERM DEBT
Q	CAPITAL STOCK
R	RETAINED EARNINGS
Q + R = S	SHAREHOLDER'S EQUITY
O + P + S = T	TOTAL LIABILITIES & EQUITY

Total Liabilities

- Note: There is not a separate line for **total liabilities** in most Balance Sheet formats.

- A company's **total liabilities** are just the sum of its *current liabilities* and its *long-term debt*.

- *Long-term debt* is any loan to the company to be repaid more than 12 months after the date of the Balance Sheet.

- Common types of long-term debt include mortgages for land and buildings and so-called *chattel mortgages* for machinery and equipment.

Balance Sheet Format
as of a specific date

	LIABILITIES & EQUITY
K	ACCOUNTS PAYABLE
L	ACCRUED EXPENSES
M	CURRENT PORTION OF DEBT
N	INCOME TAXES PAYABLE
K + L + M + N = O	CURRENT LIABILITIES
P	LONG-TERM DEBT
Q	CAPITAL STOCK
R	RETAINED EARNINGS
Q + R = S	**SHAREHOLDER'S EQUITY**
O + P + S = T	TOTAL LIABILITIES & EQUITY

Shareholders' Equity

- If you subtract what the company owes *(total liabilities)* from what it has *(total assets)*, you are left with the company's value to its owners...its **shareholders' equity.**

- **Shareholders' equity** has two components:

  1. *Capital stock:* The original amount of money the owners contributed as their investment in the stock of the company.
  2. *Retained earnings:* All the earnings of the company that have been retained, that is, not paid out as dividends to owners.

- Note: Both *"net worth"* and *"book value"* mean the same thing as **shareholders' equity.**

Balance Sheet Format
as of a specific date

	LIABILITIES & EQUITY
K	ACCOUNTS PAYABLE
L	ACCRUED EXPENSES
M	CURRENT PORTION OF DEBT
N	INCOME TAXES PAYABLE
K + L + M + N = O	CURRENT LIABILITIES
P	LONG-TERM DEBT
Q	**CAPITAL STOCK**
R	RETAINED EARNINGS
Q + R = S	SHAREHOLDER'S EQUITY
O + P + S = T	TOTAL LIABILITIES & EQUITY

Capital Stock

- The original money to start and any add-on money invested in the business is represented by shares of **capital stock** held by owners of the enterprise.

- So-called *common stock* is the regular *"denomination of ownership"* for all corporations. All companies issue common stock, but they may issue other kinds of stock, too.

- Companies often issue *preferred stock* that have certain contractual rights or *"preferences"* over the common stock. These rights may include a specified dividend and/or a preference over common stock to receive company assets if the company is liquidated.

Balance Sheet Format
as of a specific date

	LIABILITIES & EQUITY
K	ACCOUNTS PAYABLE
L	ACCRUED EXPENSES
M	CURRENT PORTION OF DEBT
N	INCOME TAXES PAYABLE
K + L + M + N = O	CURRENT LIABILITIES
P	LONG-TERM DEBT
Q	CAPITAL STOCK
R	**RETAINED EARNINGS**
Q + R = S	SHAREHOLDER'S EQUITY
O + P + S = T	TOTAL LIABILITIES & EQUITY

Retained Earnings

- All of the company's profits that have not been returned to the shareholders as dividends are called **retained earnings.**

  retained earnings = sum of all profits − sum of all dividends

- **Retained earnings** can be viewed as a "pool" of money from which future dividends could be paid. In fact, dividends cannot be paid to shareholders unless sufficient retained earnings are on the Balance Sheet to cover the total amount of the dividend checks.

- If the company has not made a profit but rather has sustained losses, it has *"negative retained earnings"* that are called its accumulated deficit.

Balance Sheet Format
as of a specific date

	LIABILITIES & EQUITY
K	ACCOUNTS PAYABLE
L	ACCRUED EXPENSES
M	CURRENT PORTION OF DEBT
N	INCOME TAXES PAYABLE
K + L + M + N = O	CURRENT LIABILITIES
P	LONG-TERM DEBT
Q	CAPITAL STOCK
R	RETAINED EARNINGS
Q + R = S	**SHAREHOLDER'S EQUITY**
O + P + S = T	TOTAL LIABILITIES & EQUITY

Changes in Shareholders' Equity

- **Shareholders' equity** is just the sum of the investment made in the stock of the company plus any profits (less any losses) minus any dividends that have been paid to shareholders.

- The value of **shareholders' equity** increases when the company: (1) *makes a profit,* thereby increasing retained earnings, or (2) *sells new stock* to investors, thereby increasing capital stock.

- The value of **shareholders' equity** decreases when the company: (1) *has a loss,* thereby lowering retained earnings, or (2) *pays dividends* to shareholders, thereby lowering retained earnings.

Balance Sheet Format
as of a specific date

ASSETS	LIABILITIES & EQUITY
CASH	ACCOUNTS PAYABLE
ACCOUNTS RECEIVABLE	ACCRUED EXPENSES
INVENTORY	CURRENT PORTION OF DEBT
PREPAID EXPENSES	INCOME TAXES PAYABLE
CURRENT ASSETS	CURRENT LIABILITIES
OTHER ASSETS	LONG-TERM DEBT
FIXED ASSETS AT COST	CAPITAL STOCK
ACCUMULATED DEPRECIATION	RETAINED EARNINGS
NET FIXED ASSETS	SHAREHOLDER'S EQUITY
TOTAL ASSETS	TOTAL LIABILITIES & EQUITY

Balance Sheet Summary

- The **Balance Sheet** presents the financial picture of the enterprise on one particular day, an instant in time.

  "have today"   *"owe today"*   *"worth today"*

  Assets = Liabilities + Shareholders' Equity

- By definition, this equation must always be *in balance* with assets equaling the sum of liabilities and equity.

- The Balance Sheet along with the **Income Statement** form the two major financial statements of the company.

Chapter 3. The Income Statement

One of the two main financial statements

of a business...the other is the **Balance Sheet.**

Income Statement Format
for the period x through y

NET SALES	1
COST OF GOODS SOLD	2
GROSS MARGIN	$1 - 2 = 3$
SALES & MARKETING	4
RESEARCH & DEVELOPMENT	5
GENERAL & ADMINISTRATIVE	6
OPERATING EXPENSES	$4 + 5 + 6 = 7$
INCOME FROM OPERATIONS	$3 - 7 = 8$
INTEREST INCOME	9
INCOME TAXES	10
NET INCOME	$8 + 9 - 10 = 11$

The Income Statement

- The **Income Statement** gives one important perspective on the health of a business—its *profitability*.

- Note: The **Income Statement** does not tell the whole picture about a company's financial health.

  The **Balance Sheet** reports on *assets, liabilities* and *equity*. The **Cash Flow Statement** reports on *cash movements*.

- Also note: The **Income Statement** says nothing about when the company receives cash or how much cash it has on hand.

The Income Statement (continued)

- The Income Statement reports on making and selling activities of a business over a period of time:

what's **sold** in the period

minus

what it **cost** to make

minus

selling & general **expenses** for the period

equals

income for the period.

- The **Income Statement** documents for a specific period (a month, quarter or year) the *second basic equation of accounting:*

Sales – Costs & Expenses = Income

minus

equals

Income Statement Format
for the period x through y

NET SALES	1
COST OF GOODS SOLD	2
GROSS MARGIN	$1 - 2 = 3$
SALES & MARKETING	4
RESEARCH & DEVELOPMENT	5
GENERAL & ADMINISTRATIVE	6
OPERATING EXPENSES	$4 + 5 + 6 = 7$
INCOME FROM OPERATIONS	$3 - 7 = 8$
INTEREST INCOME	9
INCOME TAXES	10
NET INCOME	$8 + 9 - 10 = 11$

Net Sales

- **Sales** are recorded on the Income Statement when the company actually ships products to customers. Customers now have an obligation to pay for the product and the company has the right to collect.

- When the company ships a product to a customer, it also sends an invoice (a bill). The company's right to collect is called an *account receivable* and is entered on the company's Balance Sheet.

- Note: **Net sales** means the total amount the company will ultimately collect from a sale—that is, list price less any discounts offered to the customer to induce purchase.

Sales vs. Orders

- A **sale** is made when the company actually ships a product to a customer. **Orders,** however, are something different.

- **Orders** become **sales** only when the products ordered have left the company's loading dock and are en route to the customer.

- When a **sale** is made, *income is generated* on the Income Statement. **Orders** only increase the "backlog" of products to be shipped and do not have an impact on the Income Statement in any way. Simply receiving an order does not result in income.

Costs

- **Costs** are expenditures for raw materials, workers' wages, manufacturing overhead and so forth. **Costs** are what you spend when you buy (or make) products for inventory.

- When this inventory is sold, that is, shipped to customers, its total **cost** is taken out of inventory and entered in the Income Statement as a special type of expense called *cost of goods sold.*

- **Costs** lower cash and increase inventory values on the Balance Sheet. Only when inventory is sold does its value move from the Balance Sheet to the Income Statement as *cost of goods sold.*

Income Statement Format
for the period x through y

NET SALES	1
COST OF GOODS SOLD	2
GROSS MARGIN	$1 - 2 = 3$
SALES & MARKETING	4
RESEARCH & DEVELOPMENT	5
GENERAL & ADMINISTRATIVE	6
OPERATING EXPENSES	$4 + 5 + 6 = 7$
INCOME FROM OPERATIONS	$3 - 7 = 8$
INTEREST INCOME	9
INCOME TAXES	10
NET INCOME	$8 + 9 - 10 = 11$

Cost of Goods Sold

- When a product is shipped and a sale is booked, the company records the total cost of manufacturing the product as **cost of goods sold** on the Income Statement.

- Remember: When the company made the product, it took all the product's costs and added them to the value of inventory.

- The costs to manufacture products are accumulated in inventory until the products are sold. Then these costs are *"expensed"* through the Income Statement as **cost of goods sold.**

Income Statement Format

for the period x through y

NET SALES	1
COST OF GOODS SOLD	2
GROSS MARGIN	$1 - 2 = 3$
SALES & MARKETING	4
RESEARCH & DEVELOPMENT	5
GENERAL & ADMINISTRATIVE	6
OPERATING EXPENSES	$4 + 5 + 6 = 7$
INCOME FROM OPERATIONS	$3 - 7 = 8$
INTEREST INCOME	9
INCOME TAXES	10
NET INCOME	$8 + 9 - 10 = 11$

Gross Margin

- **Gross margin** is the amount left over from sales after product manufacturing costs (cost of goods sold) are subtracted. **Gross margin** is sometimes called *gross profit* or the company's *manufacturing margin*.

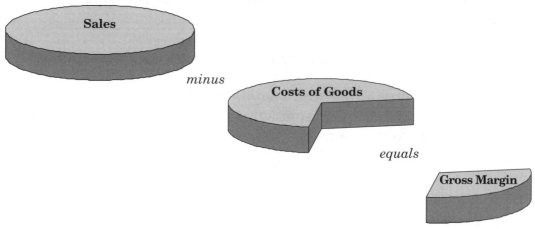

Cost vs. Expense

- Two different terms, **cost** and **expense,** are used to describe how the company spends its money:

  > *Manufacturing expenditures* to build inventories are called **costs.**

  All other business expenditures are called **expenses.**

- Note: Using the terms **cost** and **expense** correctly will make it easier to understand how the Income Statement and Balance Sheet work together.

- Also note: An *expenditure* can be either a cost or an expense. Expenditure simply means the use of cash to pay for an item purchased.

Expenses

- **Expenses** pay for developing and selling products and for running the "general and administrative" aspects of the business.

- Examples of **expenses** are paying legal fees and a sales person's salary, buying chemicals for the R&D laboratory and so forth.

- **Expenses** directly lower *income* on the Income Statement.

- Note: The words *profit* and *income* mean the same thing; that is, what's left over from sales after you have subtracted all the costs and expenses.

Income Statement Format
for the period x through y

NET SALES	1
COST OF GOODS SOLD	2
GROSS MARGIN	$1 - 2 = 3$
SALES & MARKETING	4
RESEARCH & DEVELOPMENT	5
GENERAL & ADMINISTRATIVE	6
OPERATING EXPENSES	$\mathbf{4 + 5 + 6 = 7}$
INCOME FROM OPERATIONS	$3 - 7 = 8$
INTEREST INCOME	9
INCOME TAXES	10
NET INCOME	$8 + 9 - 10 = 11$

Operating Expenses

- **Operating expenses** are those expenditures (that is, cash out) that a company makes to generate income.

- Common groupings of **operating expense** are:

  1. Sales & Marketing expense.
  2. Research & Development ("R&D") expenses.
  3. General & Administrative ("G&A") expenses.

- **Operating expenses** are also called SG&A expenses, meaning *"sales, general* and *administrative expenses."*

Income or (Loss)

- If sales exceed costs plus expenses (as reported on the Income Statement), the business has earned **income.** If costs plus expenses exceed sales, then a **loss** has occurred.

- The terms *income* and *profit* and *earnings* all have the same meaning—what's left over when you subtract expenses and costs from sales.

  Note: The Income Statement is often referred to as the *Profit & Loss Statement,* the *Earnings Statement,* or simply the *P&L.*

- Remember: **Income** is the difference between two very large numbers: *sales* less *costs* and *expenses.* Slightly lower *sales* and/or slightly higher *costs* and *expenses* can eliminate any expected profit and result in a **loss.**

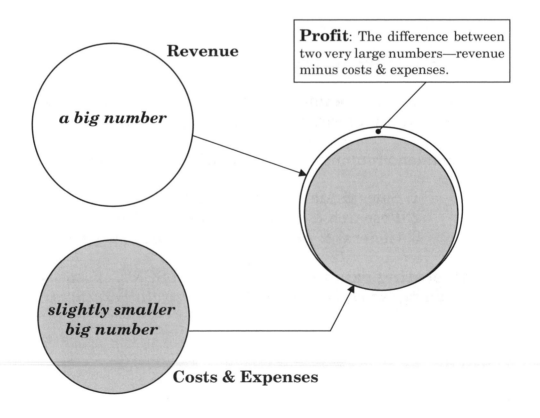

Revenue

a big number

Profit: The difference between two very large numbers—revenue minus costs & expenses.

slightly smaller big number

Costs & Expenses

Income Statement Format
for the period x through y

NET SALES	1
COST OF GOODS SOLD	2
GROSS MARGIN	$1 - 2 = 3$
SALES & MARKETING	4
RESEARCH & DEVELOPMENT	5
GENERAL & ADMINISTRATIVE	6
OPERATING EXPENSES	$4 + 5 + 6 = 7$
INCOME FROM OPERATIONS	$\mathbf{3 - 7 = 8}$
INTEREST INCOME	9
INCOME TAXES	10
NET INCOME	$8 + 9 - 10 = 11$

Income From Operations

- A manufacturing company's *operations* are all its actions taken in making and selling products, resulting in both expenses and costs. The term **income from operations** refers to what is left over after expenses and costs are subtracted from sales.

- Note: Companies can also generate income and have expenses from financial (non-operating) activities. For example, a manufacturing company selling a piece of real estate for a profit.

Income Statement Format
for the period x through y

NET SALES	1
COST OF GOODS SOLD	2
GROSS MARGIN	$1 - 2 = 3$
SALES & MARKETING	4
RESEARCH & DEVELOPMENT	5
GENERAL & ADMINISTRATIVE	6
OPERATING EXPENSES	$4 + 5 + 6 = 7$
INCOME FROM OPERATIONS	$3 - 7 = 8$
INTEREST INCOME	9
INCOME TAXES	**10**
NET INCOME	$8 + 9 - 10 = 11$

Non-operating Income & Expense

- Paying interest on a loan is a so-called **non-operating expense.** Likewise, receiving interest on cash balances in the company's bank account is **non-operating income.**

- Because it is from non-operating sources, interest income (or expense) is reported on the Income Statement just below the *Income from Operations* line. Likewise taxes.

- Note: A company's operations can be producing income, but the company as a whole can still show an overall loss. This sad state of affairs comes about when **non-operating expenses** (such as very high interest expenses) exceed the total operating income.

Income Statement Format
for the period x through y

NET SALES	1
COST OF GOODS SOLD	2
GROSS MARGIN	$1 - 2 = 3$
SALES & MARKETING	4
RESEARCH & DEVELOPMENT	5
GENERAL & ADMINISTRATIVE	6
OPERATING EXPENSES	$4 + 5 + 6 = 7$
INCOME FROM OPERATIONS	$3 - 7 = 8$
INTEREST INCOME	9
INCOME TAXES	10
NET INCOME	$8 + 9 - 10 = 11$

Net Income

- **Income** is the difference between two large numbers: (1) *sales* and (2) *costs* plus *expenses*. More *costs* plus *expenses* than sales and the company will show a loss. Less *costs* plus *expenses* than *sales* and the company will show a profit.

- Remember: **Income** is not cash. In fact, a very profitable company with lots of **net income** can also be insolvent; that is, with no cash left to pay its bills.

- Often rapidly growing companies are short of cash—even though they are highly profitable. They simply cannot supply out of earnings the capital required for such rapid growth.

Income Statement Format
for the period x through y

Top Line →

NET SALES	1
COST OF GOODS SOLD	2
GROSS MARGIN	$1 - 2 = 3$
SALES & MARKETING	4
RESEARCH & DEVELOPMENT	5
GENERAL & ADMINISTRATIVE	6
OPERATING EXPENSES	$4 + 5 + 6 = 7$
INCOME FROM OPERATIONS	$3 - 7 = 8$
INTEREST INCOME	9
INCOME TAXES	10
NET INCOME	$8 + 9 - 10 = 11$

Bottom Line →

Income (Profits) vs. Sales (Revenue)

- The words **income** and **revenue** are often confused. They mean very different things:

   Profit and *income* do mean the same thing.
   Sales and *revenue* do mean the same thing.

- **Income** (also called **profits**) is at the BOTTOM of the Income Statement. **Sales** (also called **revenue**) is at the TOP of the Income Statement.

- **Income** is often referred to as *the bottom line* because it is the last line of the Income Statement.

- **Sales** are often referred to as *the top line* because it is at the top of the Income Statement.

Income Statement Format
for the period x through y

NET SALES	1
COST OF GOODS SOLD	2
GROSS MARGIN	$1 - 2 = 3$
SALES & MARKETING	4
RESEARCH & DEVELOPMENT	5
GENERAL & ADMINISTRATIVE	6
OPERATING EXPENSES	$4 + 5 + 6 = 7$
INCOME FROM OPERATIONS	$3 - 7 = 8$
INTEREST INCOME	9
INCOME TAXES	10
NET INCOME	$8 + 9 - 10 = 11$

Income Statement Summary

- The Income Statement summarizes and displays the financial impact of:

> movement of goods to customers (**sales**)
> *minus*
> efforts to make and sell those goods (**costs** and **expenses**)
> *equals*
> any value created in the process (**income**)

- All business activities that generate income or result in a loss for a company—*that is, all transactions that change the value of shareholders' equity*—are recorded on the Income Statement.

Accrual Basis vs. Cash Basis

- The two major ways of running a company's books—*cash basis* or *accrual basis*—differ on when the company records expenses and income.

- If income is measured when cash is received and expenses are measured when cash is spent, the business is said to be operating on a cash basis—just like your checkbook.

- If income and expenses are measured when the transactions occur—regardless of the physical flow of cash—the business is said to be operating on an accrual basis. More later.

Cash Basis

- **Cash basis** books are the simplest...functioning just like the proverbial cookie jar. When the books are on a **cash basis,** accounting transactions are triggered only by the movement of cash.

- With the books on a **cash basis,** the *Income Statement* and the *Cash Flow Statement* are the same.

- In general, people run their lives on a **cash basis**, but most businesses run their books on an accrual basis. All businesses that maintain inventories of product for sale must use accrual accounting to report income—so says the IRS.

Accrual Basis

- In **accrual basis** accounting, the Income Statement does not reflect the movement of cash, but rather, the generation of obligations (payables) to pay cash in the future.

- With **accrual basis** accounting, expenses occur when the company incurs the obligation to pay, not when it actually parts with the cash. In **accrual basis** accounting, sales and costs are recorded when the goods are shipped and customers incur the obligation to pay, not when they actually pay.

- For example, under **accrual basis** accounting you would lower your net worth when you use your charge card rather than when you ultimately paid the bill.

Income Statement & Balance Sheet

- The enterprise's **Income Statement** and **Balance Sheet** are inexorably linked:

  If the enterprise's **Income Statement** shows income, then retained earnings are *increased* on the **Balance Sheet.**

  Then, also, either the enterprise's *assets* must increase or its *liabilities* decrease for the **Balance Sheet** to remain in balance.

- Thus, the **Income Statement** shows for a period all the actions taken by the enterprise to either *increase assets* or *decrease liabilities* on the **Balance Sheet.**

Chapter 4. The Cash Flow Statement

Where the company gets cash,

and where that cash goes

Cash Flow Statement Format
for the period x through y

BEGINNING CASH BALANCE	a
CASH RECEIPTS	b
CASH DISBURSEMENTS	c
CASH FROM OPERATIONS	$b - c = d$
FIXED ASSET PURCHASES	e
NET BORROWINGS	f
INCOME TAXES PAID	g
SALE OF STOCK	h
ENDING CASH BALANCE	$a + d - e + f - g + h = i$

Cash Flow Statement

- The **Cash Flow Statement** tracks the *movement of cash* through the business over *a period of time.*

- A company's **Cash Flow Statement** is just like a check register...recording all the company's transactions that use cash *(checks)* or supply cash *(deposits)*.

- The **Cash Flow Statement** shows:

    cash on hand at the start of a period
    plus
    cash received in the period
    minus
    cash spent in the period
    equals
    cash on hand at the end of the period.

Cash Transactions

- So-called **cash transactions** affect cash flow. For example:

  Paying salaries lowers **cash.**
  Paying for equipment lowers **cash.**
  Paying off a loan lowers **cash.**

  Receiving money borrowed from a bank raises **cash.**
  Receiving money from investors for stock raises **cash.**
  Receiving money from customers raises **cash.**

- Notice the use of the words "paying" and "receive money" in those transactions where cash actually changes hands.

Non-cash Transactions

- So-called **non-cash transactions** are company activities where no cash moves into or out of the company's accounts. **Non-cash transactions** have no effect on the *Cash Flow Statement* but they can affect the *Income Statement* and *Balance Sheet*.

- Examples of **non-cash transactions** include: shipping product to a customer, receiving supplies from a vendor and receiving raw materials required to make the product. For these material transfer transactions, no cash actually changes hands during the transaction proper, only later.

- Note: Cash comes into the company when the customer pays for the product, not when the company ships it. Cash moves out of the company when it pays for materials, not when the company orders or receives them.

Cash Flow

- A **positive cash flow** for a period means the company has more cash at the end of the period than at the beginning.

- A **negative cash flow** for a period means that the company has less cash at the end of the period than at the beginning.

- If a company has a continuing negative **cash flow**, it runs the risk of running out of cash and not being able to pay its bills when due—just another way of saying:

  ### *broke...tapped-out...insolvent.*

Sources and Uses of Cash

- **Cash** comes into the business *(sources)* in two major ways:

  1. *Operating activities* such as receiving payment from customers.
  2. *Financing activities* such as selling stock or borrowing money.

- **Cash** goes out of the business *(uses)* in four major ways:

  1. *Operating activities* such as paying suppliers and employees.
  2. *Financial activities* such as paying interest and principal on debt or paying dividends to shareholders.
  3. Making major *capital investments* in long-lived productive assets like machines.
  4. *Paying income taxes* to the government.

Cash Flow Statement Format
for the period x through y

BEGINNING CASH BALANCE	a
CASH RECEIPTS	b
CASH DISBURSEMENTS	c
CASH FROM OPERATIONS	**b – c = d**
FIXED ASSET PURCHASES	e
NET BORROWINGS	f
INCOME TAXES PAID	g
SALE OF STOCK	h
ENDING CASH BALANCE	a + d – e + f – g + h = i

Cash from Operations

- The normal day-to-day business activities (making and selling product) of a business are called its *operations*.

- The Cash Flow Statement shows **cash from operations** separately from other cash flows.

- *Cash receipts* are inflows of money coming from operating the business.

- *Cash disbursements* are outflows of money used in operating the business.

- *Cash receipts* (money in) minus *cash disbursements* (money out) equals **cash from operations.**

Cash Flow Statement Format
for the period x through y

BEGINNING CASH BALANCE	a
CASH RECEIPTS	**b**
CASH DISBURSEMENTS	c
CASH FROM OPERATIONS	b − c = d
FIXED ASSET PURCHASES	e
NET BORROWINGS	f
INCOME TAXES PAID	g
SALE OF STOCK	h
ENDING CASH BALANCE	a + d − e + f − g + h = i

Cash Receipts

- **Cash receipts** (also called *collections* or simply *receipts*) come from collecting money from customers.

- **Cash receipts** increase the amount of cash the company has on hand.

  Note: Receiving cash from customers decreases the amount that is due the company as accounts receivable shown on the *Balance Sheet.*

- **Cash receipts** are not profits. Profits are something else altogether. Don't confuse the two. Profits are reported on the *Income Statement.*

Cash Flow Statement Format
for the period x through y

BEGINNING CASH BALANCE	a
CASH RECEIPTS	b
CASH DISBURSEMENTS	**c**
CASH FROM OPERATIONS	$b - c = d$
FIXED ASSET PURCHASES	e
NET BORROWINGS	f
INCOME TAXES PAID	g
SALE OF STOCK	h
ENDING CASH BALANCE	$a + d - e + f - g + h = i$

Cash Disbursements

- A **cash disbursement** is writing a check to pay for the rent, for inventory and supplies or for a worker's salary. **Cash disbursements** *lower* the amount of cash the company has on hand.

- **Cash disbursements** (payments) to suppliers lower the amount the company owes as reported in *accounts payable* on the *Balance Sheet*.

- **Cash disbursements** are also called *payments* or simply *disbursements*.

Other elements of cash flow

- **Cash from operations** reports the flow of money into and out of the business from the making and selling of products.

- **Cash from operations** is a good measure of how well the enterprise is doing in its day-to-day business activities, its so-called *operations*.

- But remember, **cash from operations** is just one of the important elements of cash flow. Other major cash flows are:

    1. *Investment in fixed assets* such as buying a manufacturing facility and machinery to make product.

    2. *Financial activities* such as selling stock to investors, borrowing money from banks, paying dividends, or paying taxes to the government.

Cash Flow Statement Format
for the period x through y

BEGINNING CASH BALANCE	a
CASH RECEIPTS	b
CASH DISBURSEMENTS	c
CASH FROM OPERATIONS	$b - c = d$
FIXED ASSET PURCHASES	**e**
NET BORROWINGS	f
INCOME TAXES PAID	g
SALE OF STOCK	h
ENDING CASH BALANCE	$a + d - e + f - g + h = i$

Fixed Asset Purchases

- Money spent to buy *property, plant* and *equipment* (PP&E) is an investment in the long-term capability of the company to manufacture and sell product.

- Paying for PP&E is not considered part of operations and thus is not reported in *cash disbursements from operations.* Cash payments for PP&E are reported on a separate line on the Cash Flow Statement. PP&E purchases are *investments* in productive assets.

- Needless to say, after paying for PP&E the business has less cash. Cash is used when the PP&E is purchased originally. Note, however, when the enterprise *depreciates* a fixed asset, it does not use any cash at that time. No check is written to anyone.

Cash Flow Statement Format
for the period x through y

BEGINNING CASH BALANCE	a
CASH RECEIPTS	b
CASH DISBURSEMENTS	c
CASH FROM OPERATIONS	b – c = d
FIXED ASSET PURCHASES	e
NET BORROWINGS	**f**
INCOME TAXES PAID	g
SALE OF STOCK	h
ENDING CASH BALANCE	a + d – e + f – g + h = i

Net Borrowings

- Borrowing money *increases* the amount of cash the company has on hand.

- Conversely, paying back a loan *decreases* the company's supply of cash on hand.

- The difference between any new borrowings in a period and the amount paid back in the period is called **net borrowings.** **Net borrowings** are reported for the period on a separate line in the *Cash Flow Statement.*

Cash Flow Statement Format
for the period x through y

BEGINNING CASH BALANCE	a
CASH RECEIPTS	b
CASH DISBURSEMENTS	c
CASH FROM OPERATIONS	$b - c = d$
FIXED ASSET PURCHASES	e
NET BORROWINGS	f
INCOME TAXES PAID	**g**
SALE OF STOCK	h
ENDING CASH BALANCE	$a + d - e + f - g + h = i$

Income Taxes Paid

- Owing *income taxes* is different from paying them. The business owes some more *income tax* every time it sells something for a profit.

- But just owing taxes does not reduce cash. *Only writing a check to the government and thus paying the taxes due actually reduces the company's cash on hand.*

- Paying *income taxes* to the government decreases the company's supply of cash. **Income taxes paid** are reported on the *Cash Flow Statement*.

Cash Flow Statement Format
for the period x through y

BEGINNING CASH BALANCE	a
CASH RECEIPTS	b
CASH DISBURSEMENTS	c
CASH FROM OPERATIONS	$b - c = d$
FIXED ASSET PURCHASES	e
NET BORROWINGS	f
INCOME TAXES PAID	g
SALE OF STOCK	**h**
ENDING CASH BALANCE	$a + d - e + f - g + h = i$

Sale of Stock: New Equity

- When people invest in a company's **stock**, they exchange one piece of paper for another: real U.S. currency for a fancy stock certificate.

- When a company sells **stock** to investors, it receives money and increases the amount of cash it has on hand.

- Selling **stock** is the closest thing to *printing money* that a company can do...and it's perfectly legal—unless you mislead widows and orphans as to the real value of the **stock,** in which case the S.E.C. (U.S. Securities and Exchange Commission) will send you to jail. Really.

Cash Flow Statement Format
for the period x through y

BEGINNING CASH BALANCE	a
CASH RECEIPTS	b
CASH DISBURSEMENTS	c
CASH FROM OPERATIONS	$b - c = d$
FIXED ASSET PURCHASES	e
NET BORROWINGS	f
INCOME TAXES PAID	g
SALE OF STOCK	h
ENDING CASH BALANCE	$a + d - e + f - g + h = i$

Ending Cash Balance

- The beginning cash balance (at the start of the period) plus or minus all cash transactions that took place during the period equals the **ending cash balance.**

- Thus: *beginning* **cash** *on hand*

    plus **cash** *received*

    minus **cash** *spent*

    equals ending **cash** *on hand.*

Cash Flow Statement Format
for the period x through y

BEGINNING CASH BALANCE	a
CASH RECEIPTS	b
CASH DISBURSEMENTS	c
CASH FROM OPERATIONS	$b - c = d$
FIXED ASSET PURCHASES	e
NET BORROWINGS	f
INCOME TAXES PAID	g
SALE OF STOCK	h
ENDING CASH BALANCE	$a + d - e + f - g + h = i$

Cash Flow Statement Summary

- Think of the company's **Cash Flow Statement** as a check register reporting all the company's payments *(cash outflows)* and deposits *(cash inflows)* for a period of time.

- If no actual cash changes hands in a particular transaction, then the **Cash Flow Statement** is not changed.

- Note, however, that the *Balance Sheet* and *Income Statement* may be changed by a *non-cash transaction*.

- Note also that cash transactions—those reported on the **Cash Flow Statement**—usually do have some effect on the *Income Statement* and *Balance Sheet* as well.

Chapter 5. Connections

These pages will begin our formal study of how the three major financial statements interact—how they work in concert to give a true picture of the enterprise's financial health.

In the prior chapters, we studied separately the vocabulary and structure of the three main financial statements. What follows here is an opportunity to put the statements together as a financial reporting tool. We will see how the *Income Statement* relates to the *Balance Sheet* and vice versa and how changes to each can effect the *Cash Flow Statement*.

Remember the fundamental reporting function of each of the three main financial statements:

1. The *Income Statement* shows the manufacturing and selling actions of the enterprise that results in profit or loss.

2. The *Cash Flow Statement* details the movements of cash into and out of the coffers of the enterprise.

3. The *Balance Sheet* records what the company owns and what it owes, including the owner's stake.

Each statement views the enterprise's financial health from a different—and very necessary—perspective. And also, each statement relates to the other two. Review these examples of the natural "connections" between the three main financial statements on the following pages.

Balance Sheet Connections. First shown are several structural connections between the Balance Sheet and the other two statements.

Sales Cycle. Next shown is the sale cycle describing those repeating financial statement entries that the company must make in order to report a sale and receive payment.

Expense Cycle. Then follows the documenting entries for SG&A expenses and their subsequent payment.

Investment Cycle. Next shown are the connection entries relating to the investment of capital and the acquisition of debt.

Asset Purchase/Depreciation. Last shown are entries for asset purchases and depreciation.

~

Here is a hint for you as you study the reporting of two things entering or leaving the business (and the statements):

1. ***Watch the flow of cash money.***

2. ***Watch the flow of goods and services.***

Fundamentally, the financial statements document the movement of cash and goods and services into and out of the enterprise. That is all the financial statements are about. It is no more complicated. Everything else is in the details. Don't sweat the details.

Read on. We're making real progress!

Financial statements document the movement of cash and goods and services into and out of the enterprise. That is all financial statements are about. It is no more complicated. Everything else is details. Don't sweat the details.

Income Statement

for the period

1	NET SALES	$3,055,560
2	COST OF GOODS SOLD	2,005,830
1 - 2 = 3	GROSS MARGIN	1,049,730
4	SALES & MARKETING	328,523
5	RESEARCH & DEVELOPMENT	26,000
6	GENERAL & ADMINISTRATIVE	203,520
4 + 5 + 6 = 7	OPERATING EXPENSE	558,043
3 - 7 = 8	INCOME FROM OPERATIONS	491,687
9	NET INTEREST INCOME	(100,000)
10	INCOME TAXES	139,804
8 + 9 - 10 = 11	NET INCOME	$251,883

Cash Flow Statement

for the period

a	BEGINNING CASH BALANCE	$155,000
b	CASH RECEIPTS	2,584,900
c	CASH DISBURSEMENTS	2,796,438
b - c = d	CASH FLOW FROM OPERATIONS	(211,538)
e	PP&E PURCHASE	1,750,000
f	NET BOROWINGS	900,000
g	INCOME TAXES PAID	0
h	SALE OF CAPITAL STOCK	1,550,000
a + d - e + f - g + h = i	ENDING CASH BALANCES	$643,462

> **Balance Sheet Connections**

> **ENDING CASH** on the *Cash Flow Statement* always equals **CASH** on the *Balance Sheet*.

Balance Sheet

as of period end

A	CASH	$643,462
B	ACCOUNTS RECEIVABLE	454,760
C	INVENTORIES	414,770
D	PREPAID EXPENSES	0
A + B + C + D = E	CURRENT ASSETS	1,512,992
F	OTHER ASSETS	0
G	FIXED ASSETS @ COST	1,750,000
H	ACCUMULATED DEPRECIATION	78,573
G - H = I	NET FIXED ASSETS	1,671,427
E + F + I = J	TOTAL ASSETS	$3,184,419
K	ACCOUNTS PAYABLE	$236,297
L	ACCRUED EXPENSES	26,435
M	CURRENT PORTION OF DEBT	100,000
N	INCOME TAXES PAYABLE	139,804
K + L + M + N = O	CURRENT LIABILITIES	502,536
P	LONG-TERM DEBT	800,000
Q	CAPITAL STOCK	1,550,000
R	RETAINED EARNINGS	331,883
Q + R = S	SHAREHOLDERS' EQUITY	1,881,883
O + P + S = T	TOTAL LIABILITIES & EQUITY	$3,184,419

> According to the basic equation of accounting, **TOTAL ASSETS** equals **TOTAL LIABILITIES** plus **SHAREHOLDERS' EQUITY**. Then by definition, the *Balance Sheet* must always be "in balance."

Income Statement
for the period

1	NET SALES	$3,055,560	
2	COST OF GOODS SOLD	2,005,830	
1 - 2 = 3	GROSS MARGIN	1,049,730	
4	SALES & MARKETING	328,523	
5	RESEARCH & DEVELOPMENT	26,000	
6	GENERAL & ADMINISTRATIVE	203,520	
4 + 5 + 6 = 7	OPERATING EXPENSE	558,043	
3 - 7 = 8	INCOME FROM OPERATIONS	491,687	
9	NET INTEREST INCOME	(100,000)	
10	INCOME TAXES	139,804	
8 + 9 - 10 = 11	NET INCOME	$251,883	

Cash Flow Statement
for the period

a	BEGINNING CASH BALANCE	$155,000	
b	CASH RECEIPTS	2,584,900	
c	CASH DISBURSEMENTS	2,796,438	
b - c = d	CASH FLOW FROM OPERATIONS	(211,538)	
e	PP&E PURCHASE	1,750,000	
f	NET BOROWINGS	900,000	
g	INCOME TAXES PAID	0	
h	SALE OF CAPITAL STOCK	1,550,000	
a + d - e + f - g + h = i	ENDING CASH BALANCES	$643,462	

> **Balance Sheet Connections**

Balance Sheet
as of period end

A	CASH	$643,462	
B	ACCOUNTS RECEIVABLE	454,760	
C	INVENTORIES	414,770	
D	PREPAID EXPENSES	0	
A + B + C + D = E	CURRENT ASSETS	1,512,992	
F	OTHER ASSETS	0	
G	FIXED ASSETS @ COST	1,750,000	
H	ACCUMULATED DEPRECIATION	78,573	
G - H = I	NET FIXED ASSETS	1,671,427	
E + F + I = J	TOTAL ASSETS	$3,184,419	
K	ACCOUNTS PAYABLE	$236,297	
L	ACCRUED EXPENSES	26,435	
M	CURRENT PORTION OF DEBT	100,000	
N	INCOME TAXES PAYABLE	139,804	
K + L + M + N = O	CURRENT LIABILITIES	502,536	
P	LONG-TERM DEBT	800,000	
Q	CAPITAL STOCK	1,550,000	
R	RETAINED EARNINGS	331,883	
Q + R = S	SHAREHOLDERS' EQUITY	1,881,883	
O + P + S = T	TOTAL LIABILITIES & EQUITY	$3,184,419	

> For the *Balance Sheet* to stay "in balance," when you **subtract** from an asset account, you must also ...

> ... either **add** the same amount to another asset account **or subtract** it from a liability account.

Financial Statements

Income Statement
for the period

1	NET SALES	$3,055,560
2	COST OF GOODS SOLD	2,005,830
1 - 2 = 3	GROSS MARGIN	1,049,730
4	SALES & MARKETING	328,523
5	RESEARCH & DEVELOPMENT	26,000
6	GENERAL & ADMINISTRATIVE	203,520
4 + 5 + 6 = 7	OPERATING EXPENSE	558,043
3 - 7 = 8	INCOME FROM OPERATIONS	491,687
9	NET INTEREST INCOME	(100,000)
10	INCOME TAXES	139,804
8 + 9 - 10 = 11	NET INCOME	$251,883

Cash Flow Statement
for the period

a	BEGINNING CASH BALANCE	$155,000
b	CASH RECEIPTS	2,584,900
c	CASH DISBURSEMENTS	2,796,438
b - c = d	CASH FLOW FROM OPERATIONS	(211,538)
e	PP&E PURCHASE	1,750,000
f	NET BORROWINGS	900,000
g	INCOME TAXES PAID	0
h	SALE OF CAPITAL STOCK	1,550,000
a + d - e + f - g + h = i	ENDING CASH BALANCES	$643,462

Balance Sheet
as of period end

A	CASH	$643,462
B	ACCOUNTS RECEIVABLE	454,760
C	INVENTORIES	414,770
D	PREPAID EXPENSES	0
A + B + C + D = E	CURRENT ASSETS	1,512,992
F	OTHER ASSETS	0
G	FIXED ASSETS @ COST	1,750,000
H	ACCUMULATED DEPRECIATION	78,573
G - H = I	NET FIXED ASSETS	1,671,427
E + F + I = J	TOTAL ASSETS	$3,184,419
K	ACCOUNTS PAYABLE	$236,297
L	ACCRUED EXPENSES	26,435
M	CURRENT PORTION OF DEBT	100,000
N	INCOME TAXES PAYABLE	139,804
K + L + M + N = O	CURRENT LIABILITIES	502,536
P	LONG-TERM DEBT	800,000
Q	CAPITAL STOCK	1,550,000
R	RETAINED EARNINGS	331,883
Q + R = S	SHAREHOLDERS' EQUITY	1,881,883
O + P + S = T	TOTAL LIABILITIES & EQUITY	$3,184,419

Balance Sheet Connections

NET INCOME from the *Income Statement* is added to RETAINED EARNINGS on the Balance Sheet and thus SHAREHOLDERS' EQUITY increases.

Income Statement
for the period

1	NET SALES	$3,055,560	⬆
2	COST OF GOODS SOLD	2,005,830	
1 - 2 = 3	GROSS MARGIN	1,049,730	
4	SALES & MARKETING	328,523	
5	RESEARCH & DEVELOPMENT	26,000	
6	GENERAL & ADMINISTRATIVE	203,520	
4 + 5 + 6 = 7	OPERATING EXPENSE	558,043	
3 - 7 = 8	INCOME FROM OPERATIONS	491,687	
9	NET INTEREST INCOME	(100,000)	
10	INCOME TAXES	139,804	
8 + 9 - 10 = 11	NET INCOME	$251,883	

Cash Flow Statement
for the period

a	BEGINNING CASH BALANCE	$155,000
b	CASH RECEIPTS	2,584,900
c	CASH DISBURSEMENTS	2,796,438
b - c = d	CASH FLOW FROM OPERATIONS	(211,538)
e	PP&E PURCHASE	1,750,000
f	NET BORROWINGS	900,000
g	INCOME TAXES PAID	0
h	SALE OF CAPITAL STOCK	1,550,000
a + d - e + f - g + h = i	ENDING CASH BALANCES	$643,462

① Sales Cycle
When a sale is made on credit, **NET SALES** increases at the top of the *Income Statement* and **ACCOUNTS RECEIVABLE** increases on the *Balance Sheet* by the same amount.

Balance Sheet
as of period end

A	CASH	$643,462	
B	ACCOUNTS RECEIVABLE	454,760	⬆
C	INVENTORIES	414,770	
D	PREPAID EXPENSES	0	
A + B + C + D = E	CURRENT ASSETS	1,512,992	
F	OTHER ASSETS	0	
G	FIXED ASSETS @ COST	1,750,000	
H	ACCUMULATED DEPRECIATION	78,573	
G - H = I	NET FIXED ASSETS	1,671,427	
E + F + I = J	TOTAL ASSETS	$3,184,419	
K	ACCOUNTS PAYABLE	$236,297	
L	ACCRUED EXPENSES	26,435	
M	CURRENT PORTION OF DEBT	100,000	
N	INCOME TAXES PAYABLE	139,804	
K + L + M + N = O	CURRENT LIABILITIES	502,536	
P	LONG-TERM DEBT	800,000	
Q	CAPITAL STOCK	1,550,000	
R	RETAINED EARNINGS	331,883	
Q + R = S	SHAREHOLDERS' EQUITY	1,881,883	
O + P + S = T	TOTAL LIABILITIES & EQUITY	$3,184,419	

Income Statement
for the period

1	NET SALES	$3,055,560	
2	COST OF GOODS SOLD	2,005,830	
1 - 2 = 3	GROSS MARGIN	1,049,730	
4	SALES & MARKETING	328,523	
5	RESEARCH & DEVELOPMENT	26,000	
6	GENERAL & ADMINISTRATIVE	203,520	
4 + 5 + 6 = 7	OPERATING EXPENSE	558,043	
3 - 7 = 8	INCOME FROM OPERATIONS	491,687	
9	NET INTEREST INCOME	(100,000)	
10	INCOME TAXES	139,804	
8 + 9 - 10 = 11	NET INCOME	$251,883	

Cash Flow Statement
for the period

a	BEGINNING CASH BALANCE	$155,000
b	CASH RECEIPTS	2,584,900
c	CASH DISBURSEMENTS	2,796,438
b - c = d	CASH FLOW FROM OPERATIONS	(211,538)
e	PP&E PURCHASE	1,750,000
f	NET BORROWINGS	900,000
g	INCOME TAXES PAID	0
h	SALE OF CAPITAL STOCK	1,550,000
a + d - e + f - g + h = i	ENDING CASH BALANCES	$643,462

Balance Sheet
as of period end

A	CASH	$643,462
B	ACCOUNTS RECEIVABLE	454,760
C	INVENTORIES	414,770
D	PREPAID EXPENSES	0
A + B + C + D = E	CURRENT ASSETS	1,512,992
F	OTHER ASSETS	0
G	FIXED ASSETS @ COST	1,750,000
H	ACCUMULATED DEPRECIATION	78,573
G - H = I	NET FIXED ASSETS	1,671,427
E + F + I = J	TOTAL ASSETS	$3,184,419
K	ACCOUNTS PAYABLE	$236,297
L	ACCRUED EXPENSES	26,435
M	CURRENT PORTION OF DEBT	100,000
N	INCOME TAXES PAYABLE	139,804
K + L + M + N = O	CURRENT LIABILITIES	502,536
P	LONG-TERM DEBT	800,000
Q	CAPITAL STOCK	1,550,000
R	RETAINED EARNINGS	331,883
Q + R = S	SHAREHOLDERS' EQUITY	1,881,883
O + P + S = T	TOTAL LIABILITIES & EQUITY	$3,184,419

2

Sales Cycle
When a sale is made, product value is moved from **INVENTORY** on the *Balance Sheet* to **COST OF GOODS SOLD** on the *Income Statement*.

Income Statement

for the period

1	NET SALES	$3,055,560
2	COST OF GOODS SOLD	2,005,830
1 - 2 = 3	GROSS MARGIN	1,049,730
4	SALES & MARKETING	328,523
5	RESEARCH & DEVELOPMENT	26,000
6	GENERAL & ADMINISTRATIVE	203,520
4 + 5 + 6 = 7	OPERATING EXPENSE	558,043
3 - 7 = 8	INCOME FROM OPERATIONS	491,687
9	NET INTEREST INCOME	(100,000)
10	INCOME TAXES	139,804
8 + 9 - 10 = 11	NET INCOME	$251,883

Cash Flow Statement

for the period

a	BEGINNING CASH BALANCE	$155,000
b	CASH RECEIPTS	2,584,900
c	CASH DISBURSEMENTS	2,796,438
b - c = d	CASH FLOW FROM OPERATIONS	(211,538)
e	PP&E PURCHASE	1,750,000
f	NET BORROWINGS	900,000
g	INCOME TAXES PAID	0
h	SALE OF CAPITAL STOCK	1,550,000
a + d - e + f - g + h = i	ENDING CASH BALANCES	$643,462

3

Sales Cycle
When the customer pays for products shipped, the **ACCOUNT RECEIVABLE** on the *Balance Sheet* becomes a **CASH RECEIPT** in the *Cash Flow Statement.*

Balance Sheet

as of period end

A	CASH	$643,462
B	ACCOUNTS RECEIVABLE	454,760
C	INVENTORIES	414,770
D	PREPAID EXPENSES	0
A + B + C + D = E	CURRENT ASSETS	1,512,992
F	OTHER ASSETS	0
G	FIXED ASSETS @ COST	1,750,000
H	ACCUMULATED DEPRECIATION	78,573
G - H = I	NET FIXED ASSETS	1,671,427
E + F + I = J	TOTAL ASSETS	$3,184,419
K	ACCOUNTS PAYABLE	$236,297
L	ACCRUED EXPENSES	26,435
M	CURRENT PORTION OF DEBT	100,000
N	INCOME TAXES PAYABLE	139,804
K + L + M + N = O	CURRENT LIABILITIES	502,536
P	LONG-TERM DEBT	800,000
Q	CAPITAL STOCK	1,550,000
R	RETAINED EARNINGS	331,883
Q + R = S	SHAREHOLDERS' EQUITY	1,881,883
O + P + S = T	TOTAL LIABILITIES & EQUITY	$3,184,419

Income Statement

for the period

	1	NET SALES	$3,055,560
	2	COST OF GOODS SOLD	2,005,830
1 - 2 = 3	3	GROSS MARGIN	1,049,730
	4	SALES & MARKETING	328,523
	5	RESEARCH & DEVELOPMENT	26,000
	6	GENERAL & ADMINISTRATIVE	203,520
4 + 5 + 6 = 7	7	OPERATING EXPENSE	558,043
3 - 7 = 8	8	INCOME FROM OPERATIONS	491,687
	9	NET INTEREST INCOME	(100,000)
	10	INCOME TAXES	139,804
8 + 9 - 10 = 11	11	NET INCOME	$251,883

Cash Flow Statement

for the period

	a	BEGINNING CASH BALANCE	$155,000
	b	CASH RECEIPTS	2,584,900
	c	CASH DISBURSEMENTS	2,796,438
b - c = d	d	CASH FLOW FROM OPERATIONS	(211,538)
	e	PP&E PURCHASE	1,750,000
	f	NET BORROWINGS	900,000
	g	INCOME TAXES PAID	0
	h	SALE OF CAPITAL STOCK	1,550,000
a + d - e + f - g + h = i	i	ENDING CASH BALANCES	$643,462

4

Sales Cycle

When a sale is entered on the *Income Statement* NET INCOME (LOSS) is generated and is added to RETAINED EARNINGS on the Balance Sheet.

Balance Sheet

as of period end

	A	CASH	$643,462
	B	ACCOUNTS RECEIVABLE	454,760
	C	INVENTORIES	414,770
	D	PREPAID EXPENSES	0
A + B + C + D = E	E	CURRENT ASSETS	1,512,992
	F	OTHER ASSETS	0
	G	FIXED ASSETS @ COST	1,750,000
	H	ACCUMULATED DEPRECIATION	78,573
G - H = I	I	NET FIXED ASSETS	1,671,427
E + F + I = J	J	TOTAL ASSETS	$3,184,419
	K	ACCOUNTS PAYABLE	$236,297
	L	ACCRUED EXPENSES	26,435
	M	CURRENT PORTION OF DEBT	100,000
	N	INCOME TAXES PAYABLE	139,804
K + L + M + N = O	O	CURRENT LIABILITIES	502,536
	P	LONG-TERM DEBT	800,000
	Q	CAPITAL STOCK	1,550,000
	R	RETAINED EARNINGS	331,883
Q + R = S	S	SHAREHOLDERS' EQUITY	1,881,883
O + P + S = T	T	TOTAL LIABILITIES & EQUITY	$3,184,419

Income Statement
for the period

1	NET SALES	$3,055,560
2	COST OF GOODS SOLD	2,005,830
1 - 2 = 3	GROSS MARGIN	1,049,730
4	SALES & MARKETING	328,523 ⬆
5	RESEARCH & DEVELOPMENT	26,000 ⬆
6	GENERAL & ADMINISTRATIVE	203,520 ⬆
4 + 5 + 6 = 7	OPERATING EXPENSE	558,043
3 - 7 = 8	INCOME FROM OPERATIONS	491,687
9	NET INTEREST INCOME	(100,000)
10	INCOME TAXES	139,804
8 + 9 - 10 = 11	NET INCOME	$251,883 ⬇

Cash Flow Statement
for the period

a	BEGINNING CASH BALANCE	$155,000
b	CASH RECEIPTS	2,584,900
c	CASH DISBURSEMENTS	2,796,438
b - c = d	CASH FLOW FROM OPERATIONS	(211,538)
e	PP&E PURCHASE	1,750,000
f	NET BORROWINGS	900,000
g	INCOME TAXES PAID	0
h	SALE OF CAPITAL STOCK	1,550,000
a + d - e + f - g + h = i	ENDING CASH BALANCES	$643,462

Balance Sheet
as of period end

A	CASH	$643,462
B	ACCOUNTS RECEIVABLE	454,760
C	INVENTORIES	414,770
D	PREPAID EXPENSES	0
A + B + C + D = E	CURRENT ASSETS	1,512,992
F	OTHER ASSETS	0
G	FIXED ASSETS @ COST	1,750,000
H	ACCUMULATED DEPRECIATION	78,573
G - H = I	NET FIXED ASSETS	1,671,427
E + F + I = J	TOTAL ASSETS	$3,184,419
K	ACCOUNTS PAYABLE	$236,297 ⬆
L	ACCRUED EXPENSES	26,435
M	CURRENT PORTION OF DEBT	100,000
N	INCOME TAXES PAYABLE	139,804
K + L + M + N = O	CURRENT LIABILITIES	502,536
P	LONG-TERM DEBT	800,000
Q	CAPITAL STOCK	1,550,000
R	RETAINED EARNINGS	331,883 ⬇
Q + R = S	SHAREHOLDERS' EQUITY	1,881,883
O + P + S = T	TOTAL LIABILITIES & EQUITY	$3,184,419

1 Expense Cycle EXPENSES, when incurred and entered on the *Income Statement,* become ACCOUNTS PAYABLE on the *Balance Sheet.*

EXPENSES reduce NET INCOME on the *Income Statement* and also in RETAINED EARNINGS on the *Balance Sheet.*

Income Statement
for the period

1	NET SALES	$3,055,560
2	COST OF GOODS SOLD	2,005,830
1 - 2 = 3	GROSS MARGIN	1,049,730
4	SALES & MARKETING	328,523
5	RESEARCH & DEVELOPMENT	26,000
6	GENERAL & ADMINISTRATIVE	203,520
4 + 5 + 6 = 7	OPERATING EXPENSE	558,043
3 - 7 = 8	INCOME FROM OPERATIONS	491,687
9	NET INTEREST INCOME	(100,000)
10	INCOME TAXES	139,804
8 + 9 - 10 = 11	NET INCOME	$251,883

Cash Flow Statement
for the period

a	BEGINNING CASH BALANCE	$155,000
b	CASH RECEIPTS	2,584,900
c	CASH DISBURSEMENTS	2,796,438
b - c = d	CASH FLOW FROM OPERATIONS	(211,538)
e	PP&E PURCHASE	1,750,000
f	NET BORROWINGS	900,000
g	INCOME TAXES PAID	0
h	SALE OF CAPITAL STOCK	1,550,000
a + d - e + f - g + h = i	ENDING CASH BALANCES	$643,462

Balance Sheet
as of period end

A	CASH	$643,462
B	ACCOUNTS RECEIVABLE	454,760
C	INVENTORIES	414,770
D	PREPAID EXPENSES	0
A + B + C + D = E	CURRENT ASSETS	1,512,992
F	OTHER ASSETS	0
G	FIXED ASSETS @ COST	1,750,000
H	ACCUMULATED DEPRECIATION	78,573
G - H = I	NET FIXED ASSETS	1,671,427
E + F + I = J	TOTAL ASSETS	$3,184,419
K	ACCOUNTS PAYABLE	$236,297
L	ACCRUED EXPENSES	26,435
M	CURRENT PORTION OF DEBT	100,000
N	INCOME TAXES PAYABLE	139,804
K + L + M + N = O	CURRENT LIABILITIES	502,536
P	LONG-TERM DEBT	800,000
Q	CAPITAL STOCK	1,550,000
R	RETAINED EARNINGS	331,883
Q + R = S	SHAREHOLDERS' EQUITY	1,881,883
O + P + S = T	TOTAL LIABILITIES & EQUITY	$3,184,419

2 **Expense Cycle**
When paid, ACCOUNTS PAYABLE on the *Balance Sheet* become CASH DISBURSEMENTS and lower CASH.

Income Statement

for the period

1	NET SALES		$3,055,560
2	COST OF GOODS SOLD		2,005,830
1 - 2 = 3	GROSS MARGIN		1,049,730
4	SALES & MARKETING		328,523
5	RESEARCH & DEVELOPMENT		26,000
6	GENERAL & ADMINISTRATIVE		203,520
4 + 5 + 6 = 7	OPERATING EXPENSE		558,043
3 - 7 = 8	INCOME FROM OPERATIONS		491,687
9	NET INTEREST INCOME		(100,000)
10	INCOME TAXES		139,804
8 + 9 - 10 = 11	NET INCOME		$251,883

Cash Flow Statement

for the period

a	BEGINNING CASH BALANCE	$155,000
b	CASH RECEIPTS	2,584,900
c	CASH DISBURSEMENTS	2,796,438
b - c = d	CASH FLOW FROM OPERATIONS	(211,538)
e	PP&E PURCHASE	1,750,000
f	NET BORROWINGS	900,000 ⬆
g	INCOME TAXES PAID	0
h	SALE OF CAPITAL STOCK	1,550,000
a + d - e + f - g + h = i	ENDING CASH BALANCES	$643,462 ⬆

① Investment Cycle
NET BORROWINGS, when entered on the *Cash Flow Statement,* increase both **CASH** and **DEBT** on the *Balance Sheet.*

Repayment in *less* than one year

or

Repayment in *more* than one year

Balance Sheet

as of period end

A	CASH	$643,462 ⬆
B	ACCOUNTS RECEIVABLE	454,760
C	INVENTORIES	414,770
D	PREPAID EXPENSES	0
A + B + C + D = E	CURRENT ASSETS	1,512,992
F	OTHER ASSETS	0
G	FIXED ASSETS @ COST	1,750,000
H	ACCUMULATED DEPRECIATION	78,573
G - H = I	NET FIXED ASSETS	1,671,427
E + F + I = J	TOTAL ASSETS	$3,184,419
K	ACCOUNTS PAYABLE	$236,297
L	ACCRUED EXPENSES	26,435
M	CURRENT PORTION OF DEBT	100,000 ⬆
N	INCOME TAXES PAYABLE	139,804
K + L + M + N = O	CURRENT LIABILITIES	502,536
P	LONG-TERM DEBT	800,000 ⬆
Q	CAPITAL STOCK	1,550,000
R	RETAINED EARNINGS	331,883
Q + R = S	SHAREHOLDERS' EQUITY	1,881,883
O + P + S = T	TOTAL LIABILITIES & EQUITY	$3,184,419

Income Statement

for the period

	1	NET SALES	$3,055,560
	2	COST OF GOODS SOLD	2,005,830
1 - 2 = 3		GROSS MARGIN	1,049,730
	4	SALES & MARKETING	328,523
	5	RESEARCH & DEVELOPMENT	26,000
	6	GENERAL & ADMINISTRATIVE	203,520
4 + 5 + 6 = 7		OPERATING EXPENSE	558,043
3 - 7 = 8		INCOME FROM OPERATIONS	491,687
	9	NET INTEREST INCOME	(100,000)
	10	INCOME TAXES	139,804
8 + 9 - 10 = 11		NET INCOME	$251,883

Cash Flow Statement

for the period

	a	BEGINNING CASH BALANCE	$155,000
	b	CASH RECEIPTS	2,584,900
	c	CASH DISBURSEMENTS	2,796,438
b - c = d		CASH FLOW FROM OPERATIONS	(211,538)
	e	PP&E PURCHASE	1,750,000
	f	NET BORROWINGS	900,000
	g	INCOME TAXES PAID	0
	h	SALE OF CAPITAL STOCK	1,550,000 ↑
a + d - e + f - g + h = i		ENDING CASH BALANCES	$643,462 ↑

2

Investment Cycle
Selling stock increases both
CASH and **CAPITAL STOCK** on
the *Balance Sheet.*

Balance Sheet

as of period end

	A	CASH	$643,462 ↑
	B	ACCOUNTS RECEIVABLE	454,760
	C	INVENTORIES	414,770
	D	PREPAID EXPENSES	0
A + B + C + D = E		CURRENT ASSETS	1,512,992
	F	OTHER ASSETS	0
	G	FIXED ASSETS @ COST	1,750,000
	H	ACCUMULATED DEPRECIATION	78,573
G - H = I		NET FIXED ASSETS	1,671,427
E + F + I = J		TOTAL ASSETS	$3,184,419
	K	ACCOUNTS PAYABLE	$236,297
	L	ACCRUED EXPENSES	26,435
	M	CURRENT PORTION OF DEBT	100,000
	N	INCOME TAXES PAYABLE	139,804
K + L + M + N = O		CURRENT LIABILITIES	502,536
	P	LONG-TERM DEBT	800,000
	Q	CAPITAL STOCK	1,550,000 ↑
	R	RETAINED EARNINGS	331,883
Q + R = S		SHAREHOLDERS' EQUITY	1,881,883
O + P + S = T		TOTAL LIABILITIES & EQUITY	$3,184,419

Income Statement
for the period

1		NET SALES	$3,055,560
2		COST OF GOODS SOLD	2,005,830
1 - 2 = 3		GROSS MARGIN	1,049,730
4		SALES & MARKETING	328,523
5		RESEARCH & DEVELOPMENT	26,000
6		GENERAL & ADMINISTRATIVE	203,520
4 + 5 + 6 = 7		OPERATING EXPENSE	558,043
3 - 7 = 8		INCOME FROM OPERATIONS	491,687
9		NET INTEREST INCOME	(100,000)
10		INCOME TAXES	139,804
8 + 9 - 10 = 11		NET INCOME	$251,883

> Over time, depreciation expenses on the *Income Statement* increases **ACCUMULATED DEPRECIATION** lowering **NET ASSET VALUE.**

Cash Flow Statement
for the period

a		BEGINNING CASH BALANCE	$155,000
b		CASH RECEIPTS	2,584,900
c		CASH DISBURSEMENTS	2,796,438
b - c = d		CASH FLOW FROM OPERATIONS	(211,538)
e		PP&E PURCHASE	1,750,000
f		NET BOROWINGS	900,000
g		INCOME TAXES PAID	0
h		SALE OF CAPITAL STOCK	1,550,000
a + d - e + f - g + h = i		ENDING CASH BALANCES	$643,462

> When equipment (**PP&E**) is purchased, **FIXED ASSETS @ COST** increases and cash decreases.

Balance Sheet
as of period end

A		CASH	$643,462
B		ACCOUNTS RECEIVABLE	454,760
C		INVENTORIES	414,770
D		PREPAID EXPENSES	0
A + B + C + D = E		CURRENT ASSETS	1,512,992
F		OTHER ASSETS	0
G		FIXED ASSETS @ COST	1,750,000
H		ACCUMULATED DEPRECIATION	78,573
G - H = I		NET FIXED ASSETS	1,671,427
E + F + I = J		TOTAL ASSETS	$3,184,419
K		ACCOUNTS PAYABLE	$236,297
L		ACCRUED EXPENSES	26,435
M		CURRENT PORTION OF DEBT	100,000
N		INCOME TAXES PAYABLE	139,804
K + L + M + N = O		CURRENT LIABILITIES	502,536
P		LONG-TERM DEBT	800,000
Q		CAPITAL STOCK	1,550,000
R		RETAINED EARNINGS	331,883
Q + R = S		SHAREHOLDERS' EQUITY	1,881,883
O + P + S = T		TOTAL LIABILITIES & EQUITY	$3,184,419

> **Fixed Asset Cycle**

Section B. Transactions:
Exploits of AppleSeed Enterprises, Inc.

About This Section

We are now at the heart of learning how financial statements work. In the previous section, we reviewed financial statement structure and vocabulary, and saw examples of how the three main financial statements interact.

> **To give a real-life flavor to our study of accounting and financial reporting, we will draft the books of a hypothetical company, *AppleSeed Enterprises, Inc.***

The following pages chronicle 33 specific business transactions in Appleseed's financial life. We'll show how Appleseed constructs and maintains its books to report accurately the company's financial position. In addition, we will discuss additional financial terms and then show examples of applying financial concepts required to keep a company's books.

Each new business transaction means new "postings" to AppleSeed's financial statements as our company goes about its business of making and selling delicious applesauce. As we discuss each transaction, you'll get a hands-on feel for how a company's books are constructed. Each transaction is described in a two-page spread. See the "annotated" transaction spread on the next two pages.

Right-Hand Page. The right-hand page of each two-page transaction spread describes an AppleSeed business transaction, discussing both business rationale and financial effect. Note that numbered shadowboxes are placed beside descriptions of specific financial postings for the transaction. These shadowboxes correspond to the entries beside the smaller numbered shadowboxes on the left-hand page showing the company's three main financial statements.

As you begin to study each new transaction, first read and understand the right-hand page description. Then go to the left-hand page to see actual postings to Apple-Seed's three financial statements.

Left-Hand Page. The left-hand page of each transaction spread shows Apple-Seed's Income Statement, Balance Sheet and Cash Flow *prior* to the transaction and then *after* the transaction. Depending on the type of transaction, all three financial statements may be changed, or just two, or one or none may change.

Individual account changes are shown on left-hand pages this way:

1. The *first numeric column* shows all prior account values as of the last transaction.

2. The *second numeric column* (with small shadowboxes) shows account values posted for the transaction as described on the right-hand page.

3. The *third numeric column* shows the account values after the transaction has been posted, that is, after the second column numbers are added to the first.

Note these last values are those that will appear as the "prior" values for the next transaction

∼

That is all there is to accounting and financial reporting. It is really not rocket science at all, just a little addition and subtraction. With some effort and this book, you will find enlightenment.

However, remember, our analysis is just an overview. If you need details (and there are many), just ask an accountant associate a good question based upon the knowledge you have acquired from this book. They will be so happy to get an intelligent question from a non-financial type, they will bend over backward to answer.

Welcome to AppleSeed Enterprises!

Transaction Spread
Left-Hand Page

> Amounts to be posted for each account in this transaction.

> Account values prior to posting this transaction.

> Account values after posting transaction.

Financial Statements

Income Statement

for the period including Transactions 1 through 4		prior	+	transaction	=	sum
1	NET SALES	$0		—		$0
2	COST OF GOODS SOLD	0		—		0
1 - 2 = 3	GROSS MARGIN	0				0
4	SALES & MARKETING	0		—		0
5	RESEARCH & DEVELOPMENT	0		—		0
6	GENERAL & ADMINISTRATIVE	6,230		—		6,230
4 + 5 + 6 = 7	OPERATING EXPENSE	6,230				6,230
3 - 7 = 8	INCOME FROM OPERATIONS	(6,230)				(6,230)
9	NET INTEREST INCOME	0		—		0
10	INCOME TAXES	0		—		0
8 + 9 - 10 = 11	NET INCOME	($6,230)		0		($6,230)

IS Transaction Sum

Cash Flow Statement

for the period including Transactions 1 through 4		prior	+	transaction	=	sum
a	BEGINNING CASH BALANCE	$0				$0
b	CASH RECEIPTS	0		—		0
c	CASH DISBURSEMENTS	3,370		—		3,370
b - c = d	CASH FLOW FROM OPERATIONS	(3,370)				(3,370)
e	PP&E PURCHASE	0	[1]	1,500,000		1,500,000
f	NET BORROWINGS	1,000,000		—		1,000,000
g	INCOME TAXES PAID	0		—		0
h	SALE OF CAPITAL STOCK	1,550,000		—		1,550,000
a + d - e + f - g + h = i	ENDING CASH BALANCES	$2,546,630		(1,500,000)		$1,046,630

CF Transaction Sum

Balance Sheet

as of this Transaction 4		prior	+	transaction	=	sum
A	CASH	$2,546,630	[2]	(1,500,000)		$1,046,630
B	ACCOUNTS RECEIVABLE	0		—		0
C	INVENTORIES	0		—		0
D	PREPAID EXPENSES	0		—		0
A + B + C + D = E	CURRENT ASSETS	2,546,630				1,046,630
F	OTHER ASSETS	0		—		0
G	FIXED ASSETS @ COST	0	[3]	1,500,000		1,500,000
H	ACCUMULATED DEPRECIATION	0		—		0
G - H = I	NET FIXED ASSETS	0				1,500,000
E + F + I = J	TOTAL ASSETS	$2,546,630		0		$2,546,630

Assets Sum

K	ACCOUNTS PAYABLE			—		0
L	ACCRUED EXPENSES			—		2,860
M	CURRENT PORTION OF DEBT			—		100,000
N	INCOME TAXES PAYABLE			—		0
K + L + M + N = O	CURRENT LIABILITIES					102,860
P	LONG-TERM DEBT			—		900,000
Q	CAPITAL STOCK			—		1,550,000
R	RETAINED EARNINGS			—		(6,230)
Q + R = S	SHAREHOLDERS' EQUITY					1,543,770
O + P + S = T	TOTAL LIABILITIES & EQ			0		$2,546,630

Liabilities & Equity Sum

> Amounts to be posted as described on the facing page beside the corresponding shadowbox number.

> **Transactions are described in detail at the top of right-hand pages.**

T4. Pay $ illion for a building to be used for office, n facturing and warehouse space. Set up a d eciation schedule.

You ha found just the perfect building for AppleSeed Enterprises. The 1 0,000 square foot building is appraised at $1.1 million and the land at $550,000. The building is nicely laid out with 90,000 square feet of manufacturing and warehouse space and 10,000 square feet for offices.

You negotiate well and drive a hard bargain. You and the seller agree on a sales price for building and land of $1.5 million, a good deal for AppleSeed.

In this transaction we will buy the building, AppleSeed Enterprises' first *fixed asset*. Fixed assets (also called *"PP&E"* for *Property, Plant & Equipment*) are long-lived productive assets such as buildings, machinery

and fixtures, that are used to make, store, ship and sell product. Fixed assets are also sometimes called *capital equipment*. When you acquire a fixed asset, you add its value to the *Balance Sheet* as an asset.

Accounting convention and IRS regulations do not allow you to immediately "expense" the cost of acquiring a fixed asset. Because fixed assets have a long productive life, you can expense only a portion of their purchase price each year as you use them. **This yearly expense is called depreciation.**

We will deal with the depreciation concept in much more detail in later transactions.

Transaction: Purchase 100,000 square foot building and land for $1.5 million in cash. This facility will serve as AppleSeed Enterprises' headquarters, manufacturing facility and warehouse.

1 Write a check for $1.5 million to the seller of the building. Record this cash transaction under **PP&E PURCHASE** in the *Cash Flow Statement*.

2 Then, lower **CASH** in the *Balance Sheet* by the $1.5 million check that you wrote to buy the building.

3 Now you must make another entry to bring the *Balance Sheet* b ck into balance. Increase **FIXED ASSETS @ COST** on the *Balance Shee* the $1.5 million purchase price of the building. Note that th t is recorded at actual cost, not at the appraised or any oth tion.

> **Read the account posting descriptions. Then look at the corresponding shadowboxes in the financial statements on the left-hand page to see how the changes are made.**

Chapter 6. Startup Financing and Staffing

Welcome to our little business—AppleSeed Enterprises, Inc. Imagine that you are AppleSeed's entrepreneurial CEO. You also double as treasurer and chief financial officer.

You have just incorporated (in Delaware) and invested $50,000 of your own money into the company—well, actually it's your Great Aunt Lillian's money. You're going to need much more capital to get into production, but these initial transactions will start up the business. Follow along...we have a lot to do.

$\sim$

Transaction 1.   Sell 150,000 shares of AppleSeed's common stock ($1 par value) for $10 per share.

Transaction 2.   Pay yourself your first month's salary. Book all payroll-associated fringe benfits and taxes.

Transaction 3.   Borrow $1 million to buy a building. Terms of this 10-year mortgage are 10% per annum.

Transaction 4.   Pay $1.5 million for a building to be used for office, manufacturing and warehouse space. Set up a depreciation schedule.

Transaction 5.   Hire administrative and sales staff. Pay first month's salaries and book fringe benefits and taxes.

Transaction 6.   Pay employee health, life and disability insurance premiums plus FICA, unemployment and also withholding taxes.

Income Statement

for the period including Transactions 1 through 1	prior	+	transaction	=	sum
1 NET SALES	$0		—		$0
2 COST OF GOODS SOLD	0		—		0
1 - 2 = 3 GROSS MARGIN	0				0
4 SALES & MARKETING	0		—		0
5 RESEARCH & DEVELOPMENT	0		—		0
6 GENERAL & ADMINISTRATIVE	0		—		0
4 + 5 + 6 = 7 OPERATING EXPENSE	0				0
3 - 7 = 8 INCOME FROM OPERATIONS	0				0
9 NET INTEREST INCOME	0		—		0
10 INCOME TAXES	0		—		0
8 + 9 - 10 = 11 NET INCOME	$0		0		$0

IS Transaction Sum

Cash Flow Statement

for the period including Transactions 1 through 1	prior	+	transaction	=	sum
a BEGINNING CASH BALANCE	$0				$0
b CASH RECEIPTS	0		—		0
c CASH DISBURSEMENTS	0		—		0
b - c = d CASH FLOW FROM OPERATIONS	0				0
e PP&E PURCHASE	0		—		0
f NET BORROWINGS	0		—		0
g INCOME TAXES PAID	0		—		0
h SALE OF CAPITAL STOCK	50,000		☐1 1,500,000		1,550,000
a + d - e + f - g + h = i ENDING CASH BALANCES	$50,000		1,500,000		$1,550,000

CF Transaction Sum

Balance Sheet

as of this Transaction 1	prior	+	transaction	=	sum
A CASH	$50,000		☐2 1,500,000		$1,550,000
B ACCOUNTS RECEIVABLE	0		—		0
C INVENTORIES	0		—		0
D PREPAID EXPENSES	0		—		0
A + B + C + D = E CURRENT ASSETS	50,000				1,550,000
F OTHER ASSETS	0		—		0
G FIXED ASSETS @ COST	0		—		0
H ACCUMULATED DEPRECIATION	0		—		0
G - H = I NET FIXED ASSETS	0				0
E + F + I = J TOTAL ASSETS	$50,000		1,500,000		$1,550,000

Assets Sum

	prior	+	transaction	=	sum
K ACCOUNTS PAYABLE	$0		—		0
L ACCRUED EXPENSES	0		—		0
M CURRENT PORTION OF DEBT	0		—		0
N INCOME TAXES PAYABLE	0		—		0
K + L + M + N = O CURRENT LIABILITIES	0				0
P LONG-TERM DEBT	0		—		0
Q CAPITAL STOCK	50,000		☐3 1,500,000		1,550,000
R RETAINED EARNINGS	0		—		0
Q + R = S SHAREHOLDERS' EQUITY	50,000				1,550,000
O + P + S = T TOTAL LIABILITIES & EQUITY	$50,000		1,500,000		$1,550,000

Liabilities & Equity Sum

T1. Sell 150,000 shares of AppleSeed's common stock ($1 par value) for $10 per share.

Shares of stock represent *ownership* in a corporation. A corporation can issue a single class or multiple classes of stock, each with different rights and privileges.

Common stock has the lowest preference to receive assets if the corporation is liquidated. Common stockholders vote for the board of directors.

Preferred stock has a preference over common stock when the corporation pays a dividend or distributes assets in liquidation. Usually, preferred stockholders do not have the right to vote for directors.

Note that claims of both the common and preferred stockholders are junior to claims of bondholders or other creditors of the company.

Par value is the dollar amount that is assigned to shares by the company's charter. Par value has little significance other than to keep track of stock splits.

There is no connection between the stated par value and any *underlying worth* of the stock or the enterprise.

Transaction: A group of investors is willing to exchange their $1.5 million in cash for stock certificates representing 150,000 common shares of AppleSeed Enterprises, Inc.

Note: When you formed the company, you bought 50,000 shares of "founder's stock" at $1 per share for a total investment of $50,000 in cash. Thus, after this sale to the investor group, there will be 200,000 shares outstanding. They will own 75% of AppleSeed and you will own the rest

1 Take the money, issue the investors common stock certificates and run to the bank to deposit the check in AppleSeed's checking account. The company has received cash, so on the *Cash Flow Statement* record the $1.5 million as **SALE OF CAPITAL STOCK**.

2 This $1.5 million in cash is a new asset for the corporation, so increase **CASH** in the *Balance Sheet* by the amount received from the investors.

3 Each new asset must create a corresponding liability (or offsetting asset) or the *Balance Sheet* will be out of balance. Issuing stock creates a liability for the company. In effect, AppleSeed "owes" the new stockholders a portion of its assets. So, increase the liability **CAPITAL STOCK** on the *Balance Sheet* by $1.5 million.

Financial Statements

Income Statement

for the period including Transactions 1 through 2	prior	+	transaction	=	sum
1 NET SALES	$0		—		$0
2 COST OF GOODS SOLD	0		—		0
1 - 2 = 3 GROSS MARGIN	0				0
4 SALES & MARKETING	0		—		0
5 RESEARCH & DEVELOPMENT	0		—		0
6 GENERAL & ADMINISTRATIVE	0	**1A**	6,230		6,230
4 + 5 + 6 = 7 OPERATING EXPENSE	0				6,230
3 - 7 = 8 INCOME FROM OPERATIONS	0				(6,230)
9 NET INTEREST INCOME	0		—		0
10 INCOME TAXES	0		—		0
8 + 9 - 10 = 11 NET INCOME	$0		(6,230)		($6,230)

IS Transaction Sum

Cash Flow Statement

for the period including Transactions 1 through 2	prior	+	transaction	=	sum
a BEGINNING CASH BALANCE	$0				$0
b CASH RECEIPTS	0		—		0
c CASH DISBURSEMENTS	0	**2A**	3,370		3,370
b - c = d CASH FLOW FROM OPERATIONS	0				(3,370)
e PP&E PURCHASE	0		—		0
f NET BORROWINGS	0		—		0
g INCOME TAXES PAID	0		—		0
h SALE OF CAPITAL STOCK	1,550,000		—		1,550,000
a + d - e + f - g + h = i ENDING CASH BALANCES	$1,550,000		(3,370)		$1,546,630

CF Transaction Sum

Balance Sheet

as of this Transaction 2	prior	+	transaction	=	sum
A CASH	$1,550,000	**2B**	(3,370)		$1,546,630
B ACCOUNTS RECEIVABLE	0		—		0
C INVENTORIES	0		—		0
D PREPAID EXPENSES	0		—		0
A + B + C + D = E CURRENT ASSETS	1,550,000				1,546,630
F OTHER ASSETS	0		—		0
G FIXED ASSETS @ COST	0		—		0
H ACCUMULATED DEPRECIATION	0		—		0
G - H = I NET FIXED ASSETS	0				0
E + F + I = J TOTAL ASSETS	$1,550,000		(3,370)		$1,546,630

Assets Sum

	prior	+	transaction	=	sum
K ACCOUNTS PAYABLE	$0		—		0
L ACCRUED EXPENSES	0	**3**	2,860		2,860
M CURRENT PORTION OF DEBT	0		—		0
N INCOME TAXES PAYABLE	0		—		0
K + L + M + N = O CURRENT LIABILITIES	0				2,860
P LONG-TERM DEBT	0		—		0
Q CAPITAL STOCK	1,550,000		—		1,550,000
R RETAINED EARNINGS	0	**1B**	(6,230)		(6,230)
Q + R = S SHAREHOLDERS' EQUITY	1,550,000				1,543,770
O + P + S = T TOTAL LIABILITIES & EQUITY	$1,550,000		(3,370)		$1,546,630

Liabilities & Equity Sum

T2. Pay yourself a month's salary. Book all payroll associated fringe benefits and taxes.

Congratulations! The board of directors of AppleSeed Enterprises, Inc., has hired you to manage the company at the grand salary of $5,000 per month.

Before you spend all your newfound wealth, let's calculate: (1) your actual take-home pay; (2) the cut for taxes; and (3) the total expense to the company for fringe benefits and payroll taxes.

See the table at right. It costs Apple-Seed a total of $6,230 to pay your $5,000 in salary, even though you only receive $3,370 in your paycheck.

Salary & Employment Expenses

	PAY TO EMPLOYEES	PAY TO OTHERS
MONTHLY SALARY	$5,000	
EMPLOYEE'S FICA	$(380)	$380
FEDERAL/STATE WITHHOLDING	$(1,250)	$1,250
EMPLOYER'S FICA		$380
WORKMEN'S COMPENSATION		$100
UNEMPLOYMENT INSURANCE		$250
HEALTH & LIFE INSURANCE		$500
TOTALS PER MONTH	$3,370	$2,860
TOTAL PAID TO EMPLOYEES & OTHERS		$6,230

Transaction: Book all payroll-associated company expenses totaling $6,230 including salary, employer's contribution to FICA (Social Security) and various insurance expenses. Issue yourself a payroll check for $3,370 (your $5,000 monthly salary minus $1,250 in federal and state withholding tax and $380 for your own contribution to FICA).

1 (1A) Salary and fringes are expenses that decrease income. Add the total monthly payroll expense of $6,230 to GENERAL & ADMINISTRATIVE expenses in the *Income Statement*. (1B) Also decrease RETAINED EARNINGS in the *Balance Sheet* by the same amount.

2 (2A) So far your payroll check is the only cash that has left the company. List the $3,370 check under CASH DISBURSEMENTS in the *Cash Flow Statement*. (2B) Also decrease CASH in the *Balance Sheet* by the same amount.

3 The remaining $2,860 in expenses—due to the government and to various insurance companies—is an obligation of the company not yet discharged (that is, owed but not yet paid). Enter this amount under ACCRUED EXPENSES in the liability section of the *Balance Sheet*.

$\sim$

Income Statement

for the period including Transactions 1 through 3		prior	+	transaction	=	sum
1	NET SALES	$0		—		$0
2	COST OF GOODS SOLD	0		—		0
1 - 2 = 3	GROSS MARGIN	0				0
4	SALES & MARKETING	0		—		0
5	RESEARCH & DEVELOPMENT	0		—		0
6	GENERAL & ADMINISTRATIVE	6,230		—		6,230
4 + 5 + 6 = 7	OPERATING EXPENSE	6,230				6,230
3 - 7 = 8	INCOME FROM OPERATIONS	(6,230)				(6,230)
9	NET INTEREST INCOME	0		—		0
10	INCOME TAXES	0		—		0
8 + 9 - 10 = 11	NET INCOME	($6,230)		0		($6,230)

IS Transaction Sum

Cash Flow Statement

for the period including Transactions 1 through 3		prior	+	transaction	=	sum
a	BEGINNING CASH BALANCE	$0				$0
b	CASH RECEIPTS	0		—		0
c	CASH DISBURSEMENTS	3,370		—		3,370
b - c = d	CASH FLOW FROM OPERATIONS	(3,370)				(3,370)
e	PP&E PURCHASE	0		—		0
f	NET BORROWINGS	0	**1A**	1,000,000		1,000,000
g	INCOME TAXES PAID	0		—		0
h	SALE OF CAPITAL STOCK	1,550,000		—		1,550,000
a + d - e + f - g + h = i	ENDING CASH BALANCES	$1,546,630		1,000,000		$2,546,630

CF Transaction Sum

Balance Sheet

as of this Transaction 3		prior	+	transaction	=	sum
A	CASH	$1,546,630	**1B**	1,000,000		$2,546,630
B	ACCOUNTS RECEIVABLE	0		—		0
C	INVENTORIES	0		—		0
D	PREPAID EXPENSES	0		—		0
A + B + C + D = E	CURRENT ASSETS	1,546,630				2,546,630
F	OTHER ASSETS	0		—		0
G	FIXED ASSETS @ COST	0		—		0
H	ACCUMULATED DEPRECIATION	0		—		0
G - H = I	NET FIXED ASSETS	0				0
E + F + I = J	TOTAL ASSETS	$1,546,630		1,000,000		$2,546,630
				Assets Sum		
K	ACCOUNTS PAYABLE	$0		—		0
L	ACCRUED EXPENSES	2,860		—		2,860
M	CURRENT PORTION OF DEBT	0	**2**	100,000		100,000
N	INCOME TAXES PAYABLE	0		—		0
K + L + M + N = O	CURRENT LIABILITIES	2,860				102,860
P	LONG-TERM DEBT	0	**3**	900,000		900,000
Q	CAPITAL STOCK	1,550,000		—		1,550,000
R	RETAINED EARNINGS	(6,230)		—		(6,230)
Q + R = S	SHAREHOLDERS' EQUITY	1,543,770				1,543,770
O + P + S = T	TOTAL LIABILITIES & EQUITY	$1,546,630		1,000,000		$2,546,630

Liabilities & Equity Sum

T3. Borrow $1 million to buy a building. Terms of this 10-year mortgage are 10% interest per annum.

Go to the bank and apply for a loan to buy a building to (1) manufacture and warehouse applesauce, and (2) house the administrative and sales activities of the company.

The friendly loan officer agrees that AppleSeed has a strong equity capital base and good prospects. She agrees to lend you a cool million to buy the building but demands that you pledge all the assets of the company to collateralize the loan.

She also asks for your personal guarantee to repay the loan if the company can not. What do you say? The correct answer is no. If the business fails, you don't want to lose your home too.

You and your friendly banker agree on a 10-year loan amortization (that is, payback) schedule shown on the right.

Loan Amortization Schedule

YEAR	INTEREST PAYMENTS	PRINCIPAL PAYMENTS	OUTSTANDING PRINCIPAL
1	$100,000	$100,000	$900,000
2	$90,000	$100,000	$800,000
3	$80,000	$100,000	$700,000
4	$70,000	$100,000	$600,000
5	$60,000	$100,000	$500,000
6	$50,000	$100,000	$400,000
7	$40,000	$100,000	$300,000
8	$30,000	$100,000	$200,000
9	$20,000	$100,000	$100,000
10	$10,000	$100,000	$0
TOTAL	$550,000	$1,000,000	

Transaction: Borrow $1 million to purchase an all-purpose building. This term note will run for 10 years, calling for yearly principal payments of $100,000 plus interest at a rate of 10% per annum.

1 (1A) At the loan closing the friendly banker deposits $1 million in your checking account, thus increasing NET BORROWINGS in the *Cash Flow Statement*. (1B) Remember also, CASH increases by $1 million in the assets section of the *Balance Sheet*.

2 The CURRENT PORTION OF DEBT (that is, the amount that will be repaid this year) is $100,000 and is listed in the current liabilities section of the *Balance Sheet*.

3 The remaining debt of $900,000 will be repaid more than one year in the future and thus is listed as long-term debt in the *Balance Sheet*.

∼

Income Statement

	for the period including Transactions 1 through 4	*prior*	+	*transaction*	=	*sum*
1	NET SALES	$0		—		$0
2	COST OF GOODS SOLD	0		—		0
1 - 2 = 3	GROSS MARGIN	0				0
4	SALES & MARKETING	0		—		0
5	RESEARCH & DEVELOPMENT	0		—		0
6	GENERAL & ADMINISTRATIVE	6,230		—		6,230
4 + 5 + 6 = 7	OPERATING EXPENSE	6,230				6,230
3 - 7 = 8	INCOME FROM OPERATIONS	(6,230)				(6,230)
9	NET INTEREST INCOME	0		—		0
10	INCOME TAXES	0		—		0
8 + 9 - 10 = 11	NET INCOME	($6,230)		0		($6,230)

IS Transaction Sum

Cash Flow Statement

	for the period including Transactions 1 through 4	*prior*	+	*transaction*	=	*sum*
a	BEGINNING CASH BALANCE	$0				$0
b	CASH RECEIPTS	0		—		0
c	CASH DISBURSEMENTS	3,370		—		3,370
b - c = d	CASH FLOW FROM OPERATIONS	(3,370)				(3,370)
e	PP&E PURCHASE	0	**1**	1,500,000		1,500,000
f	NET BORROWINGS	1,000,000		—		1,000,000
g	INCOME TAXES PAID	0		—		0
h	SALE OF CAPITAL STOCK	1,550,000		—		1,550,000
a + d - e + f - g + h = i	ENDING CASH BALANCES	$2,546,630		(1,500,000)		$1,046,630

CF Transaction Sum

Balance Sheet

	as of this Transaction 4	*prior*	+	*transaction*	=	*sum*
A	CASH	$2,546,630	**2**	(1,500,000)		$1,046,630
B	ACCOUNTS RECEIVABLE	0		—		0
C	INVENTORIES	0		—		0
D	PREPAID EXPENSES	0		—		0
A + B + C + D = E	CURRENT ASSETS	2,546,630				1,046,630
F	OTHER ASSETS	0		—		0
G	FIXED ASSETS @ COST	0	**3**	1,500,000		1,500,000
H	ACCUMULATED DEPRECIATION	0		—		0
G - H = I	NET FIXED ASSETS	0				1,500,000
E + F + I = J	TOTAL ASSETS	$2,546,630		0		$2,546,630

Assets Sum

K	ACCOUNTS PAYABLE	$0		—		0
L	ACCRUED EXPENSES	2,860		—		2,860
M	CURRENT PORTION OF DEBT	100,000		—		100,000
N	INCOME TAXES PAYABLE	0		—		0
K + L + M + N = O	CURRENT LIABILITIES	102,860				102,860
P	LONG-TERM DEBT	900,000		—		900,000
Q	CAPITAL STOCK	1,550,000		—		1,550,000
R	RETAINED EARNINGS	(6,230)		—		(6,230)
Q + R = S	SHAREHOLDERS' EQUITY	1,543,770				1,543,770
O + P + S = T	TOTAL LIABILITIES & EQUITY	$2,546,630		0		$2,546,630

Liabilities & Equity Sum

T4. Pay $1.5 million for a building to be used for office, manufacturing and warehouse space. Set up a depreciation schedule.

You have found the perfect building for AppleSeed Enterprises, Inc.. This 100,000 square-foot building is appraised at $1.1 million and the land at $550,000. The building is nicely laid out with 90,000 square feet of manufacturing and warehouse space and 10,000 square feet for offices.

You negotiate well and drive a hard bargain. You and the seller agree on a sale price for building and land of $1.5 million, a good deal for AppleSeed.

In this transaction we will buy the building, AppleSeed Enterprises's first *fixed asset*. Fixed assets (also called *PP&E* for *Property, Plant & Equipment*) are long-lived productive assets such as buildings,

machinery and fixtures, that are used to make, store, ship and sell product. Fixed assets are also sometimes called *capital equipment*. When you acquire a fixed asset, you add its value to the *Balance Sheet* as an asset.

Accounting convention and IRS regulations do not allow you to immediately "expense" the cost of acquiring a fixed asset. Because fixed assets have a long productive life, you can expense only a portion of their purchase price each year as you use them. **This yearly expense is called depreciation.**

We will deal with depreciation in much more detail in later transactions.

Transaction: Purchase 100,000 square foot building and land for $1.5 million in cash. This facility will serve as AppleSeed Enterprises' headquarters, manufacturing facility and warehouse.

1 Write a check for $1.5 million to the seller of the building. Record this cash transaction under **PP&E PURCHASE** in the *Cash Flow Statement*.

2 Then, lower **CASH** in the *Balance Sheet* by the $1.5 million check that you wrote to buy the building.

3 Now you must make another entry to bring the *Balance Sheet* back into balance. Increase **FIXED ASSETS @ COST** on the *Balance Sheet* by the $1.5 million purchase price of the building. Note that this asset is recorded at actual cost, not at the appraised or any other valuation.

~

Income Statement

for the period including Transactions 1 through 5		prior	+	transaction	=	sum
1	NET SALES	$0		—		$0
2	COST OF GOODS SOLD	0		—		0
1 - 2 = 3	GROSS MARGIN	0				0
4	SALES & MARKETING	0	**1A**	7,680		7,680
5	RESEARCH & DEVELOPMENT	0		—		0
6	GENERAL & ADMINISTRATIVE	6,230	**1B**	7,110		13,340
4 + 5 + 6 = 7	OPERATING EXPENSE	6,230				21,020
3 - 7 = 8	INCOME FROM OPERATIONS	(6,230)				(21,020)
9	NET INTEREST INCOME	0		—		0
10	INCOME TAXES	0		—		0
8 + 9 - 10 = 11	NET INCOME	($6,230)		(14,790)		($21,020)

IS Transaction Sum

Cash Flow Statement

for the period including Transactions 1 through 5		prior	+	transaction	=	sum
a	BEGINNING CASH BALANCE	$0				$0
b	CASH RECEIPTS	0		—		0
c	CASH DISBURSEMENTS	3,370	**3A**	7,960		11,330
b - c = d	CASH FLOW FROM OPERATIONS	(3,370)				(11,330)
e	PP&E PURCHASE	1,500,000		—		1,500,000
f	NET BORROWINGS	1,000,000		—		1,000,000
g	INCOME TAXES PAID	0		—		0
h	SALE OF CAPITAL STOCK	1,550,000		—		1,550,000
a + d - e + f - g + h = i	ENDING CASH BALANCES	$1,046,630		(7,960)		$1,038,670

CF Transaction Sum

Balance Sheet

as of this Transaction 5		prior	+	transaction	=	sum
A	CASH	$1,046,630	**3B**	(7,960)		$1,038,670
B	ACCOUNTS RECEIVABLE	0		—		0
C	INVENTORIES	0		—		0
D	PREPAID EXPENSES	0		—		0
A + B + C + D = E	CURRENT ASSETS	1,046,630				1,038,670
F	OTHER ASSETS	0		—		0
G	FIXED ASSETS @ COST	1,500,000		—		1,500,000
H	ACCUMULATED DEPRECIATION	0		—		0
G - H = I	NET FIXED ASSETS	1,500,000				1,500,000
E + F + I = J	TOTAL ASSETS	$2,546,630		(7,960)		$2,538,670
				Assets Sum		
K	ACCOUNTS PAYABLE	$0		—		0
L	ACCRUED EXPENSES	2,860	**4**	6,830		9,690
M	CURRENT PORTION OF DEBT	100,000		—		100,000
N	INCOME TAXES PAYABLE	0		—		0
K + L + M + N = O	CURRENT LIABILITIES	102,860				109,690
P	LONG-TERM DEBT	900,000		—		900,000
Q	CAPITAL STOCK	1,550,000		—		1,550,000
R	RETAINED EARNINGS	(6,230)	**2**	(14,790)		(21,020)
Q + R = S	SHAREHOLDERS' EQUITY	1,543,770				1,528,980
O + P + S = T	TOTAL LIABILITIES & EQUITY	$2,546,630		(7,960)		$2,538,670

Liabilities & Equity Sum

T5. Hire administrative and sales staff. Pay first month's salaries and book fringe benefits and taxes.

AppleSeed will soon be in production; you had better figure out how to sell applesauce! You will also need help with administrative tasks.

Hire some SG&A employees. SG&A stands for "sales, general and administrative." SG&A is a catchall for all expenses not involved in manufacturing; that is, not added to inventory. More on this topic later.

Add to AppleSeed's SG&A payroll a secretary at the wage of $13 per hour ($2,250 per month), a bookkeeper at a salary of $3,000 per month, salesperson at $4,000 per month and a salesclerk at $10 per hour ($1,750 per month).

The table below computes SG&A take-home pay and fringe benefit costs.

SG&A Payroll-Related Expenses

	PAY TO EMPLOYEES	PAY TO OTHERS
MONTHLY SALARY	$11,000	
EMPLOYEE'S FICA	$(840)	$840
FEDERAL/STATE WITHHOLDING	$(2,200)	$2,200
EMPLOYER'S FICA		$840
WORKMEN'S COMPENSATION		$400
UNEMPLOYMENT INSURANCE		$550
HEALTH & LIFE INSURANCE		$2,000
TOTALS PER MONTH	$7,960	$6,830
TOTAL PAID TO EMPLOYEES & OTHERS		$14,790

Transaction: Book this month's payroll-associated expenses of $14,790 (that is, $7,680 for Sales & Marketing and $7,110 for G&A). These expenses include salaries, wages, insurance and other fringe benefits. Issue payroll checks totaling $7,960 to SG&A employees.

1 (1A) On the *Income Statement* add total monthly payroll expense of $7,680 for the salesperson and clerk to **SALES & MARKETING** expense. (1B) Also add the payroll expense of $7,110 for the secretary and the bookkeeper to **GENERAL & ADMINISTRATIVE** expenses.

2 Decrease **RETAINED EARNINGS** in the *Balance Sheet* by the total SG&A payroll of $14,790.

3 (3A) Issue payroll checks totaling $7,960 and list under **CASH DISBURSEMENTS** in the *Cash Flow Statement*. (3B) Decrease **CASH** in the *Balance Sheet* by the same amount.

4 The $6,830 due to others is owed, but not yet paid. Place this amount as **ACCRUED EXPENSES** in the liability section of the *Balance Sheet*.

Income Statement

for the period including Transactions 1 through 6

		prior	+	transaction	=	sum
1	NET SALES	$0		—		$0
2	COST OF GOODS SOLD	0		—		0
1 - 2 = 3	GROSS MARGIN	0				0
4	SALES & MARKETING	7,680		—		7,680
5	RESEARCH & DEVELOPMENT	0		—		0
6	GENERAL & ADMINISTRATIVE	13,340		—		13,340
4 + 5 + 6 = 7	OPERATING EXPENSE	21,020				21,020
3 - 7 = 8	INCOME FROM OPERATIONS	(21,020)				(21,020)
9	NET INTEREST INCOME	0		—		0
10	INCOME TAXES	0		—		0
8 + 9 - 10 = 11	NET INCOME	($21,020)		0		($21,020)

IS Transaction Sum

Cash Flow Statement

for the period including Transactions 1 through 6

		prior	+	transaction	=	sum
a	BEGINNING CASH BALANCE	$0				$0
b	CASH RECEIPTS	0		—		0
c	CASH DISBURSEMENTS	11,330	**1**	9,690		21,020
b - c = d	CASH FLOW FROM OPERATIONS	(11,330)				(21,020)
e	PP&E PURCHASE	1,500,000		—		1,500,000
f	NET BORROWINGS	1,000,000		—		1,000,000
g	INCOME TAXES PAID	0		—		0
h	SALE OF CAPITAL STOCK	1,550,000		—		1,550,000
a + d - e + f - g + h = i	ENDING CASH BALANCES	$1,038,670		(9,690)		$1,028,980

CF Transaction Sum

Balance Sheet

as of this Transaction 6

		prior	+	transaction	=	sum
A	CASH	$1,038,670	**2**	(9,690)		$1,028,980
B	ACCOUNTS RECEIVABLE	0		—		0
C	INVENTORIES	0		—		0
D	PREPAID EXPENSES	0		—		0
A + B + C + D = E	CURRENT ASSETS	1,038,670				1,028,980
F	OTHER ASSETS	0		—		0
G	FIXED ASSETS @ COST	1,500,000		—		1,500,000
H	ACCUMULATED DEPRECIATION	0		—		0
G - H = I	NET FIXED ASSETS	1,500,000				1,500,000
E + F + I = J	TOTAL ASSETS	$2,538,670		(9,690)		$2,528,980
				Assets Sum		
K	ACCOUNTS PAYABLE	$0		—		0
L	ACCRUED EXPENSES	9,690	**3**	(9,690)		0
M	CURRENT PORTION OF DEBT	100,000		—		100,000
N	INCOME TAXES PAYABLE	0		—		0
K + L + M + N = O	CURRENT LIABILITIES	109,690				100,000
P	LONG-TERM DEBT	900,000				900,000
Q	CAPITAL STOCK	1,550,000		—		1,550,000
R	RETAINED EARNINGS	(21,020)		—		(21,020)
Q + R = S	SHAREHOLDERS' EQUITY	1,528,980				1,528,980
O + P + S = T	TOTAL LIABILITIES & EQUITY	$2,538,670		(9,690)		$2,528,980

Liabilities & Equity Sum

T6. Pay employee health, life and disability insurance premiums plus unemployment, FICA, and withholding taxes.

When you put yourself on AppleSeed's payroll in **Transaction 2** and then hired an SG&A staff in **Transaction 5,** you issued payroll checks to all new AppleSeed employees.

However, you did not at that time pay all the payroll-associated expenses for fringe benefits such as health and life insurance or the withholding taxes and the FICA that you deducted from all employees' paychecks.

These expenses were booked in the Income Statement at the time they were incurred, but since they were not at that time actually paid, they became accrued expenses.

If an expense is booked in the Income Statement but you do not "satisfy the obligation" by paying it immediately, then you must record the expense as "accrued" on the Balance Sheet.

Transaction: Pay all the payroll-associated expenses that were accrued in **Transaction 2** and **Transaction 5,** including FICA, withholding tax and unemployment insurance due the government. Also pay to private insurance companies the workmen's compensation and health and life insurance premiums.

1 Write checks totaling $9,690—$2,860 from **Transaction 2** plus $6,830 from **Transaction 5** for these accrued expenses. Show payments in CASH DISBURSEMENTS in the *Cash Flow Statement*.

2 Lower CASH in the asset section of the *Balance Sheet* by the same amount paid above.

3 Lower ACCRUED EXPENSES in the liabilities section of the *Balance Sheet* by the $9,690 paid above. Payment of these expenses had been deferred (accrued). Now that you have paid them you can, in effect, reverse the original deferring entry.

Note: Actually paying these accrued expenses does not affect the *Income Statement* now. The *Income Statement* was already charged when the expenses were incurred.

~

Chapter 7. Staffing and Equipping Facility; Planning for Manufacturing

Now begins the fun stuff. In a few short weeks, we will be producing thousands of cases of the best applesauce you have ever tasted.

In anticipation of beginning applesauce production, we will design our production techniques, determine raw material requirements and also our labor needs, figure our costs and establish methods to keep track of our inventories.

Finally, we will order our first raw materials and get everything ready to begin trial production in our new manufacturing plant.

∼

Transaction 7. Order $250,000 worth of manufacturing machinery. Pay 1/2 down now.

Transaction 8. Receive and install manufacturing machinery. Pay the remaining $125,000 due.

Transaction 9. Hire production workers. Expense first month's salary and wages.

- Prepare bill of materials and establish labor requirements.

- Set up plant and machinery depreciation schedules.

- Plan monthly production schedule and set standard costs.

Transaction 10. Place standing orders for raw materials with suppliers. Receive one million jar labels.

Income Statement

for the period including Transactions 1 through 7		prior	+	transaction	=	sum
1	NET SALES	$0	—			$0
2	COST OF GOODS SOLD	0	—			0
1 - 2 = 3	GROSS MARGIN	0				0
4	SALES & MARKETING	7,680	—			7,680
5	RESEARCH & DEVELOPMENT	0	—			0
6	GENERAL & ADMINISTRATIVE	13,340	—			13,340
4 + 5 + 6 = 7	OPERATING EXPENSE	21,020				21,020
3 - 7 = 8	INCOME FROM OPERATIONS	(21,020)				(21,020)
9	NET INTEREST INCOME	0	—			0
10	INCOME TAXES	0	—			0
8 + 9 - 10 = 11	NET INCOME	($21,020)		0		($21,020)

IS Transaction Sum

Cash Flow Statement

for the period including Transactions 1 through 7		prior	+	transaction	=	sum
a	BEGINNING CASH BALANCE	$0				$0
b	CASH RECEIPTS	0				0
c	CASH DISBURSEMENTS	21,020	—			21,020
b - c = d	CASH FLOW FROM OPERATIONS	(21,020)				(21,020)
e	PP&E PURCHASE	1,500,000	**1**	125,000		1,625,000
f	NET BORROWINGS	1,000,000	—			1,000,000
g	INCOME TAXES PAID	0	—			0
h	SALE OF CAPITAL STOCK	1,550,000	—			1,550,000
a + d - e + f - g + h = i	ENDING CASH BALANCES	$1,028,980		(125,000)		$903,980

CF Transaction Sum

Balance Sheet

as of this Transaction 7		prior	+	transaction	=	sum
A	CASH	$1,028,980	**2**	(125,000)		$903,980
B	ACCOUNTS RECEIVABLE	0	—			0
C	INVENTORIES	0	—			0
D	PREPAID EXPENSES	0	—			0
A + B + C + D = E	CURRENT ASSETS	1,028,980				903,980
F	OTHER ASSETS	0	**3**	125,000		125,000
G	FIXED ASSETS @ COST	1,500,000	—			1,500,000
H	ACCUMULATED DEPRECIATION	0	—			0
G - H = I	NET FIXED ASSETS	1,500,000				1,500,000
E + F + I = J	TOTAL ASSETS	$2,528,980		0		$2,528,980

Assets Sum

K	ACCOUNTS PAYABLE	$0	—			0
L	ACCRUED EXPENSES	0	—			0
M	CURRENT PORTION OF DEBT	100,000	—			100,000
N	INCOME TAXES PAYABLE	0	—			0
K + L + M + N = O	CURRENT LIABILITIES	100,000				100,000
P	LONG-TERM DEBT	900,000	—			900,000
Q	CAPITAL STOCK	1,550,000	—			1,550,000
R	RETAINED EARNINGS	(21,020)	—			(21,020)
Q + R = S	SHAREHOLDERS' EQUITY	1,528,980				1,528,980
O + P + S = T	TOTAL LIABILITIES & EQUITY	$2,528,980		0		$2,528,980

Liabilities & Equity Sum

T7. Order $250,000 worth of manufacturing machinery. Pay 1/2 down now.

We will need a lot of specialized machinery to make our special applesauce: presses, large stainless steel holding tanks, bottling machines, a labeling machine and so forth.

We contract with ABC AppleCrushing Machinery Inc. (ABCACM, Inc., for short) to construct and install our equipment at total cost to AppleSeed of $250,000 including delivery charges.

Before beginning all its important work, ABCACM demands a prepayment of $125,000 in cash. The remaining payment of $125,000 will be due upon the completion of installation and qualification of the equipment.

Transaction: Place an order for $250,000 worth of applesauce-making machinery. Make a prepayment of $125,000 with the balance due upon successful installation.

1 Enclose a check for $125,000 with the purchase order to the machinery contractor. Show this prepayment as a **PROPERTY, PLANT & EQUIPMENT** purchase the *Cash Flow Statement*.

2 Lower **CASH** in the assets section of the *Balance Sheet* by the $125,000 contractor prepayment.

3 This prepayment is an asset that AppleSeed "owns." It can be viewed as a "right" to receive in the future $250,000 of equipment and only have to issue another $125,000 check to the equipment builder. Since this asset does not fit into the any of the other asset categories, increase **OTHER ASSETS** by the $125,000 machinery prepayment.

~

Income Statement

for the period including Transactions 1 through 8		prior	+	transaction	=	sum
1	NET SALES	$0		—		$0
2	COST OF GOODS SOLD	0		—		0
1 - 2 = 3	GROSS MARGIN	0				0
4	SALES & MARKETING	7,680		—		7,680
5	RESEARCH & DEVELOPMENT	0		—		0
6	GENERAL & ADMINISTRATIVE	13,340		—		13,340
4 + 5 + 6 = 7	OPERATING EXPENSE	21,020				21,020
3 - 7 = 8	INCOME FROM OPERATIONS	(21,020)				(21,020)
9	NET INTEREST INCOME	0		—		0
10	INCOME TAXES	0		—		0
8 + 9 - 10 = 11	NET INCOME	($21,020)		0		($21,020)

IS Transaction Sum

Cash Flow Statement

for the period including Transactions 1 through 8		prior	+	transaction	=	sum
a	BEGINNING CASH BALANCE	$0				$0
b	CASH RECEIPTS	0		—		0
c	CASH DISBURSEMENTS	21,020		—		21,020
b - c = d	CASH FLOW FROM OPERATIONS	(21,020)				(21,020)
e	PP&E PURCHASE	1,625,000	**1**	125,000		1,750,000
f	NET BORROWINGS	1,000,000		—		1,000,000
g	INCOME TAXES PAID	0		—		0
h	SALE OF CAPITAL STOCK	1,550,000		—		1,550,000
a + d - e + f - g + h = i	ENDING CASH BALANCES	$903,980		(125,000)		$778,980

CF Transaction Sum

Balance Sheet

as of this Transaction 8		prior	+	transaction	=	sum
A	CASH	$903,980	**2**	(125,000)		$778,980
B	ACCOUNTS RECEIVABLE	0		—		0
C	INVENTORIES	0		—		0
D	PREPAID EXPENSES	0		—		0
A + B + C + D = E	CURRENT ASSETS	903,980				778,980
F	OTHER ASSETS	125,000	**3**	(125,000)		0
G	FIXED ASSETS @ COST	1,500,000	**4**	250,000		1,750,000
H	ACCUMULATED DEPRECIATION	0		—		0
G - H = I	NET FIXED ASSETS	1,500,000				1,750,000
E + F + I = J	TOTAL ASSETS	$2,528,980		0		$2,528,980
				Assets Sum		
K	ACCOUNTS PAYABLE	$0		—		0
L	ACCRUED EXPENSES	0		—		0
M	CURRENT PORTION OF DEBT	100,000		—		100,000
N	INCOME TAXES PAYABLE	0		—		0
K + L + M + N = O	CURRENT LIABILITIES	100,000				100,000
P	LONG-TERM DEBT	900,000		—		900,000
Q	CAPITAL STOCK	1,550,000		—		1,550,000
R	RETAINED EARNINGS	(21,020)		—		(21,020)
Q + R = S	SHAREHOLDERS' EQUITY	1,528,980				1,528,980
O + P + S = T	TOTAL LIABILITIES & EQUITY	$2,528,980		0		$2,528,980

Liabilities & Equity Sum

T8. Receive and install applesauce-making machinery. Pay the $125,000 balance due.

ABCACM does a super job—on time and on budget. They submit an invoice for their work and you are happy to pay. Our applesauce machinery is installed and ready for operation.

These new machines are a productive asset...so-called because they will be used to produce our product and make a profit for AppleSeed.

Note that when you paid for these machines you just shifted money from one asset category on the Balance Sheet into another, from cash to fixed assets. The Income Statement was not affected. When we use and then depreciate these assets, the Income Statement will take a hit. More later.

Transaction: Make final payment of $125,000, the balance due on our new applesauce-making machinery.

1 Everything is working well. Accept delivery on the machinery and write a check for the $125,000 balance due. Show this payment as a **PROPERTY, PLANT & EQUIPMENT** purchase in the *Cash Flow Statement.*

2 Lower **CASH** in the assets section of the *Balance Sheet* by the $125,000 paid to the contractor.

3 Lower **OTHER ASSETS** by the $125,000 prepayment that now will be converted (below) to a fixed asset.

4 Increase **FIXED ASSETS @ COST** by the total $250,000 cost of the machinery. Half of this amount comes from this transaction (payment of the $125,000 balance due) and half from reversing the **OTHER ASSETS** account (prepayment of $125,000 in Transaction 7) now that we have received the machinery.

∼

Income Statement

for the period including Transactions 1 through 9		prior	+	transaction	=	sum
1	NET SALES	$0		—		$0
2	COST OF GOODS SOLD	0		—		0
1 - 2 = 3	GROSS MARGIN	0				0
4	SALES & MARKETING	7,680		—		7,680
5	RESEARCH & DEVELOPMENT	0		—		0
6	GENERAL & ADMINISTRATIVE	13,340	**1A**	4,880		18,220
4 + 5 + 6 = 7	OPERATING EXPENSE	21,020				25,900
3 - 7 = 8	INCOME FROM OPERATIONS	(21,020)				(25,900)
9	NET INTEREST INCOME	0		—		0
10	INCOME TAXES	0		—		0
8 + 9 - 10 = 11	NET INCOME	($21,020)		(4,880)		($25,900)

IS Transaction Sum

Cash Flow Statement

for the period including Transactions 1 through 9		prior	+	transaction	=	sum
a	BEGINNING CASH BALANCE	$0				$0
b	CASH RECEIPTS	0		—		0
c	CASH DISBURSEMENTS	21,020	**2A**	2,720		23,740
b - c = d	CASH FLOW FROM OPERATIONS	(21,020)				(23,740)
e	PP&E PURCHASE	1,750,000		—		1,750,000
f	NET BORROWINGS	1,000,000		—		1,000,000
g	INCOME TAXES PAID	0		—		0
h	SALE OF CAPITAL STOCK	1,550,000		—		1,550,000
a + d - e + f - g + h = i	ENDING CASH BALANCES	$778,980		(2,720)		$776,260

CF Transaction Sum

Balance Sheet

as of this Transaction 9		prior	+	transaction	=	sum
A	CASH	$778,980	**2B**	(2,720)		$776,260
B	ACCOUNTS RECEIVABLE	0		—		0
C	INVENTORIES	0		—		0
D	PREPAID EXPENSES	0		—		0
A + B + C + D = E	CURRENT ASSETS	778,980				776,260
F	OTHER ASSETS	0		—		0
G	FIXED ASSETS @ COST	1,750,000		—		1,750,000
H	ACCUMULATED DEPRECIATION	0		—		0
G - H = I	NET FIXED ASSETS	1,750,000				1,750,000
E + F + I = J	TOTAL ASSETS	$2,528,980		(2,720)		$2,526,260
				Assets Sum		
K	ACCOUNTS PAYABLE	$0		—		0
L	ACCRUED EXPENSES	0	**3**	2,160		2,160
M	CURRENT PORTION OF DEBT	100,000		—		100,000
N	INCOME TAXES PAYABLE	0		—		0
K + L + M + N = O	CURRENT LIABILITIES	100,000				102,160
P	LONG-TERM DEBT	900,000		—		900,000
Q	CAPITAL STOCK	1,550,000		—		1,550,000
R	RETAINED EARNINGS	(21,020)	**1B**	(4,880)		(25,900)
Q + R = S	SHAREHOLDERS' EQUITY	1,528,980				1,524,100
O + P + S = T	TOTAL LIABILITIES & EQUITY	$2,528,980		(2,720)		$2,526,260

Liabilities & Equity Sum

T9. Hire production workers. Expense first month's salary and wages.

The plant is shaping up and we need manufacturing workers and a supervisor to guide them along.

Hire the supervisor at a salary of $3,750 per month and have her start immediately. Using similar calculations to those in the table for **Transaction 5**, the supervisor will receive $2,720 per month in take-home pay. The company will also pay $2,160 in fringes and various taxes to the government. Salary and fringes for the supervisor total $4,880 per month.

We will begin paying the supervisor right away. However, since we have not yet started production, we will charge this month's salary to G&A as a start-up expense. Normally the manufacturing salary and wage expense is charged to inventory. More later.

The supervisor starts interviewing hourly production workers. Wages will be $12.50 per hour plus fringes with an expected 40-hour week. Hire five workers and tell them to report next month when we expect to start production.

AppleSeed's manufacturing payroll now totals $17,180 per month: $4,880 for the supervisor and $12,300 for the five hourly workers.

Production Labor Costs	TAKE-HOME PAY TO EMPLOYEES	FRINGE BENEFITS AND TAXES	TOTALS
SUPERVISOR	$2,720	$2,160	$4,880
HOURLY WORKERS	$6,300	$6,000	$12,300
MANUFACTURING PAYROLL	$9,020	$8,160	$17,180

Transaction: Book supervisor's salary and associated payroll expenses as a General & Administrative expense since we have not yet started production. Issue first month's salary check. Make no entries for hourly workers since they have not yet reported for work.

1 (1A) On the *Income Statement* add $4,880 (the total salary and payroll costs for the supervisor) to GENERAL & ADMINISTRATIVE EXPENSE. (1B) Decrease RETAINED EARNINGS in the liabilities section of the *Balance Sheet* by the same amount.

2 (2A) Issue a payroll check totaling $2,720 and list under CASH DISBURSEMENTS in the *Cash Flow Statement*. (2B) Decrease CASH in the *Balance Sheet* by the same amount.

3 The remaining $2,160 in benefits and taxes is owed but not yet paid. Place this amount in ACCRUED EXPENSES on the *Balance Sheet*.

Manufacturing Costing

How much will it cost to make our fine applesauce? How should we account for manufacturing costs? How will we correctly value our inventory? These are essential questions for managing the books of our business

~

Manufacturing businesses such as AppleSeed Enterprises, Inc., compute product cost by determining and then adding three separate cost elements. The three common cost elements are: (1) raw material costs, (2) direct labor costs, and (3) overhead costs.

Overhead costs is a catchall category for costs that cannot be assigned to a specific product, but rather are ongoing costs required just to keep the plant open. Examples of overhead costs include costs for plant space, heat, light, power, supervisory labor, depreciation and so forth.

We will discuss so-called *direct costs* first and then overhead costs. Direct costs (basically materials and labor) are simple and easy to understand.

After discussing each element of manufacturing cost separately, we will then summarize them into a product "standard" cost for use in (1) inventory valuation on the Balance Sheet, and (2) computing the cost of product sold for entry on the Income Statement.

Cost of Raw Materials. See AppleSeed's applesauce "Bill of Materials" below. This table lists all of the materials that go into our product and the unit cost of these materials in normal commercial purchase quantities. Also shown is the amount and cost of materials that go into a single shipping "unit" of our product, in this instance a case containing 12 jars of applesauce.

From the Bill of Materials below we see that we buy apples in ton quantities at a price of $120 per ton delivered to our plant. Also, each 12-jar case of our applesauce takes 33 lbs. of apples to produce. Because 2,000 lbs. of apples cost us $120, we will pay $1.98 for the 33 lbs. of apples that will go into a case of applesauce.

AppleSeed Enterprises' Applesauce Bill of Materials

	PRICE PER UNIT OF RAW MATERIAL	UNIT OF MEASURE FOR RAW MATERIAL	QUANTITY REQUIRED PER CASE OF 12 JARS	EXTENDED COST PER CASE OF 12 JARS
APPLES	$120	TON	33.00 LBS.	$1.98
SUGAR	$140	1000 LBS.	2.30 LBS.	$0.32
CINNAMON	$280	100 LBS.	0.35 OZ.	$0.06
GLASS JAR	$55	GROSS	12	$4.60
JAR CAP	$10	GROSS	12	$0.83
JAR LABEL	$200	10,000	12	$0.24
LARGE BOX	$75	GROSS	1	$0.52
			COST PER CASE	$8.55

Using a similar calculation for all the other raw materials in our product yields a total materials cost of $8.55 per 12-jar case of applesauce.

Cost of Direct Labor. We have designed our plant to manufacture up to 20,000 cases of applesauce each month. Because the plant is highly automated, we will need only five hourly workers to achieve this production level.

Our total hourly labor payroll for a single month is $12,300 (as computed in **Transaction 9**). Divide this labor cost by the 20,000 cases we plan to produce each month. We compute a direct labor cost of $0.62 for each case of applesauce made.

Manufacturing Labor Cost per Case

Hourly payroll per month	$12,000.00
÷ Cases produced	20,000
= hourly payroll per case	$0.62

We have just estimated the first two elements of product cost—materials and direct labor. They were easy compared to what follows: overhead and depreciation.

Overhead

It is not difficult to see how material cost should be added as a part of product costs. Same for direct labor. However, "overhead" is not so simple.

It takes more than just materials and labor to make a product. It takes a manufacturing building; it takes machinery; it takes heat, light and power; and it takes supervisors to make things run properly. These costs don't go "directly" into the product as do materials and labor, but they are costs to make the product nonetheless.

~

We will next study depreciation charges for AppleSeed and then come back to compute total overhead costs and total manufacturing costs for making our applesauce.

Depreciation

A major cost for AppleSeed is the depreciation of machinery and buildings used to make our product. Basically, depreciation is a way of charging to current activities a pro-rata portion of the original purchase price of long-lived assets.

For example, suppose we purchase a $100,000 machine. Over its useful life, it will make 500,000 jars of applesauce. Therefore, each jar should be charged a $0.20 cost for its pro-rata use of that machine. Thus, we would add $0.20 to the cost of each jar as a depreciation charge.

To simplify, both accounting practice and tax laws say that fixed assets such as buildings and machinery can be "written off" or "depreciated" each year by a certain specified portion of their value. Some assets are written off over a longer useful life (buildings over 20 to 30 years) or a shorter useful life (automobiles over 5 years).

Depreciation Schedule. Look at the AppleSeed Enterprises' fixed asset depreciation schedule on the facing page. Listed in the left-most column are AppleSeed's fixed assets. Note that the total amount under "original purchase price" is the same amount shown on AppleSeed's Balance Sheet for Fixed Assets @ Cost.

Depreciation is just a method of dribbling the costs of fixed assets through the Income Statement over time as you use the assets.

AppleSeed Enterprises's Fixed Asset Depreciation Schedule

	ORIGINAL PURCHASE PRICE	YEARS OF USEFUL LIFE	DEPRECIATION CHARGE EACH YEAR	BOOK VALUE AT END OF YEAR 1	BOOK VALUE AT END OF YEAR 2	BOOK VALUE AT END OF YEAR 3
BUILDING	$1,000,000	20	$50,000	$950,000	$900,000	$850,000
LAND	$500,000	forever	$0	$500,000	$500,000	$500,000
MACHINERY	$250,000	7	$357,14	$214,286	$178,572	$142,858
TOTALS	$1,750,000		$85,714	$1,664,286	$1,578,572	$1,492,858

The next column lists the useful life that AppleSeed will use to compute depreciation for each asset class. In the next column, we list the actual yearly depreciation amount when using the "straight-line" method to compute depreciation. Straight-line yearly depreciation equals original cost divided by years of useful life.

Note that with straight-line depreciation, the same amount of depreciation is taken for each year of useful life. "Accelerated" depreciation methods allow you to depreciate more in early years.

Book Value. The remaining three columns show the "book value" of Apple-Seed's fixed assets at the end of each of the next three years. Book value is just the original purchase price of a fixed asset less all the depreciation charges taken over the years—the so-called "accumulated depreciation." The book value of the fixed assets is shown on the Balance Sheet as *Net Fixed Assets*.

Note that book value is an accounting definition of "value." It does not necessarily correspond to any actual resale value or replacement value.

Effect on Income. Each year Apple-Seed will add $85,714 (or $7,143 per month) to its costs to account for its use of fixed assets throughout the year. This charge will hit the Income Statement as an element of product costs shown in *Cost of Goods Sold*. More later.

Effect on Cash. Unlike most other expenses, you do not pay a depreciation charge with cash. That is to say, cash balance and cash flow are not affected as you depreciate a fixed asset. Why is this so? Sounds like a free lunch?

Depreciation is not free. When you originally purchased the fixed asset, you paid its total cost with cash. The Cash Flow Statement showed the payment at full purchase price. However, this purchase price did not go through Income Statement as an expense *at that time*. We depreciate the full cost of a long-lived asset over time in the Income Statement.

Depreciation is just a method of dribbling the costs of fixed assets through the Income Statement over time, as you use the assets.

Overhead Continued

AppleSeed Enterprises's manufacturing overhead is made up of the supervisor's salary, depreciation charges and other odds and ends such as heat, light and power, and general supplies. Most of these costs must be paid regardless of the production volume. That is, these costs are generally the same whether we produce a lot or a little applesauce.

Let's compute AppleSeed's manufacturing overhead. From **Transaction 9,** we see that the supervisor's total payroll cost is $4,880 per month. From computations on the prior page, we see that depreciation

Product Cost @ Three Different Production Levels

	COSTS PER CASE	COSTS PER MONTH	TOTAL COSTS FOR 10,000 CASES PER MONTH PRODUCTION	TOTAL COSTS FOR 20,000 CASES PER MONTH PRODUCTION	TOTAL COSTS FOR 30,000 CASES PER MONTH PRODUCTION
RAW MATERIALS	$8.55		$85,500	$171,000	$256,500
DIRECT LABOR	$0.62		$6,150	$12,300	$18,450
OVERHEAD— SUPERVISOR		$4,880	$4,880	$4,880	$4,880
DEPRECIATION		$7,143	$7,143	$7,143	$7,143
ALL OTHER		$8,677	$8,677	$8,677	$8,677
TOTAL MANUFACTURING $ COST IN MONTH			$112,350	$204,000	$295,650
CASES MANUFACTURED IN MONTH			10,000	20,000	30,000
$ MANUFACTURING COST PER CASE			$11.24	$10.20	$9.86

is $7,143 per month. Let's assume that all other elements of overhead (heat, power, etc.) will cost $8,677 per month. Thus, AppleSeed's total manufacturing overhead is $20,700 each and every month as shown below:

Supervisory payroll	$4,880
Depreciation	$7,143
all other costs	$8,677
Total monthly overhead	$20,700

But note that it all does not go out as cash each month. Remember, depreciation is a non-cash expense—just a bookkeeping entry. The actual cash outlay for overhead is only the supervisor's salary and the "all other" expense that totals $13,577 each month.

Fixed and Variable Costs

Some of AppleSeed's manufacturing costs get larger (in total) with each additional case the company makes. For example, with more cases produced, more raw material is consumed. Ten cases require $85.50 worth of raw materials; 100 cases require $855 worth of raw materials. This type of cost, one that varies directly and proportionally with production volume, is called a ***variable cost.*** Direct labor is another example of a variable cost.

A cost that does not normally change with the volume level of production is called a ***fixed cost.*** Examples of AppleSeed fixed costs are supervisory labor costs and depreciation. Generally, the elements of overhead are fixed costs.

What is important about the concept of fixed and variable costs? Costs to produce a manufactured product can vary greatly depending on the: (1) production volume and (2) proportion of fixed versus variable costs elements in product cost.

Thus, when we talk about the cost of an individual case of applesauce to manufacture, we must also state a production volume. Then the total fixed manufacturing costs can be "allocated" proportionally to each individual unit of production. Thus, we can establish a cost for inventory valuation and cost of goods sold computation.

See the table above. It shows different product costs at different production volumes. Actual costs to produce a case of applesauce vary between $11.24 and $9.86, depending on whether we produce 10,000 or up to 30,000 cases. The lower case cost is at the higher volume. When we talk about what an individual case of applesauce costs us to make, we must also state a production volume.

Now we are ready to compute Apple-Seed's product costs and determine how to value our inventory.

Standard Cost System

Okay, let's pull all the manufacturing costs together and compute what a case of applesauce costs to make. But remember, we cannot compute the unit cost of a case of applesauce until we set a monthly level of production.

In the production costing chart shown on the previous page, we have computed the total monthly costs to produce apple-sauce at three different production volumes: 10,000, 20,000 or 30,000 cases per month. We have also computed for these production volumes AppleSeed's cost per case. Depending on our monthly production volume, a single case of apple-sauce can cost between $11.24 (at 10,000 cases per month) and $9.86 (at 30,000 cases per month). Quite a significant difference!

The so-called *standard cost* is an estimate of product unit cost assuming a certain production volume. Accountants use standard cost as a good estimate of real costs to simplify day-to-day accounting transactions.

Establishing a standard cost will be useful for maintaining AppleSeed Enterprises's books. We will use this standard cost to value Inventory and to establish Cost of Goods Sold (COGS) when we sell our product.

AppleSeed's planned production is 20,000 cases per month. From the table on the previous page, we expect our actual costs will be $10.20 per case of applesauce we manufacture. The table shows this standard cost broken down by element of cost. We will be using this breakdown in later transactions.

Variances. What happens if at the end of a period we find that we manufactured either more (or less) than 20,000 cases per month? Won't the "costs" then change? Yes, costs will change. We will account for this overestimate or underestimate of costs by making manufacturing variance adjustments to the books. More on this topic later on pages 138-9.

AppleSeed Enterprises's Standard Cost Calculations by Cost Element @ 20,000 Cases per Month Production Level

	TOTAL COST PER MONTH AT 20,000 CASE PRODUCTION	COST PER CASE	TO EMPLOYEES	FRINGES AND TAXES	TO SUPPLIERS	DEPRECIATION CHARGE
RAW MATERIALS	$171,000	$8.55			$8.55	
DIRECT LABOR	$12,300	$0.62	$0.32	$0.30		
OVERHEAD—SUPERVISOR	$4,880	$0.24	$0.14	$0.10		
DEPRECIATION	$7,143	$0.36				$0.36
ALL OTHER	$8,677	$0.43			$0.43	
	$204,000	$10.20	$.46	$0.40	$8.98	$0.36

			TO EMPLOYEES	FRINGES AND TAXES	TO SUPPLIERS	DEPRECIATION CHARGE
TOTALS PER MONTH			$9,020	$8,160	$179,677	$7,143

Income Statement

for the period including Transactions 1 through 10	*prior*	+	*transaction*	=	*sum*
1 NET SALES	$0		—		$0
2 COST OF GOODS SOLD	0		—		0
1 - 2 = 3 GROSS MARGIN	0				0
4 SALES & MARKETING	7,680		—		7,680
5 RESEARCH & DEVELOPMENT	0		—		0
6 GENERAL & ADMINISTRATIVE	18,220		—		18,220
4 + 5 + 6 = 7 OPERATING EXPENSE	25,900				25,900
3 - 7 = 8 INCOME FROM OPERATIONS	(25,900)				(25,900)
9 NET INTEREST INCOME	0		—		0
10 INCOME TAXES	0		—		0
8 + 9 - 10 = 11 NET INCOME	($25,900)		0		($25,900)

IS Transaction Sum

Cash Flow Statement

for the period including Transactions 1 through 10	*prior*	+	*transaction*	=	*sum*
a BEGINNING CASH BALANCE	$0				$0
b CASH RECEIPTS	0		—		0
c CASH DISBURSEMENTS	23,740		—		23,740
b - c = d CASH FLOW FROM OPERATIONS	(23,740)				(23,740)
e PP&E PURCHASE	1,750,000		—		1,750,000
f NET BORROWINGS	1,000,000		—		1,000,000
g INCOME TAXES PAID	0		—		0
h SALE OF CAPITAL STOCK	1,550,000		—		1,550,000
a + d - e + f - g + h = i ENDING CASH BALANCES	$776,260		0		$776,260

CF Transaction Sum

Balance Sheet

as of this Transaction 10	*prior*	+	*transaction*	=	*sum*
A CASH	$776,260		—		$776,260
B ACCOUNTS RECEIVABLE	0		—		0
C INVENTORIES	0	1	20,000		20,000
D PREPAID EXPENSES	0		—		0
A + B + C + D = E CURRENT ASSETS	776,260				796,260
F OTHER ASSETS	0		—		0
G FIXED ASSETS @ COST	1,750,000		—		1,750,000
H ACCUMULATED DEPRECIATION	0		—		0
G - H = I NET FIXED ASSETS	1,750,000				1,750,000
E + F + I = J TOTAL ASSETS	$2,526,260		20,000		$2,546,260

Assets Sum

	prior	+	*transaction*	=	*sum*
K ACCOUNTS PAYABLE	$0	2	20,000		20,000
L ACCRUED EXPENSES	2,160		—		2,160
M CURRENT PORTION OF DEBT	100,000		—		100,000
N INCOME TAXES PAYABLE	0		—		0
K + L + M + N = O CURRENT LIABILITIES	102,160				122,160
P LONG-TERM DEBT	900,000		—		900,000
Q CAPITAL STOCK	1,550,000		—		1,550,000
R RETAINED EARNINGS	(25,900)		—		(25,900)
Q + R = S SHAREHOLDERS' EQUITY	1,524,100				1,524,100
O + P + S = T TOTAL LIABILITIES & EQUITY	$2,526,260		20,000		$2,546,260

Liabilities & Equity Sum

T10. Place an order for raw materials (apples, spices and packaging materials). Receive one million specially printed jar labels at $0.02 each.

We must order and receive raw materials before AppleSeed can start production. The table below shows the quantities of various materials required for our monthly planned production level of 20,000 cases. Place a standing order with your suppliers for delivery of these quantities of raw materials each month. To get a good price on very special four-color labels, the printer demands a press run of one million labels at $0.02 each. Place the label order and receive the labels from the printer.

Raw Material Costs and Monthly Production Requirements

	QUANTITY PER CARTON	COST PER CARTON	QUANTITY NEEDED FOR 20,000 CARTONS	EXTENDED COST FOR 20,000 CARTONS
APPLES	33.00 LBS.	$1.98	330 TONS	$39,600
SUGAR	2.30 LBS.	$0.32	52 TONS	$6,400
CINNAMON	0.35 OZ.	$0.06	438 LBS.	$1,200
GLASS JAR	12	$4.60	1,667 GROSS	$92,000
JAR CAP	12	$0.83	1,667 GROSS	$16,600
JAR LABEL	12	$0.24	1,667 GROSS	$4,800
LARGE BOX	1	$0.52	139 GROSS	$10,400
	TOTALS	$8.55		$171,000

Transaction: Order and receive one million applesauce jar labels at a cost of $0.02 each for a total of $20,000 to be paid 30 days after delivery.

1 Place the labels in raw material inventory for use when we start production. Increase INVENTORIES by $20,000 in the assets section of the *Balance Sheet.*

2 We owe our printer for the labels, but we will pay the bill later. Increase ACCOUNTS PAYABLE by $20,000 in the liabilities section of the *Balance Sheet.*

Note: Simply placing an order for raw materials has no effect on any of the three financial statements. However, when you do receive materials, the *Balance Sheet* is modified to account for these new assets and the balancing new liabilities—what you owe for the materials is listed as an ACCOUNTS PAYABLE.

Chapter 8. Startup of Manufacturing Operations

We are ready to start producing applesauce. The machinery is up and running, the workers are hired and we are about to receive a supply of raw materials.

While manufacturing goes fairly smoothly, we do botch a half-day's production and have to scrap it. We will learn how to value our inventory "at standard" and book our first manufacturing variance. Raw materials keep rolling in.

～

Transaction 11. Receive two months' supply of raw materials.

Transaction 12. Start up production. Pay workers and supervisor for the month.

Transaction 13. Book depreciation and other manufacturing overhead costs for the month.

Transaction 14. Pay for the labels received in Transaction 10.

Transaction 15. Finish manufacturing 19,500 cases of applesauce and move them into finished goods inventory.

Transaction 16. Scrap 500 cases worth of work-in-process inventory.

- Manufacturing variances: what can go wrong; what can go right.

Transaction 17. Pay for the two months' supply of raw materials received in Transaction 11 above.

Transaction 18. Manufacture another month's supply of applesauce.

Income Statement

for the period including Transactions 1 through 11		prior	+	transaction	=	sum
1	NET SALES	$0	—			$0
2	COST OF GOODS SOLD	0	—			0
1 - 2 = 3	GROSS MARGIN	0				0
4	SALES & MARKETING	7,680	—			7,680
5	RESEARCH & DEVELOPMENT	0	—			0
6	GENERAL & ADMINISTRATIVE	18,220	—			18,220
4 + 5 + 6 = 7	OPERATING EXPENSE	25,900				25,900
3 - 7 = 8	INCOME FROM OPERATIONS	(25,900)				(25,900)
9	NET INTEREST INCOME	0	—			0
10	INCOME TAXES	0	—			0
8 + 9 - 10 = 11	NET INCOME	($25,900)		0		($25,900)

IS Transaction Sum

Cash Flow Statement

for the period including Transactions 1 through 11		prior	+	transaction	=	sum
a	BEGINNING CASH BALANCE	$0				$0
b	CASH RECEIPTS	0	—			0
c	CASH DISBURSEMENTS	23,740	—			23,740
b - c = d	CASH FLOW FROM OPERATIONS	(23,740)				(23,740)
e	PP&E PURCHASE	1,750,000	—			1,750,000
f	NET BORROWINGS	1,000,000	—			1,000,000
g	INCOME TAXES PAID	0	—			0
h	SALE OF CAPITAL STOCK	1,550,000	—			1,550,000
a + d - e + f - g + h = i	ENDING CASH BALANCES	$776,260		0		$776,260

CF Transaction Sum

Balance Sheet

as of this Transaction 11		prior	+	transaction	=	sum
A	CASH	$776,260	—			$776,260
B	ACCOUNTS RECEIVABLE	0	—			0
C	INVENTORIES	20,000	**1**	332,400		352,400
D	PREPAID EXPENSES	0	—			0
A + B + C + D = E	CURRENT ASSETS	796,260				1,128,660
F	OTHER ASSETS	0	—			0
G	FIXED ASSETS @ COST	1,750,000	—			1,750,000
H	ACCUMULATED DEPRECIATION	0	—			0
G - H = I	NET FIXED ASSETS	1,750,000				1,750,000
E + F + I = J	TOTAL ASSETS	$2,546,260		332,400		$2,878,660

Assets Sum

		prior	+	transaction	=	sum
K	ACCOUNTS PAYABLE	$20,000	**2**	332,400		352,400
L	ACCRUED EXPENSES	2,160	—			2,160
M	CURRENT PORTION OF DEBT	100,000	—			100,000
N	INCOME TAXES PAYABLE	0	—			0
K + L + M + N = O	CURRENT LIABILITIES	122,160				454,560
P	LONG-TERM DEBT	900,000	—			900,000
Q	CAPITAL STOCK	1,550,000	—			1,550,000
R	RETAINED EARNINGS	(25,900)	—			(25,900)
Q + R = S	SHAREHOLDERS' EQUITY	1,524,100				1,524,100
O + P + S = T	TOTAL LIABILITIES & EQUITY	$2,546,260		332,400		$2,878,660

Liabilities & Equity Sum

T11. Receive two months' supply of raw materials.

Receive two months' supply of the rest of the raw materials necessary to manufacture our splendid applesauce. We will buy them on credit. Our suppliers will ship the materials to us now and not expect payment for a little while.

> Now is the time for AppleSeed to set up an *Inventory Valuation Worksheet.* (See table below.) This worksheet will help us compute the value of our inventory as we make and sell applesauce.
>
> The worksheet will list the effects of all transactions that change inventory values. The "Total Inventory" value at the bottom of the worksheet will always equal the **INVENTORY** value shown on our *Balance Sheet.*
>
> ~

Our inventory will be divided into three groups depending on where it is in the manufacturing process. These categories will not show up on the *Balance Sheet.* The *Balance Sheet* lists only the total inventory figure. You'll see in future transactions how useful it is to account for inventory valuation using these three classifications:

Raw Material Inventory is just that, "raw" purchased goods unmodified by us and waiting to be processed.

Work-In-Process ("WIP") refers to materials that are being processed by our machines and by our labor force. Work-in-process has added value because of our processing. More on this concept later.

Finished Goods Inventory is product finished and ready to ship. For inventory valuation purposes we will use the "standard cost" we computed earlier to value our finished goods.

Transaction: Receive two months' supply of all raw materials (apples, sugar, cinnamon, jars, caps, boxes) worth $332,400 in total. (That is, $8.55 total materials per case less $0.24 for the already received labels times 40,000 cases.)

1 Increase **INVENTORIES** account on the *Balance Sheet* by the $332,400 cost of these materials.

2 Increase **ACCOUNTS PAYABLE** on the *Balance Sheet* by the value of the materials received.

Inventory Valuation Worksheet	RAW MATERIAL	WORK IN PROCESS	FINISHED GOODS
INVENTORY VALUES AT STARTUP (PRIOR TO T10)	$0	$0	$0
A. Receive labels (**T10**)	$20,000	$0	$0
B. Receive 2 months' supply of other raw materials (**T11**)	$332,400	$0	$0
INVENTORY SUBTOTALS (AS OF THIS TRANSACTION)	$352,400	$0	$0
TOTAL INVENTORY =	$352,400		

Financial Statements

Income Statement

for the period including Transactions 1 through 12

		prior	+	transaction	=	sum
1	NET SALES	$0		—		$0
2	COST OF GOODS SOLD	0		—		0
1 - 2 = 3	GROSS MARGIN	0				0
4	SALES & MARKETING	7,680		—		7,680
5	RESEARCH & DEVELOPMENT	0		—		0
6	GENERAL & ADMINISTRATIVE	18,220		—		18,220
4 + 5 + 6 = 7	OPERATING EXPENSE	25,900				25,900
3 - 7 = 8	INCOME FROM OPERATIONS	(25,900)				(25,900)
9	NET INTEREST INCOME	0		—		0
10	INCOME TAXES	0		—		0
8 + 9 - 10 = 11	NET INCOME	($25,900)		0		($25,900)

IS Transaction Sum

Cash Flow Statement

for the period including Transactions 1 through 12

		prior	+	transaction	=	sum
a	BEGINNING CASH BALANCE	$0				$0
b	CASH RECEIPTS	0		—		0
c	CASH DISBURSEMENTS	23,740	**1A**	9,020		32,760
b - c = d	CASH FLOW FROM OPERATIONS	(23,740)				(32,760)
e	PP&E PURCHASE	1,750,000		—		1,750,000
f	NET BORROWINGS	1,000,000		—		1,000,000
g	INCOME TAXES PAID	0		—		0
h	SALE OF CAPITAL STOCK	1,550,000		—		1,550,000
a + d - e + f - g + h = i	ENDING CASH BALANCES	$776,260		(9,020)		$767,240

CF Transaction Sum

Balance Sheet

as of this Transaction 12

		prior	+	transaction	=	sum
A	CASH	$776,260	**1B**	(9,020)		$767,240
B	ACCOUNTS RECEIVABLE	0		—		0
C	INVENTORIES	352,400	**3**	17,180		369,580
D	PREPAID EXPENSES	0		—		0
A + B + C + D = E	CURRENT ASSETS	1,128,660				1,136,820
F	OTHER ASSETS	0		—		0
G	FIXED ASSETS @ COST	1,750,000		—		1,750,000
H	ACCUMULATED DEPRECIATION	0		—		0
G - H = I	NET FIXED ASSETS	1,750,000				1,750,000
E + F + I = J	TOTAL ASSETS	$2,878,660		8,160		$2,886,820

Assets Sum

		prior	+	transaction	=	sum
K	ACCOUNTS PAYABLE	$352,400		—		$352,400
L	ACCRUED EXPENSES	2,160	**2**	8,160		10,320
M	CURRENT PORTION OF DEBT	100,000		—		100,000
N	INCOME TAXES PAYABLE	0		—		0
K + L + M + N = O	CURRENT LIABILITIES	454,560				462,720
P	LONG-TERM DEBT	900,000		—		900,000
Q	CAPITAL STOCK	1,550,000		—		1,550,000
R	RETAINED EARNINGS	(25,900)		—		(25,900)
Q + R = S	SHAREHOLDERS' EQUITY	1,524,100				1,524,100
O + P + S = T	TOTAL LIABILITIES & EQUITY	$2,878,660		8,160		$2,886,820

Liabilities & Equity Sum

T12. Start production. Pay supervisor and workers for the month. Book payroll-associated fringes and taxes.

We are finally ready to produce applesauce. The plant is ready and the workers have just shown up for work.

A month's supply of raw material ($8.55 per case times 20,000 cases equals a total of $171,000) is on its way from storage onto the plant floor to await processing. On the inventory worksheet we will "move" this raw material into work-in-process.

Also, with this transaction we will pay our workers and the supervisor a month's salary and wages. Because these salary and wages go toward producing product, they are called costs. These manufacturing costs will be accounted for by adding them to our work-in-process inventory. Thus, our inventory will increase in value by the amount of labor that we add while we process our product.

Transaction 9 showed the detail amounts for our manufacturing payroll. Because we were not yet in production then, we charged the Income Statement with the expense covering the supervisor's salary. Now that we are manufacturing product, these salary and wages are costs that increase the value of our product, and are shown as an increase in the value of inventory.

Transaction: Pay production workers' wages and supervisor's salary for the month. Book associated fringe benefits and payroll taxes.

1 Cut checks for $9,020 for take-home salary and workers' wages. (1A) Increase CASH DISBURSEMENTS by that amount in the *Cash Flow Statement*. (1B) Lower CASH by that amount in the *Balance Sheet*.

2 Book payroll-associated fringes and taxes of $8,160 as ACCRUED EXPENSES on the *Balance Sheet*.

3 Increase INVENTORIES on the *Balance Sheet* by $17,180; that is, $9,020 in salary and wages plus $8,160 in benefits and taxes.

Inventory Valuation Worksheet	RAW MATERIAL	WORK IN PROCESS	FINISHED GOODS
INVENTORY VALUES FROM T11.	$352,400	$0	$0
C. Move material to make 20,000 cases from raw materials to WIP.	($171,000)	$171,000	$0
D. Pay supervisor and workers for the month. See **T9**.	$0	$17,180	$0
INVENTORY SUBTOTALS (AS OF THIS TRANSACTION)	$181,400	$188,180	$0
	TOTAL INVENTORY =		$369,580

Financial Statements

Income Statement

for the period including Transactions 1 through 13

		prior	+	transaction	=	sum
1	NET SALES	$0		—		$0
2	COST OF GOODS SOLD	0		—		0
1 - 2 = 3	GROSS MARGIN	0				0
4	SALES & MARKETING	7,680		—		7,680
5	RESEARCH & DEVELOPMENT	0		—		0
6	GENERAL & ADMINISTRATIVE	18,220		—		18,220
4 + 5 + 6 = 7	OPERATING EXPENSE	25,900				25,900
3 - 7 = 8	INCOME FROM OPERATIONS	(25,900)				(25,900)
9	NET INTEREST INCOME	0		—		0
10	INCOME TAXES	0		—		0
8 + 9 - 10 = 11	NET INCOME	($25,900)		0		($25,900)

IS Transaction Sum

Cash Flow Statement

for the period including Transactions 1 through 13

		prior	+	transaction	=	sum
a	BEGINNING CASH BALANCE	$0				$0
b	CASH RECEIPTS	0		—		0
c	CASH DISBURSEMENTS	32,760		—		32,760
b - c = d	CASH FLOW FROM OPERATIONS	(32,760)				(32,760)
e	PP&E PURCHASE	1,750,000		—		1,750,000
f	NET BORROWINGS	1,000,000		—		1,000,000
g	INCOME TAXES PAID	0		—		0
h	SALE OF CAPITAL STOCK	1,550,000		—		1,550,000
a + d - e + f - g + h = i	ENDING CASH BALANCES	$767,240		0		$767,240

CF Transaction Sum

Balance Sheet

as of this Transaction 13

		prior	+	transaction	=	sum
A	CASH	$767,240		—		$767,240
B	ACCOUNTS RECEIVABLE	0		—		0
C	INVENTORIES	369,580	3	15,820		385,400
D	PREPAID EXPENSES	0		—		0
A + B + C + D = E	CURRENT ASSETS	1,136,820				1,152,640
F	OTHER ASSETS	0		—		0
G	FIXED ASSETS @ COST	1,750,000		—		1,750,000
H	ACCUMULATED DEPRECIATION	0	2	7,143		7,143
G - H = I	NET FIXED ASSETS	1,750,000				1,742,857
E + F + I = J	TOTAL ASSETS	$2,886,820		8,677		$2,895,497

Assets Sum

		prior	+	transaction	=	sum
K	ACCOUNTS PAYABLE	$352,400	1	8,677		$361,077
L	ACCRUED EXPENSES	10,320		—		10,320
M	CURRENT PORTION OF DEBT	100,000		—		100,000
N	INCOME TAXES PAYABLE	0		—		0
K + L + M + N = O	CURRENT LIABILITIES	462,720				471,397
P	LONG-TERM DEBT	900,000		—		900,000
Q	CAPITAL STOCK	1,550,000		—		1,550,000
R	RETAINED EARNINGS	(25,900)		—		(25,900)
Q + R = S	SHAREHOLDERS' EQUITY	1,524,100				1,524,100
O + P + S = T	TOTAL LIABILITIES & EQUITY	$2,886,820		8,677		$2,895,497

Liabilities & Equity Sum

T13. Book depreciation and other manufacturing overhead costs for the month.

As we are busily working on applesauce-making, there are a few bean-counting details that must be performed.

We are using our new machines in our very beautifully refurbished building. Something has to pay for all this splendor. With this transaction we will depreciate our machinery and building.

This depreciation charge is a manufacturing cost...a legitimate cost of making our applesauce. Thus, when we book this depreciation, we will add it in as a cost of manufacturing by increasing the value of our work-in-process inventory. Remember, all the manufacturing costs go into inventory.

Depreciation is a "non-cash" transaction, so we will not alter cash or accounts payable when we book AppleSeed's depreciation charge. No such luck with the "all other" overhead charges. We will eventually have to pay for them. Thus, accounts payable will be increased by what we owe.

Transaction: Book this month's manufacturing depreciation of $7,143 and $8,677 covering "all other" overhead costs. Note that depreciation is not a cash expense and will not lower our cash balance. But, the "all other" overhead we will eventually have to pay with cash.

1 Increase **ACCOUNTS PAYABLE** on the *Balance Sheet* by $8,677 covering the "all other" manufacturing overhead.

2 Increase **ACCUMULATED DEPRECIATION** on the *Balance Sheet* by this month's $7,143 depreciation charge.

3 Increase **INVENTORIES** on the *Balance Sheet* by $15,820 covering this month's depreciation of $7,143 plus the $8,677 "all other" manufacturing overhead.

~

Inventory Valuation Worksheet	RAW MATERIAL	WORK IN PROCESS	FINISHED GOODS
INVENTORY VALUES FROM T12.	$181,400	$188,180	$0
E. Book manufacturing depreciation for the month.	$0	$7,143	$0
F. Book all other manufacturing overhead costs.	$0	$8,677	$0
INVENTORY SUBTOTALS (AS OF THIS TRANSACTION)	$181,400	$204,000	$0
		TOTAL INVENTORY =	$385,400

Income Statement

for the period including Transactions 1 through 14	prior	+	transaction	=	sum
1 NET SALES	$0		—		$0
2 COST OF GOODS SOLD	0		—		0
1 - 2 = 3 GROSS MARGIN	0				0
4 SALES & MARKETING	7,680		—		7,680
5 RESEARCH & DEVELOPMENT	0		—		0
6 GENERAL & ADMINISTRATIVE	18,220		—		18,220
4 + 5 + 6 = 7 OPERATING EXPENSE	25,900				25,900
3 - 7 = 8 INCOME FROM OPERATIONS	(25,900)				(25,900)
9 NET INTEREST INCOME	0		—		0
10 INCOME TAXES	0		—		0
8 + 9 - 10 = 11 NET INCOME	($25,900)		0		($25,900)

IS Transaction Sum

Cash Flow Statement

for the period including Transactions 1 through 14	prior	+	transaction	=	sum
a BEGINNING CASH BALANCE	$0				$0
b CASH RECEIPTS	0		—		0
c CASH DISBURSEMENTS	32,760	**1**	20,000		52,760
b - c = d CASH FLOW FROM OPERATIONS	(32,760)				(52,760)
e PP&E PURCHASE	1,750,000		—		1,750,000
f NET BORROWINGS	1,000,000		—		1,000,000
g INCOME TAXES PAID	0		—		0
h SALE OF CAPITAL STOCK	1,550,000		—		1,550,000
a + d - e + f - g + h = i ENDING CASH BALANCES	$767,240		(20,000)		$747,240

CF Transaction Sum

Balance Sheet

as of this Transaction 14	prior	+	transaction	=	sum
A CASH	$767,240	**2**	(20,000)		$747,240
B ACCOUNTS RECEIVABLE	0		—		0
C INVENTORIES	385,400		—		385,400
D PREPAID EXPENSES	0		—		0
A + B + C + D = E CURRENT ASSETS	1,152,640				1,132,640
F OTHER ASSETS	0		—		0
G FIXED ASSETS @ COST	1,750,000		—		1,750,000
H ACCUMULATED DEPRECIATION	7,143		—		7,143
G - H = I NET FIXED ASSETS	1,742,857				1,742,857
E + F + I = J TOTAL ASSETS	$2,895,497		(20,000)		$2,875,497

Assets Sum

	prior	+	transaction	=	sum
K ACCOUNTS PAYABLE	$361,077	**3**	(20,000)		$341,077
L ACCRUED EXPENSES	10,320		—		10,320
M CURRENT PORTION OF DEBT	100,000		—		100,000
N INCOME TAXES PAYABLE	0		—		0
K + L + M + N = O CURRENT LIABILITIES	471,397				451,397
P LONG-TERM DEBT	900,000		—		900,000
Q CAPITAL STOCK	1,550,000		—		1,550,000
R RETAINED EARNINGS	(25,900)		—		(25,900)
Q + R = S SHAREHOLDERS' EQUITY	1,524,100				1,524,100
O + P + S = T TOTAL LIABILITIES & EQUITY	$2,895,497		(20,000)		$2,875,497

Liabilities & Equity Sum

T14. Pay for labels received in Transaction 10.

We received our applesauce jar labels over a month ago and the printer is very anxious to get paid. When we received the jar labels we created an accounts payable. When we pay this vendor with cash we will "reverse" the payable at the same time we lower cash.

Note, paying for this raw material in no way affects the values in our Inventory Valuation Worksheet. The inventory was increased by the cost of the labels when we received them and created an accounts payable.

Transaction: Pay for 1 million labels received in **Transaction 10**. Issue a check to our vendor for $20,000 as payment in full.

1 Cut a check for $20,000 to pay the label printer. Increase CASH DISBURSEMENTS by that amount in the *Cash Flow Statement.*

2 Lower cash by $20,000 in the assets section of the *Balance Sheet* since we wrote the check.

3 Lower ACCOUNTS PAYABLE in the liabilities section of the *Balance Sheet* by the $20,000 that we no longer owe (since we just paid as described above).

$\sim$

Inventory Valuation Worksheet	RAW MATERIAL	WORK IN PROCESS	FINISHED GOODS
INVENTORY VALUES FROM **T13**.	$181,400	$204,000	$0
G. Pay for labels received on **T10**.	$0	$0	$0
INVENTORY SUBTOTALS (AS OF THIS TRANSACTION)	$181,400	$204,000	$0
		TOTAL INVENTORY =	$385,400

Income Statement

for the period including Transactions 1 through 15		prior	+	transaction	=	sum
1	NET SALES	0		—		$0
2	COST OF GOODS SOLD	0		—		0
1 - 2 = 3	GROSS MARGIN	0				0
4	SALES & MARKETING	7,680		—		7,680
5	RESEARCH & DEVELOPMENT	0		—		0
6	GENERAL & ADMINISTRATIVE	18,220		—		18,220
4 + 5 + 6 = 7	OPERATING EXPENSE	25,900				25,900
3 - 7 = 8	INCOME FROM OPERATIONS	(25,900)				(25,900)
9	NET INTEREST INCOME	0		—		0
10	INCOME TAXES	0		—		0
8 + 9 - 10 = 11	NET INCOME	(25,900)		0		($25,900)

IS Transaction Sum

Cash Flow Statement

for the period including Transactions 1 through 15		prior	+	transaction	=	sum
a	BEGINNING CASH BALANCE	0				$0
b	CASH RECEIPTS	0		—		0
c	CASH DISBURSEMENTS	52,760		—		52,760
b - c = d	CASH FLOW FROM OPERATIONS	(52,760)				(52,760)
e	PP&E PURCHASE	1,750,000		—		1,750,000
f	NET BORROWINGS	1,000,000		—		1,000,000
g	INCOME TAXES PAID	0		—		0
h	SALE OF CAPITAL STOCK	1,550,000		—		1,550,000
a + d - e + f - g + h = i	ENDING CASH BALANCES	747,240		0		$747,240

CF Transaction Sum

Balance Sheet

as of this Transaction 15		prior	+	transaction	=	sum
A	CASH	747,240		—		$747,240
B	ACCOUNTS RECEIVABLE	0		—		0
C	INVENTORIES	385,400		—		385,400
D	PREPAID EXPENSES	0		—		0
A + B + C + D = E	CURRENT ASSETS	1,132,640				1,132,640
F	OTHER ASSETS	0		—		0
G	FIXED ASSETS @ COST	1,750,000		—		1,750,000
H	ACCUMULATED DEPRECIATION	7,143		—		7,143
G - H = I	NET FIXED ASSETS	1,742,857				1,742,857
E + F + I = J	TOTAL ASSETS	2,875,497		0		$2,875,497

Assets Sum

		prior	+	transaction	=	sum
K	ACCOUNTS PAYABLE	341,077		—		$341,077
L	ACCRUED EXPENSES	10,320		—		10,320
M	CURRENT PORTION OF DEBT	100,000		—		100,000
N	INCOME TAXES PAYABLE	0		—		0
K + L + M + N = O	CURRENT LIABILITIES	451,397				451,397
P	LONG-TERM DEBT	900,000		—		900,000
Q	CAPITAL STOCK	1,550,000		—		1,550,000
R	RETAINED EARNINGS	(25,900)		—		(25,900)
Q + R = S	SHAREHOLDERS' EQUITY	1,524,100				1,524,100
O + P + S = T	TOTAL LIABILITIES & EQUITY	2,875,497		0		$2,875,497

Liabilities & Equity Sum

T15. Finish Manufacturing 19,500 cases of our applesauce and move them from work-in-process (WIP) into finished goods inventory.

Manufacturing our product is a continuous flow of raw material and labor into work-in-process inventory and then on to finished goods.

When we have finally boxed our finished jars of applesauce and they are ready for shipping, we place them in our finished goods warehouse. We will value this inventory at "standard cost," ready to become a COST OF GOODS SOLD amount when we ship.

On our Inventory Valuation Worksheet we will decrease work-in-process inventory and also increase finished goods inventory by the same amount, the value of goods we moved from work-in-process to finished goods.

Remember, we started out to make 20,000 cases. But somewhere in the process we lost some product and only ended up with 19,500 cases. We will "move" these 19,500 cases into finished goods inventory. In the next transaction we will deal with what happened and how to account for the remaining 500 cases.

The inventory value of the 19,500 cases to be transferred is $198,900—a $10.20 standard cost times 19,500 cases. Note that while accounting entries (see below) are made in our Inventory Valuation Worksheet as we move work-in-process inventory into finished goods, no change is made in the company's *Income Statement*, *Balance Sheet* or *Cash Flow Statement*.

Inventory values will become COST OF GOODS SOLD only when we ship product to customers.

Transaction: This movement of inventory into a different class is really just an internal management control transaction as far as the financial statements are concerned. There is no effect on the three major financial statements of AppleSeed. INVENTORIES on the *Balance Sheet* remains the same. Our Inventory Valuation Worksheet, as shown below, reflects the change in inventory status.

∼

Inventory Valuation Worksheet	RAW MATERIAL	WORK IN PROCESS	FINISHED GOODS
INVENTORY VALUES FROM T14.	$181,400	$204,000	$0
H. Move 19,500 cases from WIP into FG @ standard cost.	$0	$(198,900)	$198,900
INVENTORY SUBTOTALS (AS OF THIS TRANSACTION)	$181,400	$5,100	$198,900
		TOTAL INVENTORY =	$385,400

Income Statement

for the period including Transactions 1 through 16		prior	+	transaction	=	sum
1	NET SALES	$0		—		$0
2	COST OF GOODS SOLD	0	**2**	5,100		5,100
1 - 2 = 3	GROSS MARGIN	0				(5,100)
4	SALES & MARKETING	7,680		—		7,680
5	RESEARCH & DEVELOPMENT	0		—		0
6	GENERAL & ADMINISTRATIVE	18,220		—		18,220
4 + 5 + 6 = 7	OPERATING EXPENSE	25,900				25,900
3 - 7 = 8	INCOME FROM OPERATIONS	(25,900)				(31,000)
9	NET INTEREST INCOME	0		—		0
10	INCOME TAXES	0		—		0
8 + 9 - 10 = 11	NET INCOME	($25,900)		(5,100)		($31,000)

IS Transaction Sum

Cash Flow Statement

for the period including Transactions 1 through 16		prior	+	transaction	=	sum
a	BEGINNING CASH BALANCE	$0				$0
b	CASH RECEIPTS	0		—		0
c	CASH DISBURSEMENTS	52,760		—		52,760
b - c = d	CASH FLOW FROM OPERATIONS	(52,760)				(52,760)
e	PP&E PURCHASE	1,750,000		—		1,750,000
f	NET BORROWINGS	1,000,000		—		1,000,000
g	INCOME TAXES PAID	0		—		0
h	SALE OF CAPITAL STOCK	1,550,000		—		1,550,000
a + d - e + f - g + h = i	ENDING CASH BALANCES	$747,240		0		$747,240

CF Transaction Sum

Balance Sheet

as of this Transaction 16		prior	+	transaction	=	sum
A	CASH	$747,240		—		$747,240
B	ACCOUNTS RECEIVABLE	0		—		0
C	INVENTORIES	385,400	**1**	(5,100)		380,300
D	PREPAID EXPENSES	0		—		0
A + B + C + D = E	CURRENT ASSETS	1,132,640				1,127,540
F	OTHER ASSETS	0		—		0
G	FIXED ASSETS @ COST	1,750,000		—		1,750,000
H	ACCUMULATED DEPRECIATION	7,143		—		7,143
G - H = I	NET FIXED ASSETS	1,742,857				1,742,857
E + F + I = J	TOTAL ASSETS	$2,875,497		(5,100)		$2,870,397
				Assets Sum		
K	ACCOUNTS PAYABLE	$341,077		—		$341,077
L	ACCRUED EXPENSES	10,320		—		10,320
M	CURRENT PORTION OF DEBT	100,000		—		100,000
N	INCOME TAXES PAYABLE	0		—		0
K + L + M + N = O	CURRENT LIABILITIES	451,397				451,397
P	LONG-TERM DEBT	900,000		—		900,000
Q	CAPITAL STOCK	1,550,000		—		1,550,000
R	RETAINED EARNINGS	(25,900)	**3**	(5,100)		(31,000)
Q + R = S	SHAREHOLDERS' EQUITY	1,524,100				1,519,000
O + P + S = T	TOTAL LIABILITIES & EQUITY	$2,875,497		(5,100)		$2,870,397

Liabilities & Equity Sum

T16. Scrap 500 cases' worth of work-in-process inventory.

After we moved all the product that we could find (19,500 cases) into finished goods, we looked around for the remaining 500 cases we had expected to make.

We started out with enough material to make 20,000 cases but seem to have produced only 19,500 cases. The material and labor expenditures for these remaining 500 cases still remain in work-in-process inventory—but where is the product?

Our production supervisor comes up with the answer. It seems that our workers had some trouble starting up some of the new machines. Everything is fixed now, but for the first month of production every 40th jar of applesauce got smashed in the innards of the conveyor belts!

Thus, our output was only 19,500 cases and we spoiled 500 cases. We still expended the labor to produce 20,000 cases and we used all the material required to produce 20,000 cases, but at the end we only produced 19,500 cases.

Oh well, no use crying over spilled applesauce. But how should we account for the loss? Scrap the value of 500 cases of applesauce. Lower the value of work-in-process inventory, and take a corresponding loss on the *Income Statement*.

Transaction: Scrap the value of 500 cases of applesauce from the work-in-process inventory. Take a loss on the *Income Statement* for this amount.

1 Reduce **INVENTORIES** on the *Balance Sheet* by the $5,100 value of the inventory to be scrapped (that is 500 cases times the standard cost of $10.20 each).

2 Charge $5,100 to **COST OF GOODS SOLD** for the loss in value of the inventory due to scrapping 500 cases of work-in-process inventory.

3 Remember that the resulting loss in the *Income Statement* must be reflected as a decrease in **RETAINED EARNINGS** in the *Balance Sheet*.

~

Inventory Valuation Worksheet	RAW MATERIAL	WORK IN PROCESS	FINISHED GOODS
INVENTORY VALUES FROM T15.	$181,400	$5,100	$198,900
I. Scrap 500 cases of applesauce from WIP inventory.	$0	$(5,100)	$0
INVENTORY SUBTOTALS (AS OF THIS TRANSACTION)	$181,400	$0	$198,900
		TOTAL INVENTORY =	$380,300

Manufacturing Variances

The most efficient type of cost accounting is one that makes use of predetermined costs—referred to as *standard costs*. This procedure consists of setting, in advance of production, what the unit cost *should* be, and upon completion of production, comparing the actual costs with these *standard costs*. Any differences (either positive or negative) are then applied to the financial statements as a "variance" in order to reflect reality.

Standard Costs

We at AppleSeed Enterprises use a *standard costing system* to value our inventory. It is a convenient and accurate way to run the books and to account for what our products cost.

But, remember, the standard cost is what we *expect* our product to cost if all goes according to plan. That is, all must go *exactly* as expected (or excess money spent in one area must be saved in another) if our *actual cost* is to equal our standard cost.

In using a standard costing system, the various costs for materials, labor and overhead are booked into inventory at their *actual amounts*. But when product is placed in finished goods and then is sold, the transaction is performed "at standard."

The difference between the actual and the standard cost is then booked in the accounting records. These differences, if any, are called *manufacturing variances*.

Types of Variances. For AppleSeed's product and production costs to be "at standard," that is, for no manufacturing cost variances to have occurred:

- We must produce 20,000 cases in a month—no more, no less. *Otherwise we will have a **volume variance.***

- Our raw material must cost just what we have estimated them to be—no more, no less. *Otherwise we will have a **purchase variance.***

- The amount of raw material used must be just as planned. *Otherwise we will have a **yield variance.***

- We need no more or less direct labor and no overtime to produce our 20,000 cases. *Otherwise we will have a **labor variance.***

- We don't have excess scrap produced in the production process. *Otherwise we will have a **scrap variance.***

For AppleSeed's product and production costs to be at standard, that is, for no variances to have occurred:

1. We must produce exactly 20,000 cases in a month.

2. Our raw material must cost exactly what we have estimated.

3. The amount of raw material used must be just as planned.

4. We need no more or less direct labor and no overtime to produce our 20,000 cases.

5. We don't have excess scrap produced in the production process.

Most often, everything does not come out perfectly. We will then have to apply variances to our books. Remember, our production cost accounting relied upon standard cost. We used this standard cost to apply costs to inventory and to cost of goods sold. If actual costs were different—and they always are, hopefully by just a little bit—we will have to adjust the books by entering variance amounts.

Note that while it does not apply to AppleSeed, there is one other kind of manufacturing variance, the *mix variance.* A multi-product company can make more (or less) of one product than planned. This production difference can result in more (or less) overhead "absorption" depending on the relative overhead contribution of the products actually produced. This "under" or "over absorption" is accounted for as a product mix variance.

In summary, volume variances occur when we make more or less product than we had planned. Thus we must spread our fixed costs and overhead over less product (resulting in a higher cost) or over more product (resulting in a lower cost).

Spending variances can occur when raw materials cost more or less than planned. Actual product cost reflects these differences.

Labor variances are very easy to understand. If it takes more man-hours to make our product than expected by the standard, then our product must cost more than planned.

If AppleSeed continuously books large manufacturing variances each month, we should modify our standard costs to make them conform more closely to reality.

> **If AppleSeed continuously books large manufacturing variances each month, we should modify our standard costs to make them conform more closely to reality.**

Income Statement

for the period including Transactions 1 through 17		prior	+	transaction	=	sum
1	NET SALES	$0		—		$0
2	COST OF GOODS SOLD	5,100		—		5,100
1 - 2 = 3	GROSS MARGIN	(5,100)				(5,100)
4	SALES & MARKETING	7,680		—		7,680
5	RESEARCH & DEVELOPMENT	0		—		0
6	GENERAL & ADMINISTRATIVE	18,220		—		18,220
4 + 5 + 6 = 7	OPERATING EXPENSE	25,900				25,900
3 - 7 = 8	INCOME FROM OPERATIONS	(31,000)				(31,000)
9	NET INTEREST INCOME	0		—		0
10	INCOME TAXES	0		—		0
8 + 9 - 10 = 11	NET INCOME	($31,000)		0		($31,000)

IS Transaction Sum

Cash Flow Statement

for the period including Transactions 1 through 17		prior	+	transaction	=	sum
a	BEGINNING CASH BALANCE	$0				$0
b	CASH RECEIPTS	0		—		0
c	CASH DISBURSEMENTS	52,760	**1**	150,000		202,760
b - c = d	CASH FLOW FROM OPERATIONS	(52,760)				(202,760)
e	PP&E PURCHASE	1,750,000		—		1,750,000
f	NET BORROWINGS	1,000,000		—		1,000,000
g	INCOME TAXES PAID	0		—		0
h	SALE OF CAPITAL STOCK	1,550,000		—		1,550,000
a + d - e + f - g + h = i	ENDING CASH BALANCES	$747,240		(150,000)		$597,240

CF Transaction Sum

Balance Sheet

as of this Transaction 17		prior	+	transaction	=	sum
A	CASH	$747,240	**2**	(150,000)		$597,240
B	ACCOUNTS RECEIVABLE	0		—		0
C	INVENTORIES	380,300		—		380,300
D	PREPAID EXPENSES	0		—		0
A + B + C + D = E	CURRENT ASSETS	1,127,540				977,540
F	OTHER ASSETS	0		—		0
G	FIXED ASSETS @ COST	1,750,000		—		1,750,000
H	ACCUMULATED DEPRECIATION	7,143		—		7,143
G - H = I	NET FIXED ASSETS	1,742,857				1,742,857
E + F + I = J	TOTAL ASSETS	$2,870,397		(150,000)		$2,720,397

Assets Sum

		prior	+	transaction	=	sum
K	ACCOUNTS PAYABLE	$341,077	**3**	(150,000)		$191,077
L	ACCRUED EXPENSES	10,320		—		10,320
M	CURRENT PORTION OF DEBT	100,000		—		100,000
N	INCOME TAXES PAYABLE	0		—		0
K + L + M + N = O	CURRENT LIABILITIES	451,397				301,397
P	LONG-TERM DEBT	900,000		—		900,000
Q	CAPITAL STOCK	1,550,000		—		1,550,000
R	RETAINED EARNINGS	(31,000)		—		(31,000)
Q + R = S	SHAREHOLDERS' EQUITY	1,519,000				1,519,000
O + P + S = T	TOTAL LIABILITIES & EQUITY	$2,870,397		(150,000)		$2,720,397

Liabilities & Equity Sum

T17. Pay for some of the raw materials received in Transaction 11.

With our first month's production successfully placed in our finished goods warehouse, we throw a company picnic in celebration.

Halfway through the first hot dog, an important telephone call comes in. The president of Acme Apple and Jar Supply Incorporated, our apple and jar supplier, is on the line. He is calling to see how we are doing and when we plan to pay our bill for apples and jars. He suggests $150,000 or so would be appreciated.

Because we want to remain on good terms with this important supplier, we tell him, "The check is in the mail," and rush back to our offices to put it there.

Looking at our listing of current accounts payable, we note that we owe Acme: $79,200 for apples, $184,000 for jars, and $33,200 for jar caps—a total of $296,400 outstanding.

Take out the checkbook and write the check.

Transaction: Pay a major supplier a portion of what is due for apples and jars. Cut a check for $150,000 in partial payment.

1 Cut a check for $150,000 to pay the supplier. Increase CASH DISBURSEMENTS by that amount in the *Cash Flow Statement*.

2 Lower CASH by $150,000 in the assets section of the *Balance Sheet*.

3 Lower ACCOUNTS PAYABLE in the liabilities section of the *Balance Sheet* by $150,000 that we not longer owe...since we just paid as described above.

Note: Actually paying for raw materials does not affect our inventory value in any way. Inventory value increased when we received the raw material and we created an accounts payable.

$\sim$

Inventory Valuation Worksheet	RAW MATERIAL	WORK IN PROCESS	FINISHED GOODS
INVENTORY VALUES FROM **T16**.	$181,400	$0	$198,900
J. Pay for raw materials received in **T11**.	$0	$0	$0
INVENTORY SUBTOTALS (AS OF THIS TRANSACTION)	$181,400	$0	$198,900
	TOTAL INVENTORY =		$380,300

Income Statement

for the period including Transactions 1 through 18		*prior*	+	*transaction*	=	*sum*
1	NET SALES	$0		—		$0
2	COST OF GOODS SOLD	5,100	[1]	1,530		6,630
1 - 2 = 3	GROSS MARGIN	(5,100)				(6,630)
4	SALES & MARKETING	7,680		—		7,680
5	RESEARCH & DEVELOPMENT	0		—		0
6	GENERAL & ADMINISTRATIVE	18,220		—		18,220
4 + 5 + 6 = 7	OPERATING EXPENSE	25,900				25,900
3 - 7 = 8	INCOME FROM OPERATIONS	(31,000)				(32,530)
9	NET INTEREST INCOME	0		—		0
10	INCOME TAXES	0		—		0
8 + 9 - 10 = 11	NET INCOME	($31,000)		(1,530)		($32,530)

IS Transaction Sum

Cash Flow Statement

for the period including Transactions 1 through 18		*prior*	+	*transaction*	=	*sum*
a	BEGINNING CASH BALANCE	$0				$0
b	CASH RECEIPTS	0		—		0
c	CASH DISBURSEMENTS	202,760	[2]	9,020		211,780
b - c = d	CASH FLOW FROM OPERATIONS	(202,760)				(211,780)
e	PP&E PURCHASE	1,750,000		—		1,750,000
f	NET BORROWINGS	1,000,000		—		1,000,000
g	INCOME TAXES PAID	0		—		0
h	SALE OF CAPITAL STOCK	1,550,000		—		1,550,000
a + d - e + f - g + h = i	ENDING CASH BALANCES	$597,240		(9,020)		$588,220

CF Transaction Sum

Balance Sheet

as of this Transaction 18		*prior*	+	*transaction*	=	*sum*
A	CASH	$597,240	[3]	(9,020)		$588,220
B	ACCOUNTS RECEIVABLE	0		—		0
C	INVENTORIES	380,300	[4]	197,670		577,970
D	PREPAID EXPENSES	0		—		0
A + B + C + D = E	CURRENT ASSETS	977,540				1,166,190
F	OTHER ASSETS	0		—		0
G	FIXED ASSETS @ COST	1,750,000		—		1,750,000
H	ACCUMULATED DEPRECIATION	7,143	[5]	7,143		14,286
G - H = I	NET FIXED ASSETS	1,742,857				1,735,714
E + F + I = J	TOTAL ASSETS	$2,720,397		181,507		$2,901,904

Assets Sum

K	ACCOUNTS PAYABLE	$191,077	[6]	174,877		$365,954
L	ACCRUED EXPENSES	10,320	[7]	8,160		18,480
M	CURRENT PORTION OF DEBT	100,000		—		100,000
N	INCOME TAXES PAYABLE	0		—		0
K + L + M + N = O	CURRENT LIABILITIES	301,397				484,434
P	LONG-TERM DEBT	900,000		—		900,000
Q	CAPITAL STOCK	1,550,000		—		1,550,000
R	RETAINED EARNINGS	(31,000)	[8]	(1,530)		(32,530)
Q + R = S	SHAREHOLDERS' EQUITY	1,519,000				1,517,470
O + P + S = T	TOTAL LIABILITIES & EQUITY	$2,720,397		181,507		$2,901,904

Liabilities & Equity Sum

T18. Manufacture another month's supply of our wonderful applesauce.

Things are progressing at our enterprise. With this multiple transaction we will make another month's worth of applesauce and pay a few bills. Soon we will be ready to ship applesauce to our valued customers!

Shown at the bottom of the page are the series *(K through Q)* of Inventory Valuation Worksheet entries for the rest of the month. The table below translates these actions into transactions to post to AppleSeed's financial statements.

Transactions: Make entries in the *Income Statement, Cash Flow Statement* and *Balance Sheet* as shown in the total column at below right. ***Note that for each worksheet entry (K through Q below), the change in Assets equals the change in Liabilities.***

WORKSHEET ENTRY	K.	L.	M.	N.	O.	P.	Q.	TOTALS	
COST OF GOODS SOLD							$1,530	$1,530	**1**
CASH DISBURSEMENTS			$9,020					$9,020	**2**
CASH			$(9,020)					$(9,020)	**3**
INVENTORIES	$166,200		$17,180	$7,143	$8,677		$(1,530)	$197,670	**4**
ACCUM. DEPRECIATION				$7,143				$(7,143)	**5**
CHANGE IN ASSETS	$166,200	$0	$8,160	$0	$8,677	$0	$(1,530)	$181,507	
ACCOUNTS PAYABLE	$166,200				$8,677			$174,877	**6**
ACCRUED EXPENSES			$8,160					$8,160	**7**
RETAINED EARNINGS							$(1,530)	$(1,530)	**8**
CHANGE IN LIABILITIES	$166,200	$0	$8,160	$0	$8,677	$0	$(1,530)	$181,507	

Inventory Valuation Worksheet	RAW MATERIAL	WORK IN PROCESS	FINISHED GOODS
INVENTORY VALUES FROM T17.	$181,400	$0	$198,900
K. Receive a month's raw material supply less labels. (see **T10**)	$166,200	$0	$0
L. Move a month's supply of raw materials into WIP. (see **T12**)	$(171,000)	$171,000	$0
M. Pay hourly workers/supervisor for another month. (see **T12**)	$0	$17,180	$0
N. Book manufacturing depreciation for the month. (see **T13**)	$0	$7,143	$0
O. Book "all other" mfg. overhead for another month. (see **T13**)	$0	$8,677	$0
P. Move 19,000 cases to finished goods @ standard cost.(see **T15**)	$0	$(193,800)	$193,800
Q. Scrap 150 cases from WIP. (see **T16**)	$0	$(1,530)	$0
INVENTORY SUBTOTALS (AS OF THIS TRANSACTION)	$176,600	$8,670	$392,700
	TOTAL INVENTORY =		$577,970

Chapter 9. Marketing and Selling

A wise old consultant once said to me, "Really, the only thing you need to be in business is a customer."

AppleSeed Enterprises, Inc., is ready to find customers for its super, new brand of applesauce. We will begin marketing our product and testing the receptiveness of the marketplace to a new supplier—us!

Next (unfortunately), we will suffer one major risk of doing business, the deadbeat customer.

~

Transaction 19. Produce product advertising fliers and T-shirt giveaways.

• Product pricing; break-even analysis.

Transaction 20. A new customer orders 1,000 cases of applesauce. Ship 1,000 cases at $15.90 per case.

Transaction 21. Take an order (on credit) for 15,000 cases at a discounted price of $15.66 per case.

Transaction 22. Ship and invoice customer for 15,000 cases of applesauce ordered in Transaction 21 above.

Transaction 23. Receive payment of $234,900 for shipment made in Transaction 22 and pay the broker's commission.

Transaction 24. Oops! Customer goes bankrupt. Write off cost of 1,000 cases as a bad debt.

Financial Statements

Income Statement

for the period including Transactions 1 through 19		prior	+	transaction	=	sum
1	NET SALES	$0		—		$0
2	COST OF GOODS SOLD	6,630		—		6,630
1 - 2 = 3	GROSS MARGIN	(6,630)				(6,630)
4	SALES & MARKETING	7,680	[1]	103,250		110,930
5	RESEARCH & DEVELOPMENT	0		—		0
6	GENERAL & ADMINISTRATIVE	18,220		—		18,220
4 + 5 + 6 = 7	OPERATING EXPENSE	25,900				129,150
3 - 7 = 8	INCOME FROM OPERATIONS	(32,530)				(135,780)
9	NET INTEREST INCOME	0		—		0
10	INCOME TAXES	0		—		0
8 + 9 - 10 = 11	NET INCOME	($32,530)		(103,250)		($135,780)

IS Transaction Sum

Cash Flow Statement

for the period including Transactions 1 through 19		prior	+	transaction	=	sum
a	BEGINNING CASH BALANCE	$0				$0
b	CASH RECEIPTS	0		—		0
c	CASH DISBURSEMENTS	211,780		—		211,780
b - c = d	CASH FLOW FROM OPERATIONS	(211,780)				(211,780)
e	PP&E PURCHASE	1,750,000		—		1,750,000
f	NET BORROWINGS	1,000,000		—		1,000,000
g	INCOME TAXES PAID	0		—		0
h	SALE OF CAPITAL STOCK	1,550,000		—		1,550,000
a + d - e + f - g + h = i	ENDING CASH BALANCES	$588,220		0		$588,220

CF Transaction Sum

Balance Sheet

as of this Transaction 19		prior	+	transaction	=	sum
A	CASH	$588,220		—		$588,220
B	ACCOUNTS RECEIVABLE	0		—		0
C	INVENTORIES	577,970		—		577,970
D	PREPAID EXPENSES	0		—		0
A + B + C + D = E	CURRENT ASSETS	1,166,190				1,166,190
F	OTHER ASSETS	0		—		0
G	FIXED ASSETS @ COST	1,750,000		—		1,750,000
H	ACCUMULATED DEPRECIATION	14,286		—		14,286
G - H = I	NET FIXED ASSETS	1,735,714				1,735,714
E + F + I = J	TOTAL ASSETS	$2,901,904		0		$2,901,904
				Assets Sum		
K	ACCOUNTS PAYABLE	$365,954	[3]	103,250		$469,204
L	ACCRUED EXPENSES	18,480		—		18,480
M	CURRENT PORTION OF DEBT	100,000		—		100,000
N	INCOME TAXES PAYABLE	0		—		0
K + L + M + N = O	CURRENT LIABILITIES	484,434				587,684
P	LONG-TERM DEBT	900,000		—		900,000
Q	CAPITAL STOCK	1,550,000		—		1,550,000
R	RETAINED EARNINGS	(32,530)	[2]	(103,250)		(135,780)
Q + R = S	SHAREHOLDERS' EQUITY	1,517,470				1,414,220
O + P + S = T	TOTAL LIABILITIES & EQUITY	$2,901,904		0		$2,901,904

Liabilities & Equity Sum

T19. Produce product advertising fliers and T-shirt giveaways.

The usual method of selling our type of product is through a food broker to a retail store and then ultimately to the consumer. Food brokers serve the purpose of manufacturers' representatives, convincing retailers to stock various brands of product. For their efforts, these brokers receive a commission of about 2% of sales. They do not take title to the goods, they just smooth the way.

AppleSeed engages a topflight manufacturers' representative, SlickSales & Associates, to market its products. Slick-Sales and AppleSeed negotiate a sales commission of 2% of gross revenue to be paid SlickSales for placing AppleSeed's applesauce with retailers.

SlickSales requests that AppleSeed prepare and then supply them with sales literature to be given prospective customers. Everybody agrees that a direct mail promotion would be a good idea too.

We hire an advertising agency to design, print and mail a very fancy brochure to promote AppleSeed's applesauce products.

The agency also produces 10,000 AppleSeed Applesauce T-shirts to ship to supermarkets for use as a promotional giveaway.

Transaction: Our advertising agency submits a bill for designing, printing and mailing 4,500 very fancy brochures for a $38,250 total cost. The 10,000 T-shirts cost $6.50 each for a total of $65,000. Book these amounts as an AppleSeed Enterprises marketing and selling expense.

1 Book brochure and T-shirt expenses totaling $103,250 under SALES & MARKETING expense in the *Income Statement*.

2 Lower RETAINED EARNINGS in the liabilities section of the *Balance Sheet* by this $103,250 sales and marketing expense.

3 Increase ACCOUNTS PAYABLE in the liabilities section of the *Balance Sheet* by the same amount for the bill we owe the advertising agency.

~

Product Pricing

What should we charge for our delicious applesauce? How should we price our product?

Marketing textbooks say that pricing decisions are best made in the marketplace. Price-setting should be based on a competitive understanding and on our competitive goals. Manufacturing costs should have little bearing on pricing decisions.

After we have set a competitive price, we should then look at our costs to see that an adequate profit can be made. If we can't make our desired profit selling our applesauce at a competitive price, then we have just two options: lower costs or exit the business.

Market Pricing

Who are AppleSeed's competitors? How does our product compare with their offerings? What do they all charge for their applesauce? What should *we* charge to be competitive?

The chart below shows the wholesale and retail pricing structure for several brands of applesauce sold in our market. The chart translates the various markups (manufacturer's, wholesaler's and retailer's markups) into selling and cost prices at each level of distribution. Remember that a low-level distributor's price is the next upper-level distributor's cost.

We decide to position AppleSeed's applesauce as a mid-priced brand of very high quality. We think that at a retail price of $1.905 a jar (or $22.86 for a case of 12 jars), we offer good value. But can we make a profit at this selling price? A break-even analysis will help us answer this important question.

Review the volume and costs analysis on the facing page. Then look at the break-even chart on page 151.

Comparative Applesauce Prices in Our Market

	MANUFACTURE'S SELLING PRICE *Base Price*	WHOLESALER'S SELLING PRICE *Plus 15% over manufacture's price*	RETAILER'S SELLING PRICE *Plus 25% over wholesaler's price*
% OF MFG'S SELLING PRICE	100%	115%	143%
% OF RETAILER'S SELLING PRICE	70%	80%	100%
BRAND A	$15.21	$17.49	$21.86
BRAND B	$15.40	$17.71	$22.14
BRAND C	$16.58	$19.07	$23.84
APPLESEED ENTERPRISES BRAND	$15.90	$18.29	$22.86

Break-Even Analysis

Financial types (such as AppleSeed's bankers) will ask the question, "How much will you have to sell to make a profit? "

This revenue value, where increasing volume turns losses into profits, is called the company's "break-even point." *The break-even point is that sales volume where revenues are exactly equal to costs plus expenses, and thus, the company neither makes a profit nor suffers a loss.*

Your banker is sizing-up the company's operations and gauging whether it can achieve a profitable sales volume. A break-even analysis focuses management on the inherent profitability (or lack thereof) of an enterprise.

Let's do a break-even analysis for AppleSeed. The table below shows Apple-Seed Enterprises's annual costs and expenses at various sales and production volumes.

Some of AppleSeed's costs and expenses will not change with its volume of production and sales *(fixed costs)* and some will change *(variable costs)*.

Appleseed Enterprises Proforma Annual Costs and Expenses at Various Projected Production Volumes

	VARIABLE COST PER CASE	TOTAL FIXED COST PER YEAR	ANNUAL TOTALS @ ZERO CASES PER MONTH	ANNUAL TOTALS @ 5,000 CASES PER MONTH	ANNUAL TOTALS @ 10,000 CASES PER MONTH	ANNUAL TOTALS @ 15,000 CASES PER MONTH	ANNUAL TOTALS @ 20,000 CASES PER MONTH

Total Annual Variable Costs at Several Production Volumes

	VARIABLE COST PER CASE		@ ZERO	@ 5,000	@ 10,000	@ 15,000	@ 20,000
+ MATERIAL COSTS	$8.550	—	$0	$513,000	$1,026,000	$1,539,000	$2,052,000
+ DIRECT LABOR	$0.615	—	$0	$36,900	$73,800	$110,700	$147,600
+ BROKER COM.	$0.318	—	$0	$19,080	$38,160	$57,240	$76,320
= TOTAL ANNUAL VARIABLE COSTS	$9.483	—	$0	$568,980	$1,137,960	$1,706,940	$2,275,920

Total Annual Fixed Costs (no change with increasing production volume)

		TOTAL FIXED	@ ZERO	@ 5,000	@ 10,000	@ 15,000	@ 20,000
+ MFG. SUERVISOR	—	$58,650					
+ DEPRECIATION	—	$85,714					
+ ALL OTHER MFG.	—	$104,124					
+ SG&A SALARIES	—	$251,160					
+ INTEREST	—	$100,000					
+ MARKETING	—	$223,250					
= TOTAL ANNUAL FIXED COSTS	—	$822,898	$822,898	$822,898	$822,898	$822,898	$822,898

Total fixed costs are the same at all production levels. That is why they are called "fixed costs." These fixed costs do not change if you make more or if you make less product.

Profit & Loss Statements at Several Production Volumes

	@ ZERO	@ 5,000	@ 10,000	@ 15,000	@ 20,000
+ ANNUAL REVENUE @ $15.90 PER CASE	0	$954,000	$1,908,000	$2,862,000	$3,816,000
− TOTAL ANNUAL VARIABLE COSTS	0	$568,980	$1,137,960	$1,706,940	$2,275,920
− TOTAL ANNUAL FIXED COSTS	$822,898	$822,898	$822,898	$822,898	$822,898
= TOTAL ANNUAL PROFIT (LOSS)	$(822,898)	$(437,878)	$(52,858)	$332,162	$717,182

Fixed Costs. Fixed costs will be the same for AppleSeed, month after month, whether the company makes and sells 5,000 cases, 10,000 cases or even 20,000 cases per month. This fixed cost includes manufacturing costs and also SG&A expenses that are not related to volume. As shown in the table on page 149, we can see that AppleSeed's fixed costs are $822,898 per year.

Variable Costs. Each time AppleSeed sells a case of applesauce, it spends $9.483 in variable cost as shown in the table on page 149. So, if the company sells 10,000 cases per month (120,000 cases per year), total variable cost will be $9.483 per case times 120,000 cases for a total of $1,137,960 variable cost. If AppleSeed sells 20,000 cases per month, then the total variable cost will be double to $2,275,920.

AppleSeed's break-even chart on page 151 graphically represents the relationships shown in the table on page 149 between: (1) total revenue, (2) fixed costs, (3) total variable costs and (4) profit or loss for production volumes from zero to 25,000 cases per month. Reviewing the chart on page 151 shows that AppleSeed turns a profit at a production and sales volume of about 10,700 cases per month. Profitability improves nicely as sales and production reach our 15,000 case per month target.

Note that the difference between total variable cost and total sales is often called *contribution*. That is, the dollar amount that a level of sales "contributes" toward paying for fixed costs and expenses and any profit for the enterprise. The break-even point occurs when the contribution exactly equals fixed costs.

Profit is the difference between two large numbers: (1) sales *less* (2) costs & expenses. Small changes in either can result in large swings in profit (loss). Volume, cost and price are all connected to ultimate profits, as is shown in a break-even chart.

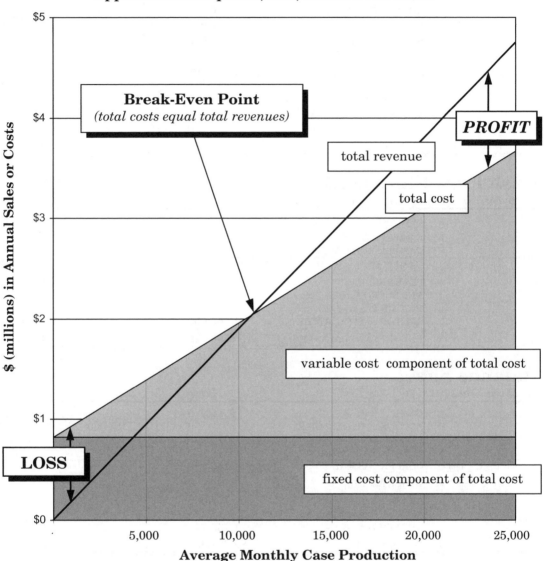

AppleSeed Enterprises, Inc., Break-Even Chart

A break-even chart is a useful, graphic way to help understand how: (1) product cost (both fixed and variable) is affected by production volume and (2) how product pricing affects profits. Volume, cost and price are all connected to ultimate profits, as is shown graphically in a break-even chart.

Income Statement

for the period including Transactions 1 through 20		prior	+	transaction	=	sum
1	NET SALES	$0	**1A**	15,900		$15,900
2	COST OF GOODS SOLD	6,630	**3B**	10,200		16,830
1 - 2 = 3	GROSS MARGIN	(6,630)				(930)
4	SALES & MARKETING	110,930	**2A**	318		111,248
5	RESEARCH & DEVELOPMENT	0		—		0
6	GENERAL & ADMINISTRATIVE	18,220		—		18,220
4 + 5 + 6 = 7	OPERATING EXPENSE	129,150				129,468
3 - 7 = 8	INCOME FROM OPERATIONS	(135,780)				(130,398)
9	NET INTEREST INCOME	0		—		0
10	INCOME TAXES	0		—		0
8 + 9 - 10 = 11	NET INCOME	($135,780)		5,382		($130,398)

IS Transaction Sum

Cash Flow Statement

for the period including Transactions 1 through 20		prior	+	transaction	=	sum
a	BEGINNING CASH BALANCE	$0				$0
b	CASH RECEIPTS	0		—		0
c	CASH DISBURSEMENTS	211,780		—		211,780
b - c = d	CASH FLOW FROM OPERATIONS	(211,780)				(211,780)
e	PP&E PURCHASE	1,750,000		—		1,750,000
f	NET BORROWINGS	1,000,000		—		1,000,000
g	INCOME TAXES PAID	0		—		0
h	SALE OF CAPITAL STOCK	1,550,000		—		1,550,000
a + d - e + f - g + h = i	ENDING CASH BALANCES	$588,220		0		$588,220

CF Transaction Sum

Balance Sheet

as of this Transaction 20		prior	+	transaction	=	sum
A	CASH	$588,220		—		$588,220
B	ACCOUNTS RECEIVABLE	0	**1B**	15,900		15,900
C	INVENTORIES	577,970	**3A**	(10,200)		567,770
D	PREPAID EXPENSES	0		—		0
A + B + C + D = E	CURRENT ASSETS	1,166,190				1,171,890
F	OTHER ASSETS	0		—		0
G	FIXED ASSETS @ COST	1,750,000		—		1,750,000
H	ACCUMULATED DEPRECIATION	14,286		—		14,286
G - H = I	NET FIXED ASSETS	1,735,714				1,735,714
E + F + I = J	TOTAL ASSETS	$2,901,904		5,700		$2,907,604

Assets Sum

K	ACCOUNTS PAYABLE	$469,204		—		$469,204
L	ACCRUED EXPENSES	18,480	**2B**	318		18,798
M	CURRENT PORTION OF DEBT	100,000		—		100,000
N	INCOME TAXES PAYABLE	0		—		0
K + L + M + N = O	CURRENT LIABILITIES	587,684				588,002
P	LONG-TERM DEBT	900,000		—		900,000
Q	CAPITAL STOCK	1,550,000		—		1,550,000
R	RETAINED EARNINGS	(135,780)	**4**	5,382		(130,398)
Q + R = S	SHAREHOLDERS' EQUITY	1,414,220				1,419,602
O + P + S = T	TOTAL LIABILITIES & EQUITY	$2,901,904		5,700		$2,907,604

Liabilities & Equity Sum

T20. A new customer orders 1,000 cases of applesauce. Ship 1,000 cases at $15.90 per case.

It's the moment we have all been waiting for—AppleSeed Enterprises' very first customer.

Your brother-in-law is the manager of a small convenience store chain. At the instigation of your spouse, he places an order for 1,000 cases to stock applesauce in his northwest region's stores.

Based on past experience, you trust your brother-in-law about as far as you can throw him...and he weighs in at 240 lbs.

You accept the order, but ask him to send a $15,900 prepayment check before you will ship. He says no. You decide to ship on credit and cross your fingers.

Transaction: Receive order for 1,000 cases of applesauce at a selling price of $15.90 per case. Ship product and send a $15,900 invoice to the customer.

1 (1A) Book your first sale of $15,900 as **NET SALES** on AppleSeed's *Income Statement*. (1B) Add an **ACCOUNTS RECEIVABLE** for the same amount in the *Balance Sheet*.

2 (2A) Book on the *Income Statement* the 2% commission ($318) for our broker as a **SALES & MARKETING** expense. (2B) Also book this $318 commission in **ACCRUED EXPENSES** on the *Balance Sheet*. The broker does not get paid until we do.

3 (3A) Reduce **INVENTORIES** on the *Balance Sheet* by $10,200— 1,000 cases times standard cost of $10.20 for each case. (3B) Corresponding to the inventory reduction above, increase **COST OF GOODS SOLD** by $10,200—the standard cost of 1,000 cases of applesauce.

4 Increase **RETAINED EARNINGS** on the *Balance Sheet* by $5,382—the sale amount, less cost of goods, less the selling commission. That amount is AppleSeed's profit on the sales

∼

Inventory Valuation Worksheet	RAW MATERIAL	WORK IN PROCESS	FINISHED GOODS
INVENTORY VALUES FROM T18.	$176,600	$8,670	$392,700
R. Ship 1,000 cases of applesauce at $10.20 standard cost/case.	$0	$0	$(10,200)
INVENTORY SUBTOTALS (AS OF THIS TRANSACTION)	$176,000	$8,670	$382,500
		TOTAL INVENTORY =	$567,770

Income Statement

for the period including Transactions 1 through 21	*prior*	+	*transaction*	=	*sum*
1 NET SALES	$15,900		—		$15,900
2 COST OF GOODS SOLD	16,830		—		16,830
1 - 2 = 3 GROSS MARGIN	(930)				(930)
4 SALES & MARKETING	111,248		—		111,248
5 RESEARCH & DEVELOPMENT	0		—		0
6 GENERAL & ADMINISTRATIVE	18,220		—		18,220
4 + 5 + 6 = 7 OPERATING EXPENSE	129,468				129,468
3 - 7 = 8 INCOME FROM OPERATIONS	(130,398)				(130,398)
9 NET INTEREST INCOME	0		—		0
10 INCOME TAXES	0		—		0
8 + 9 - 10 = 11 NET INCOME	($130,398)		0		($130,398)

IS Transaction Sum

Cash Flow Statement

for the period including Transactions 1 through 21	*prior*	+	*transaction*	=	*sum*
a BEGINNING CASH BALANCE	$0				$0
b CASH RECEIPTS	0		—		0
c CASH DISBURSEMENTS	211,780		—		211,780
b - c = d CASH FLOW FROM OPERATIONS	(211,780)				(211,780)
e PP&E PURCHASE	1,750,000		—		1,750,000
f NET BORROWINGS	1,000,000		—		1,000,000
g INCOME TAXES PAID	0		—		0
h SALE OF CAPITAL STOCK	1,550,000		—		1,550,000
a + d - e + f - g + h = i ENDING CASH BALANCES	$588,220		0		$588,220

CF Transaction Sum

Balance Sheet

as of this Transaction 21	*prior*	+	*transaction*	=	*sum*
A CASH	$588,220		—		$588,220
B ACCOUNTS RECEIVABLE	15,900		—		15,900
C INVENTORIES	567,770		—		567,770
D PREPAID EXPENSES	0		—		0
A + B + C + D = E CURRENT ASSETS	1,171,890				1,171,890
F OTHER ASSETS	0				0
G FIXED ASSETS @ COST	1,750,000		—		1,750,000
H ACCUMULATED DEPRECIATION	14,286		—		14,286
G - H = I NET FIXED ASSETS	1,735,714				1,735,714
E + F + I = J TOTAL ASSETS	$2,907,604		0		$2,907,604

Assets Sum

	prior	+	*transaction*	=	*sum*
K ACCOUNTS PAYABLE	$469,204		—		$469,204
L ACCRUED EXPENSES	18,798		—		18,798
M CURRENT PORTION OF DEBT	100,000		—		100,000
N INCOME TAXES PAYABLE	0		—		0
K + L + M + N = O CURRENT LIABILITIES	588,002				588,002
P LONG-TERM DEBT	900,000		—		900,000
Q CAPITAL STOCK	1,550,000		—		1,550,000
R RETAINED EARNINGS	(130,398)		—		(130,398)
Q + R = S SHAREHOLDERS' EQUITY	1,419,602				1,419,602
O + P + S = T TOTAL LIABILITIES & EQUITY	$2,907,604		0		$2,907,604

Liabilities & Equity Sum

T21. Take an order (on credit) for 15,000 cases at $15.66 per case.

Our broker is beginning to do his job. We may soon receive a big order from one of the largest food retailers in the area. We have the goods in inventory, so we promise to ship promptly.

To close the deal, we authorize our broker to offer the prospective customer a 1.5% discount. The retailer agrees to purchase 15,000 cases at a discounted selling price of $15.66 per case ($15.90 list less the 24¢ discount).

Transaction: Receive an order for 15,000 cases of applesauce at a selling price of $15.66 per case, $234,900 for the total order.

Note: Receiving an order has no effect on the three major financial statements. Only when the product ordered is shipped to customers do you record a SALE and the associated COST OF GOODS SOLD.

～

Income Statement

for the period including Transactions 1 through 22	prior	+	transaction	=	sum
1 NET SALES	$15,900	**1A**	234,900		$250,800
2 COST OF GOODS SOLD	16,830	**2A**	153,000		169,830
1 - 2 = 3 GROSS MARGIN	(930)				80,970
4 SALES & MARKETING	111,248	**3A**	4,698		115,946
5 RESEARCH & DEVELOPMENT	0		—		0
6 GENERAL & ADMINISTRATIVE	18,220		—		18,220
4 + 5 + 6 = 7 OPERATING EXPENSE	129,468				134,166
3 - 7 = 8 INCOME FROM OPERATIONS	(130,398)				(53,196)
9 NET INTEREST INCOME	0		—		0
10 INCOME TAXES	0		—		0
8 + 9 - 10 = 11 NET INCOME	($130,398)		77,202		($53,196)

IS Transaction Sum

Cash Flow Statement

for the period including Transactions 1 through 22	prior	+	transaction	=	sum
a BEGINNING CASH BALANCE	$0				$0
b CASH RECEIPTS	0		—		0
c CASH DISBURSEMENTS	211,780		—		211,780
b - c = d CASH FLOW FROM OPERATIONS	(211,780)				(211,780)
e PP&E PURCHASE	1,750,000		—		1,750,000
f NET BORROWINGS	1,000,000		—		1,000,000
g INCOME TAXES PAID	0		—		0
h SALE OF CAPITAL STOCK	1,550,000		—		1,550,000
a + d - e + f - g + h = i ENDING CASH BALANCES	$588,220		0		$588,220

CF Transaction Sum

Balance Sheet

as of this Transaction 22	prior	+	transaction	=	sum
A CASH	$588,220		—		$588,220
B ACCOUNTS RECEIVABLE	15,900	**1B**	234,900		250,800
C INVENTORIES	567,770	**2B**	(153,000)		414,770
D PREPAID EXPENSES	0		—		0
A + B + C + D = E CURRENT ASSETS	1,171,890				1,253,790
F OTHER ASSETS	0		—		0
G FIXED ASSETS @ COST	1,750,000		—		1,750,000
H ACCUMULATED DEPRECIATION	14,286		—		14,286
G - H = I NET FIXED ASSETS	1,735,714				1,735,714
E + F + I = J TOTAL ASSETS	$2,907,604		81,900		$2,989,504
			Assets Sum		
K ACCOUNTS PAYABLE	$469,204		—		$469,204
L ACCRUED EXPENSES	18,798	**3B**	4,698		23,496
M CURRENT PORTION OF DEBT	100,000		—		100,000
N INCOME TAXES PAYABLE	0		—		0
K + L + M + N = O CURRENT LIABILITIES	588,002				592,700
P LONG-TERM DEBT	900,000		—		900,000
Q CAPITAL STOCK	1,550,000		—		1,550,000
R RETAINED EARNINGS	(130,398)	**4**	77,202		(53,196)
Q + R = S SHAREHOLDERS' EQUITY	1,419,602				1,496,804
O + P + S = T TOTAL LIABILITIES & EQUITY	$2,907,604		81,900		$2,989,504

Liabilities & Equity Sum

T22. Ship and invoice customer for 15,000 cases of applesauce ordered in Transaction 21.

Although we did lower our price to get this large order, our costs will remain the same. Thus we will garner a lower profit in this transaction than if we had sold at full list price.

AppleSeed's net sales amount will be $234,900 versus the $238,500 if we had sold at list price—a difference of $3,600 in lower sales.

Our gross margin (that is, sales less cost of goods sold) will be $81,900 versus $85,500—again, a difference of $3,600 less margin.

In fact, this $3,600 difference in the original selling price will drop all the way to the bottom line as a lower profit. Discounts are dangerous profit-gobblers. Try to use them sparingly.

Transaction: Ship 15,000 cases of applesauce and send a $234,900 invoice to the customer.

1 (1A) Book sale of $234,900 as **NET SALES** on AppleSeed's *Income Statement*. (1B) Make a corresponding entry as **ACCOUNTS RECEIVABLE** on the *Balance Sheet*.

2 (2A) On the *Income Statement* book **COST OF GOODS SOLD** for this sale of $153,000, equaling a $10.20 standard cost per case times 15,000 cases shipped. (2B) Reduce **INVENTORIES** on the *Balance Sheet* by this same amount.

3 (3A) Book on the *Income Statement* a **SALES & MARKETING** expense of $4,698 as the 2% selling commission for our broker. (3B) Also book this expense in **ACCRUED EXPENSES** on the *Balance Sheet*.

4 Increase **RETAINED EARNINGS** on the *Balance Sheet* by $77,202—the sale amount less cost of goods sold less the selling commission.

$\sim$

Inventory Valuation Worksheet	RAW MATERIAL	WORK IN PROCESS	FINISHED GOODS
INVENTORY VALUES FROM T20.	$176,000	$8,670	$382,500
S. Ship 15,000 cases of applesauce at $10.20 standard cost.	$0	$0	$(153,000)
INVENTORY SUBTOTALS (AS OF THIS TRANSACTION)	$181,400	$8,670	$229,500
		TOTAL INVENTORY =	$414,770

Income Statement

for the period including Transactions 1 through 23	prior	+	transaction	=	sum
1	NET SALES	$250,800	—	$250,800
2	COST OF GOODS SOLD	169,830	—	169,830
1 - 2 = 3	GROSS MARGIN	80,970		80,970
4	SALES & MARKETING	115,946	—	115,946
5	RESEARCH & DEVELOPMENT	0	—	0
6	GENERAL & ADMINISTRATIVE	18,220	—	18,220
4 + 5 + 6 = 7	OPERATING EXPENSE	134,166		134,166
3 - 7 = 8	INCOME FROM OPERATIONS	(53,196)		(53,196)
9	NET INTEREST INCOME	0	—	0
10	INCOME TAXES	0	—	0
8 + 9 - 10 = 11	NET INCOME	($53,196)	0	($53,196)

IS Transaction Sum

Cash Flow Statement

for the period including Transactions 1 through 23	prior	+	transaction	=	sum
a	BEGINNING CASH BALANCE	$0			$0
b	CASH RECEIPTS	0	**1A**	234,900	234,900
c	CASH DISBURSEMENTS	211,780	**2A**	4,698	216,478
b - c = d	CASH FLOW FROM OPERATIONS	(211,780)			18,422
e	PP&E PURCHASE	1,750,000	—	1,750,000
f	NET BORROWINGS	1,000,000	—	1,000,000
g	INCOME TAXES PAID	0	—	0
h	SALE OF CAPITAL STOCK	1,550,000	—	1,550,000
a + d - e + f - g + h = i	ENDING CASH BALANCES	$588,220	230,202	$818,422

CF Transaction Sum

Balance Sheet

as of this Transaction 23	prior	+	transaction	=	sum
A	CASH	$588,220	**3**	230,202	$818,422
B	ACCOUNTS RECEIVABLE	250,800	**1B**	(234,900)	15,900
C	INVENTORIES	414,770	—	414,770
D	PREPAID EXPENSES	0	—	0
A + B + C + D = E	CURRENT ASSETS	1,253,790		1,249,092
F	OTHER ASSETS	0	—	0
G	FIXED ASSETS @ COST	1,750,000	—	1,750,000
H	ACCUMULATED DEPRECIATION	14,286	—	14,286
G - H = I	NET FIXED ASSETS	1,735,714		1,735,714
E + F + I = J	TOTAL ASSETS	$2,989,504	(4,698)	$2,984,806

Assets Sum

K	ACCOUNTS PAYABLE	$469,204	—	$469,204
L	ACCRUED EXPENSES	23,496	**2B** (4,698)	18,798
M	CURRENT PORTION OF DEBT	100,000	—	100,000
N	INCOME TAXES PAYABLE	0	—	0
K + L + M + N = O	CURRENT LIABILITIES	592,700		588,002
P	LONG-TERM DEBT	900,000	—	900,000
Q	CAPITAL STOCK	1,550,000	—	1,550,000
R	RETAINED EARNINGS	(53,196)	—	(53,196)
Q + R = S	SHAREHOLDERS' EQUITY	1,496,804		1,496,804
O + P + S = T	TOTAL LIABILITIES & EQUITY	$2,989,504	(4,698)	$2,984,806

Liabilities & Equity Sum

T23. Receive payment of $234,900 for shipment made in Transaction 22 and pay the broker's commission.

Our big customer is very happy with our applesauce. He says that our brightly colored jars are "walking off the shelves." We're extremely happy that we decided to spend so much money on very fancy packaging.

Although it is true that "all you really need to be in business is a customer," what you really need is a customer who pays. With this transaction we will collect our first accounts receivable and turn it into cash.

Transaction: Receive payment of $234,900 for shipment that was made in Transaction 22. Pay the broker his $4,698 selling commission.

1 (1A) Book $234,900 in CASH RECEIPTS in the *Cash Flow Statement*. (1B) Decrease ACCOUNTS RECEIVABLE on the *Balance Sheet* by the same amount.

2 (2A) Issue a $4,698 check to our broker and record in CASH DISBURSEMENTS in the *Cash Flow Statement*. (2B) Lower ACCRUED EXPENSES by the amount paid the broker.

3 Increase CASH by $230,202 on the *Balance Sheet* (that is, $234,900 received less $4,698 disbursed).

Note: A customer's cash payment for goods in no way changes the *Income Statement*. The *Income Statement* recorded a sale when first, we shipped the goods, and second, the customer incurred the obligation to pay (our accounts receivable).

⌣

Income Statement

for the period including Transactions 1 through 24

		prior	+	transaction	=	sum
1	NET SALES	$250,800		—		$250,800
2	COST OF GOODS SOLD	169,830		—		169,830
1 - 2 = 3	GROSS MARGIN	80,970				80,970
4	SALES & MARKETING	115,946	**2A**	(318)		115,628
5	RESEARCH & DEVELOPMENT	0		—		0
6	GENERAL & ADMINISTRATIVE	18,220	**1A**	15,900		34,120
4 + 5 + 6 = 7	OPERATING EXPENSE	134,166				149,748
3 - 7 = 8	INCOME FROM OPERATIONS	(53,196)				(68,778)
9	NET INTEREST INCOME	0		—		0
10	INCOME TAXES	0		—		0
8 + 9 - 10 = 11	NET INCOME	($53,196)		(15,582)		($68,778)

IS Transaction Sum

Cash Flow Statement

for the period including Transactions 1 through 24

		prior	+	transaction	=	sum
a	BEGINNING CASH BALANCE	$0				$0
b	CASH RECEIPTS	234,900		—		234,900
c	CASH DISBURSEMENTS	216,478		—		216,478
b - c = d	CASH FLOW FROM OPERATIONS	18,422				18,422
e	PP&E PURCHASE	1,750,000		—		1,750,000
f	NET BORROWINGS	1,000,000		—		1,000,000
g	INCOME TAXES PAID	0		—		0
h	SALE OF CAPITAL STOCK	1,550,000		—		1,550,000
a + d - e + f - g + h = i	ENDING CASH BALANCES	$818,422		0		$818,422

CF Transaction Sum

Balance Sheet

as of this Transaction 24

		prior	+	transaction	=	sum
A	CASH	$818,422		—		$818,422
B	ACCOUNTS RECEIVABLE	15,900	**1B**	(15,900)		0
C	INVENTORIES	414,770		—		414,770
D	PREPAID EXPENSES	0		—		0
A + B + C + D = E	CURRENT ASSETS	1,249,092				1,233,192
F	OTHER ASSETS	0		—		0
G	FIXED ASSETS @ COST	1,750,000		—		1,750,000
H	ACCUMULATED DEPRECIATION	14,286		—		14,286
G - H = I	NET FIXED ASSETS	1,735,714				1,735,714
E + F + I = J	TOTAL ASSETS	$2,984,806		(15,900)		$2,968,906
				Assets Sum		
K	ACCOUNTS PAYABLE	$469,204		—		$469,204
L	ACCRUED EXPENSES	18,798	**2B**	(318)		18,480
M	CURRENT PORTION OF DEBT	100,000		—		100,000
N	INCOME TAXES PAYABLE	0		—		0
K + L + M + N = O	CURRENT LIABILITIES	588,002				587,684
P	LONG-TERM DEBT	900,000		—		900,000
Q	CAPITAL STOCK	1,550,000		—		1,550,000
R	RETAINED EARNINGS	(53,196)	**3**	(15,582)		(68,778)
Q + R = S	SHAREHOLDERS' EQUITY	1,496,804				1,481,222
O + P + S = T	TOTAL LIABILITIES & EQUITY	$2,984,806		(15,900)		$2,968,906

Liabilities & Equity Sum

T24. Oops! Customer goes bankrupt. Write off cost of 1,000 cases as a bad debt.

Remember back in **Transaction 20** we shipped 1,000 cases of applesauce to your brother-in-law's company? You'll never guess what happened. They went bankrupt! Now he even wants a job.

We will never get paid. And because the goods have already been distributed and sold to applesauce lovers around the northwest, we will never get our product back, either.

Transaction: Write off the $15,900 accounts receivable that was entered when you made the 1,000 case shipment. Also, reduce the amount payable to our broker by what would have been his commission on the sale. If we don't get paid, he doesn't either!

1 (1A) Book the bad-debt expense of $15,900 against GENERAL & ADMINISTRATIVE expense on the *Income Statement*. (1B) Reduce ACCOUNTS RECEIVABLE on the *Balance Sheet* by the $15,900 we will never collect. These entries reverse the sale we had made.

2 (2A) Book a "negative expense" of minus $318 in SALES & MARKETING expense on the *Income Statement*. (2B) Decrease ACCRUED EXPENSE on the *Balance Sheet* by the same amount. These entries reverse the commission that had been due our broker.

3 Reduce RETAINED EARNINGS on the *Balance Sheet* by $15,582, the sale amount we wrote off less the commission no longer due.

Note: Our out-of-pocket loss is really just the $10,200 inventory value of the goods shipped.

Remember that in **Transaction 20** we booked a profit from this sale of $5,382—the $15,900 sale minus the $10,200 cost of goods sold minus the $318 selling commission. Thus, if you combine the $15,582 drop in RETAINED EARNINGS booked in this transaction plus the $5,382 increase in RETAINED EARNINGS from **Transaction 20**, you are left with our loss of $10,200 from this bad debt.

~

Chapter 10. Administrative Tasks

We've been busy making and selling our delicious applesauce. However, having been in business for three months, it's time to attend to some important administrative tasks.

$\sim$

Transaction 25.   Pay this year's general liability insurance.

Transaction 26.   Make principal and interest payments on three months' worth of building debts.

Transaction 27.   Pay payroll-associated taxes and insurance benefit premiums.

Transaction 28.   Pay some suppliers...especially the mean and hungry ones.

Income Statement

for the period including Transactions 1 through 25		prior	+	transaction	=	sum
1	NET SALES	$250,800		—		$250,800
2	COST OF GOODS SOLD	169,830		—		169,830
1 - 2 = 3	GROSS MARGIN	80,970				80,970
4	SALES & MARKETING	115,628		—		115,628
5	RESEARCH & DEVELOPMENT	0		—		0
6	GENERAL & ADMINISTRATIVE	34,120	**2**	6,500		40,620
4 + 5 + 6 = 7	OPERATING EXPENSE	149,748				156,248
3 - 7 = 8	INCOME FROM OPERATIONS	(68,778)				(75,278)
9	NET INTEREST INCOME	0		—		0
10	INCOME TAXES	0		—		0
8 + 9 - 10 = 11	NET INCOME	($68,778)		(6,500)		($75,278)

IS Transaction Sum

Cash Flow Statement

for the period including Transactions 1 through 25		prior	+	transaction	=	sum
a	BEGINNING CASH BALANCE	$0				$0
b	CASH RECEIPTS	234,900		—		234,900
c	CASH DISBURSEMENTS	216,478	**1A**	26,000		242,478
b - c = d	CASH FLOW FROM OPERATIONS	18,422				(7,578)
e	PP&E PURCHASE	1,750,000		—		1,750,000
f	NET BORROWINGS	1,000,000		—		1,000,000
g	INCOME TAXES PAID	0		—		0
h	SALE OF CAPITAL STOCK	1,550,000		—		1,550,000
a + d - e + f - g + h = i	ENDING CASH BALANCES	$818,422		(26,000)		$792,422

CF Transaction Sum

Balance Sheet

as of this Transaction 25		prior	+	transaction	=	sum
A	CASH	$818,422	**1B**	(26,000)		$792,422
B	ACCOUNTS RECEIVABLE	0		—		0
C	INVENTORIES	414,770		—		414,770
D	PREPAID EXPENSES	0	**3**	19,500		19,500
A + B + C + D = E	CURRENT ASSETS	1,233,192				1,226,692
F	OTHER ASSETS	0		—		0
G	FIXED ASSETS @ COST	1,750,000		—		1,750,000
H	ACCUMULATED DEPRECIATION	14,286		—		14,286
G - H = I	NET FIXED ASSETS	1,735,714				1,735,714
E + F + I = J	TOTAL ASSETS	$2,968,906		(6,500)		$2,962,406

Assets Sum

K	ACCOUNTS PAYABLE	$469,204		—		$469,204
L	ACCRUED EXPENSES	18,480		—		18,480
M	CURRENT PORTION OF DEBT	100,000		—		100,000
N	INCOME TAXES PAYABLE	0		—		0
K + L + M + N = O	CURRENT LIABILITIES	587,684				587,684
P	LONG-TERM DEBT	900,000		—		900,000
Q	CAPITAL STOCK	1,550,000		—		1,550,000
R	RETAINED EARNINGS	(68,778)	**4**	(6,500)		(75,278)
Q + R = S	SHAREHOLDERS' EQUITY	1,481,222				1,474,722
O + P + S = T	TOTAL LIABILITIES & EQUITY	$2,968,906		(6,500)		$2,962,406

Liabilities & Equity Sum

T25. Pay this year's general liability insurance.

During the first month we were in business many insurance brokers dropped by to try to sell us their wares.

We selected LightningBolt Brokers as our insurance agent. LightningBolt put together a package of building insurance, liability insurance and business interruption insurance that appeared to meet our needs.

We signed up for coverage and the broker said that she would send us a bill for the year, which we just got yesterday.

Transaction: With this transaction we will pay a full year's insurance premium of $26,000, giving us three months' prior coverage (the amount of time we have been in business) and also coverage for the remaining nine months in our fiscal year.

1 (1A) Issue a check for $26,000 to the insurance broker and book in **CASH DISBURSEMENTS** in the *Cash Flow Statement*. (1B) Lower **CASH** on the *Balance Sheet* by the amount of the check.

2 Book as a **GENERAL & ADMINISTRATIVE** expense on the *Income Statement* the $6,500 portion of the premium covering the last three months.

3 Book in **PREPAID EXPENSES** on the *Balance Sheet* the remaining $19,500 premium covering the next nine months.

Note: As time goes by, we will take this remaining $19,500 as an expense through the *Income Statement*. The transaction at that time will be to book the expense in the *Income Statement* and at the same time lower the amount of **PREPAID EXPENSES** in the *Balance Sheet*.

4 Reduce **RETAINED EARNINGS** in the Balance Sheet by the $6,500 loss due to the expense we have run through the *Income Statement*.

~

Financial Statements

Income Statement

for the period including Transactions 1 through 26

		prior	+	transaction	=	sum
1	NET SALES	$250,800		—		$250,800
2	COST OF GOODS SOLD	169,830		—		169,830
1 - 2 = 3	GROSS MARGIN	80,970				80,970
4	SALES & MARKETING	115,628		—		115,628
5	RESEARCH & DEVELOPMENT	0		—		0
6	GENERAL & ADMINISTRATIVE	40,620		—		40,620
4 + 5 + 6 = 7	OPERATING EXPENSE	156,248				156,248
3 - 7 = 8	INCOME FROM OPERATIONS	(75,278)				(75,278)
9	NET INTEREST INCOME	0	**3A**	(25,000)		(25,000)
10	INCOME TAXES	0		—		0
8 + 9 - 10 = 11	NET INCOME	($75,278)		(25,000)		($100,278)

IS Transaction Sum

Cash Flow Statement

for the period including Transactions 1 through 26

		prior	+	transaction	=	sum
a	BEGINNING CASH BALANCE	$0				$0
b	CASH RECEIPTS	234,900		—		234,900
c	CASH DISBURSEMENTS	242,478	**1B**	25,000		267,478
b - c = d	CASH FLOW FROM OPERATIONS	(7,578)				(32,578)
e	PP&E PURCHASE	1,750,000		—		1,750,000
f	NET BORROWINGS	1,000,000	**1A**	(25,000)		975,000
g	INCOME TAXES PAID	0		—		0
h	SALE OF CAPITAL STOCK	1,550,000		—		1,550,000
a + d - e + f - g + h = i	ENDING CASH BALANCES	$792,422		(50,000)		$742,422

CF Transaction Sum

Balance Sheet

as of this Transaction 26

		prior	+	transaction	=	sum
A	CASH	$792,422	**1C**	(50,000)		$742,422
B	ACCOUNTS RECEIVABLE	0		—		0
C	INVENTORIES	414,770		—		414,770
D	PREPAID EXPENSES	19,500		—		19,500
A + B + C + D = E	CURRENT ASSETS	1,226,692				1,176,692
F	OTHER ASSETS	0		—		0
G	FIXED ASSETS @ COST	1,750,000		—		1,750,000
H	ACCUMULATED DEPRECIATION	14,286		—		14,286
G - H = I	NET FIXED ASSETS	1,735,714				1,735,714
E + F + I = J	TOTAL ASSETS	$2,962,406		(50,000)		$2,912,406

Assets Sum

		prior	+	transaction	=	sum
K	ACCOUNTS PAYABLE	$469,204		—		$469,204
L	ACCRUED EXPENSES	18,480		—		18,480
M	CURRENT PORTION OF DEBT	100,000		—		100,000
N	INCOME TAXES PAYABLE	0		—		0
K + L + M + N = O	CURRENT LIABILITIES	587,684				587,684
P	LONG-TERM DEBT	900,000	**2**	(25,000)		875,000
Q	CAPITAL STOCK	1,550,000		—		1,550,000
R	RETAINED EARNINGS	(75,278)	**3B**	(25,000)		(100,278)
Q + R = S	SHAREHOLDERS' EQUITY	1,474,722				1,449,722
O + P + S = T	TOTAL LIABILITIES & EQUITY	$2,962,406		(50,000)		$2,912,406

Liabilities & Equity Sum

T26. Make principal and interest payments on three months' worth of building debts.

Review the loan amortization schedule in Transaction 3. It shows how we must pay back the money we owe on the purchase of our building. Also, the fine print in the loan documentation says we must pay the principal and interest quarterly.

Three months have gone by since we got the loan, so interest and principal payments are due. According to the amortization schedule, this year we owe a total of $100,000 in principal payments and also $100,000 in interest payments.

Transaction: Make a quarterly payment of $25,000 in principal and also a $25,000 interest payment on the building mortgage.

1 (1A) Lower **NET BORROWINGS** in the *Cash Flow Statement* by the $25,000 principal payment. (1B) Book in **CASH DISBURSEMENTS** for the $25,000 interest payment. (1C) Lower **CASH** on the *Balance Sheet* by the total $50,000 in cash that left the company.

2 Lower **LONG-TERM DEBT** on the *Balance Sheet* by the $25,000 principal payment made above.

3 (3A) Book the interest payment as a negative $25,000 under **NET INTEREST INCOME** on the *Income Statement*. (3B) Then book the resulting loss in **RETAINED EARNINGS** on the *Balance Sheet*.

Note: The interest payment entry for this transaction is booked as a negative number. If we had a category **INTEREST EXPENSE** on the *Income Statement* instead of **INTEREST INCOME**, then interest payments by the company would be booked as a positive number and interest income would be booked as a negative number.

Got that? It's important to pay attention to the exact account meaning when determining whether an entry should be positive or negative.

∿

Income Statement

for the period including Transactions 1 through 27		prior	+	transaction	=	sum
1	NET SALES	$250,800		—		$250,800
2	COST OF GOODS SOLD	169,830		—		169,830
1 - 2 = 3	GROSS MARGIN	80,970				80,970
4	SALES & MARKETING	115,628		—		115,628
5	RESEARCH & DEVELOPMENT	0		—		0
6	GENERAL & ADMINISTRATIVE	40,620		—		40,620
4 + 5 + 6 = 7	OPERATING EXPENSE	156,248				156,248
3 - 7 = 8	INCOME FROM OPERATIONS	(75,278)				(75,278)
9	NET INTEREST INCOME	(25,000)		—		(25,000)
10	INCOME TAXES	0		—		0
8 + 9 - 10 = 11	NET INCOME	($100,278)		0		($100,278)

IS Transaction Sum

Cash Flow Statement

for the period including Transactions 1 through 27		prior	+	transaction	=	sum
a	BEGINNING CASH BALANCE	$0				$0
b	CASH RECEIPTS	234,900		—		234,900
c	CASH DISBURSEMENTS	267,478	**1A**	18,480		285,958
b - c = d	CASH FLOW FROM OPERATIONS	(32,578)				(51,058)
e	PP&E PURCHASE	1,750,000		—		1,750,000
f	NET BORROWINGS	975,000		—		975,000
g	INCOME TAXES PAID	0		—		0
h	SALE OF CAPITAL STOCK	1,550,000		—		1,550,000
a + d - e + f - g + h = i	ENDING CASH BALANCES	$742,422		(18,480)		$723,942

CF Transaction Sum

Balance Sheet

as of this Transaction 27		prior	+	transaction	=	sum
A	CASH	$742,422	**1B**	(18,480)		$723,942
B	ACCOUNTS RECEIVABLE	0		—		0
C	INVENTORIES	414,770		—		414,770
D	PREPAID EXPENSES	19,500		—		19,500
A + B + C + D = E	CURRENT ASSETS	1,176,692				1,158,212
F	OTHER ASSETS	0		—		0
G	FIXED ASSETS @ COST	1,750,000		—		1,750,000
H	ACCUMULATED DEPRECIATION	14,286		—		14,286
G - H = I	NET FIXED ASSETS	1,735,714				1,735,714
E + F + I = J	TOTAL ASSETS	$2,912,406		(18,480)		$2,893,926

Assets Sum

		prior	+	transaction	=	sum
K	ACCOUNTS PAYABLE	$469,204		—		$469,204
L	ACCRUED EXPENSES	18,480	**2**	(18,480)		0
M	CURRENT PORTION OF DEBT	100,000		—		100,000
N	INCOME TAXES PAYABLE	0		—		0
K + L + M + N = O	CURRENT LIABILITIES	587,684				569,204
P	LONG-TERM DEBT	875,000		—		875,000
Q	CAPITAL STOCK	1,550,000		—		1,550,000
R	RETAINED EARNINGS	(100,278)		—		(100,278)
Q + R = S	SHAREHOLDERS' EQUITY	1,449,722				1,449,722
O + P + S = T	TOTAL LIABILITIES & EQUITY	$2,912,406		(18,480)		$2,893,926

Liabilities & Equity Sum

T27. Pay payroll-associated taxes and insurance benefit premiums.

We have some payroll-associated taxes and insurance benefit payments that are due for payment. We had better pay them! The government gets very nasty if we don't pay all withholding and FICA premiums when they are due.

These obligations are some of the few debts that cannot be erased by bankruptcy. Also, if the company does not pay these debts, the IRS often goes after officers of the company personally to collect the government's due.

Transaction: Pay payroll taxes, fringe benefits and insurance premiums. Write checks to the government and to insurance companies totaling $18,480 for payment of withholding and FICA taxes and for payroll-associated fringe benefits.

1 (1A) Book a CASH DISBURSEMENT of $18,480 in the *Cash Flow Statement*. (1B) Lower CASH on the *Balance Sheet* by the same amount.

2 Lower ACCRUED EXPENSES on the *Balance Sheet* by the $18,480 amount paid to the government and to various insurance companies.

Note: The *Income Statement* and RETAINED EARNINGS are not affected by this payment transaction. Because AppleSeed runs its books on an accrual basis, we already "expensed" these expenses when they occurred—not when the actual payment is made.

～

Income Statement

for the period including Transactions 1 through 28		prior	+	transaction	=	sum
1	NET SALES	$250,800		—		$250,800
2	COST OF GOODS SOLD	169,830		—		169,830
1 - 2 = 3	GROSS MARGIN	80,970				80,970
4	SALES & MARKETING	115,628		—		115,628
5	RESEARCH & DEVELOPMENT	0		—		0
6	GENERAL & ADMINISTRATIVE	40,620		—		40,620
4 + 5 + 6 = 7	OPERATING EXPENSE	156,248				156,248
3 - 7 = 8	INCOME FROM OPERATIONS	(75,278)				(75,278)
9	NET INTEREST INCOME	(25,000)		—		(25,000)
10	INCOME TAXES	0		—		0
8 + 9 - 10 = 11	NET INCOME	($100,278)		0		($100,278)

IS Transaction Sum

Cash Flow Statement

for the period including Transactions 1 through 28		prior	+	transaction	=	sum
a	BEGINNING CASH BALANCE	$0				$0
b	CASH RECEIPTS	234,900		—		234,900
c	CASH DISBURSEMENTS	285,958	**1**	150,000		435,958
b - c = d	CASH FLOW FROM OPERATIONS	(51,058)				(201,058)
e	PP&E PURCHASE	1,750,000		—		1,750,000
f	NET BORROWINGS	975,000		—		975,000
g	INCOME TAXES PAID	0		—		0
h	SALE OF CAPITAL STOCK	1,550,000		—		1,550,000
a + d - e + f - g + h = i	ENDING CASH BALANCES	$723,942		(150,000)		$573,942

CF Transaction Sum

Balance Sheet

as of this Transaction 28		prior	+	transaction	=	sum
A	CASH	$723,942	**2**	(150,000)		$573,942
B	ACCOUNTS RECEIVABLE	0		—		0
C	INVENTORIES	414,770		—		414,770
D	PREPAID EXPENSES	19,500		—		19,500
A + B + C + D = E	CURRENT ASSETS	1,158,212				1,008,212
F	OTHER ASSETS	0		—		0
G	FIXED ASSETS @ COST	1,750,000		—		1,750,000
H	ACCUMULATED DEPRECIATION	14,286		—		14,286
G - H = I	NET FIXED ASSETS	1,735,714				1,735,714
E + F + I = J	TOTAL ASSETS	$2,893,926		(150,000)		$2,743,926

Assets Sum

		prior	+	transaction	=	sum
K	ACCOUNTS PAYABLE	$469,204	**3**	(150,000)		$319,204
L	ACCRUED EXPENSES	0		—		0
M	CURRENT PORTION OF DEBT	100,000		—		100,000
N	INCOME TAXES PAYABLE	0		—		0
K + L + M + N = O	CURRENT LIABILITIES	569,204				419,204
P	LONG-TERM DEBT	875,000		—		875,000
Q	CAPITAL STOCK	1,550,000		—		1,550,000
R	RETAINED EARNINGS	(100,278)		—		(100,278)
Q + R = S	SHAREHOLDERS' EQUITY	1,449,722				1,449,722
O + P + S = T	TOTAL LIABILITIES & EQUITY	$2,893,926		(150,000)		$2,743,926

Liabilities & Equity Sum

T28. Pay some suppliers...especially the mean and hungry ones.

Several of our raw material suppliers have telephoned recently and asked how we are doing...and, by the way, when are we planning to pay their bills?

Because we are in a check-writing mood (and because we will shortly be asking them to send us more apples), we pay a chunk of supplier bills

---

Transaction: Pay suppliers a portion of what is due for apples and jars. Cut a check for $150,000 in partial payment.

1 Write a check for $150,000 to pay suppliers. Increase CASH DISBURSEMENTS by that amount in the *Cash Flow Statement*.

2 Lower CASH by $150,000 in the assets section of the *Balance Sheet*.

3 Lower ACCOUNTS PAYABLE in the liabilities section of the *Balance Sheet* by the $150,000 that we no longer owe, since we just paid as described above.

$\sim$

Chapter 11. Growth, Profit and Return

With these transactions we will fast-forward through the rest of Apple-Seed's first year in business. We will determine our profit for the year, compute the income taxes we owe, declare a dividend and issue our first Annual Report to Shareholders.

Taxes and dividends—one bad, one good? Actually, without taxes, there would be no dividends. Dividends are paid out of retained earnings. If the business has earnings (and can thus pay dividends), then it will have to pay taxes. Taxes with earnings; no taxes with no earnings. No earnings, then no dividends. Thus, no taxes, no dividends.

But enough of this. Some really exciting events are taking place at our now not-so-little company. We have attracted the attention of a large nationwide food-processing conglomerate. The president of the conglomerate particularly likes our applesauce. She may make us an offer to buy the company! How much is it worth?

∼

Transaction 29. Fast-forward through the rest of the year.
Record summary transactions.

Transaction 30. Book income taxes payable.

Transaction 31. Declare a $0.375 per share dividend and pay
to common shareholders

- Cash Flow Statement vs. Changes in Financial Position

- AppleSeed Enterprises, Inc. Annual Report to Shareholders

- What is AppleSeed worth? How to value a business.

Income Statement

for the period including Transactions 1 through 29		prior	+	transaction	=	sum
1	NET SALES	$250,800		2,804,760		$3,055,560
2	COST OF GOODS SOLD	169,830		1,836,000		2,005,830
1 - 2 = 3	GROSS MARGIN	80,970		968,760		1,049,730
4	SALES & MARKETING	115,628		212,895		328,523
5	RESEARCH & DEVELOPMENT	0		26,000		26,000
6	GENERAL & ADMINISTRATIVE	40,620		162,900		203,520
4 + 5 + 6 = 7	OPERATING EXPENSE	156,248		401,795		558,043
3 - 7 = 8	INCOME FROM OPERATIONS	(75,278)		566,965		491,687
9	NET INTEREST INCOME	(25,000)		(75,000)		(100,000)
10	INCOME TAXES	0		—		0
8 + 9 - 10 = 11	NET INCOME	($100,278)		491,965		$391,687

IS Transaction Sum

Cash Flow Statement

for the period including Transactions 1 through 29		prior	+	transaction	=	sum
a	BEGINNING CASH BALANCE	$0				$0
b	CASH RECEIPTS	234,900		2,350,000		2,584,900
c	CASH DISBURSEMENTS	435,958		2,285,480		2,721,438
b - c = d	CASH FLOW FROM OPERATIONS	(201,058)		64,520		(136,538)
e	PP&E PURCHASE	1,750,000		—		1,750,000
f	NET BORROWINGS	975,000		(75,000)		900,000
g	INCOME TAXES PAID	0		—		0
h	SALE OF CAPITAL STOCK	1,550,000		—		1,550,000
a + d - e + f - g + h = i	ENDING CASH BALANCES	$573,942		(10,480)		$563,462

CF Transaction Sum

Balance Sheet

as of this Transaction 29		prior	+	transaction	=	sum
A	CASH	$573,942		(10,480)		$563,462
B	ACCOUNTS RECEIVABLE	0		454,760		454,760
C	INVENTORIES	414,770		—		414,770
D	PREPAID EXPENSES	19,500		(19,500)		0
A + B + C + D = E	CURRENT ASSETS	1,008,212		424,780		1,432,992
F	OTHER ASSETS	0		—		0
G	FIXED ASSETS @ COST	1,750,000		—		1,750,000
H	ACCUMULATED DEPRECIATION	14,286		64,287		78,573
G - H = I	NET FIXED ASSETS	1,735,714		(64,287)		1,671,427
E + F + I = J	TOTAL ASSETS	$2,743,926		360,493		$3,104,419
				Assets Sum		
K	ACCOUNTS PAYABLE	$319,204		(82,907)		$236,297
L	ACCRUED EXPENSES	0		26,435		26,435
M	CURRENT PORTION OF DEBT	100,000		—		100,000
N	INCOME TAXES PAYABLE	0		—		0
K + L + M + N = O	CURRENT LIABILITIES	419,204		(56,472)		362,732
P	LONG-TERM DEBT	875,000		(75,000)		800,000
Q	CAPITAL STOCK	1,550,000		—		1,550,000
R	RETAINED EARNINGS	(100,278)		491,965		391,687
Q + R = S	SHAREHOLDERS' EQUITY	1,449,722		491,965		1,941,687
O + P + S = T	TOTAL LIABILITIES & EQUITY	$2,743,926		360,493		$3,104,419

Liabilities & Equity Sum

T29. Fast-forward through the rest of the year. Record summary transactions for the remainder the year.

AppleSeed Enterprises, Inc., has been in business for about three months now. We seem to have gotten the hang of recurding transactions and manipulating the *Income Statement, Cash Flow Statement* and *Balacne Sheet*. It is fun.

With this series of entries, we will compress and summarize all the remaining transactions that took place in AppleSeed's next nine months of operations. As you can see from the statements, we sold about $2.8 million in applesauce during the last nine months of the year and a total of $3.1 million for the year.

We also collected a little less than $2.6 million from customers during the year and paid out a little over $2.7 million to suppliers, employees, etc. Significantly, we turned cash flow positive—that is, more cash receipts than cash disbursements—to the tune of over $64,520 during the last nine months of our fiscal year. Note that we were still cash flow negative by $136,538 for the whole year.

The bookings in this summary transaction close out our first year in business. Let's review the bottom line. Income from operations amounted to $491,687. Subtract from this figure the interest paid on building debt and we have a total of $391,687 as our *pre-tax* profit for the year.

A very nice showing. Taxes next.

Transaction: Book a series of entries in the *Income Statement, Cash Flow Statement* and the *Balance Sheet* summarizing transactions that take place in the remaining nine months of AppleSeed Enterprises's first fiscal year.

～

Income Statement

		prior	+	transaction	=	sum
1	NET SALES	$3,055,560		—		$3,055,560
2	COST OF GOODS SOLD	2,005,830		—		2,005,830
1 - 2 = 3	GROSS MARGIN	1,049,730				1,049,730
4	SALES & MARKETING	328,523		—		328,523
5	RESEARCH & DEVELOPMENT	26,000		—		26,000
6	GENERAL & ADMINISTRATIVE	203,520		—		203,520
4 + 5 + 6 = 7	OPERATING EXPENSE	558,043				558,043
3 - 7 = 8	INCOME FROM OPERATIONS	491,687				491,687
9	NET INTEREST INCOME	(100,000)		—		(100,000)
10	INCOME TAXES	0	**1A**	139,804		139,804
8 + 9 - 10 = 11	NET INCOME	$391,687		(139,804)		$251,883

IS Transaction Sum

Cash Flow Statement

for the period including Transactions 1 through 30

		prior	+	transaction	=	sum
a	BEGINNING CASH BALANCE	$0				$0
b	CASH RECEIPTS	2,584,900		—		2,584,900
c	CASH DISBURSEMENTS	2,721,438		—		2,721,438
b - c = d	CASH FLOW FROM OPERATIONS	(136,538)				(136,538)
e	PP&E PURCHASE	1,750,000		—		1,750,000
f	NET BORROWINGS	900,000		—		900,000
g	INCOME TAXES PAID	0		—		0
h	SALE OF CAPITAL STOCK	1,550,000		—		1,550,000
a + d - e + f - g + h = i	ENDING CASH BALANCES	$563,462		0		$563,462

CF Transaction Sum

Balance Sheet

as of this Transaction 30

		prior	+	transaction	=	sum
A	CASH	$563,462		—		$563,462
B	ACCOUNTS RECEIVABLE	454,760		—		454,760
C	INVENTORIES	414,770		—		414,770
D	PREPAID EXPENSES	0		—		0
A + B + C + D = E	CURRENT ASSETS	1,432,992				1,432,992
F	OTHER ASSETS	0		—		0
G	FIXED ASSETS @ COST	1,750,000		—		1,750,000
H	ACCUMULATED DEPRECIATION	78,573		—		78,573
G - H = I	NET FIXED ASSETS	1,671,427				1,671,427
E + F + I = J	TOTAL ASSETS	$3,104,419		0		$3,104,419

Assets Sum

		prior	+	transaction	=	sum
K	ACCOUNTS PAYABLE	$236,297		—		$236,297
L	ACCRUED EXPENSES	26,435		—		26,435
M	CURRENT PORTION OF DEBT	100,000		—		100,000
N	INCOME TAXES PAYABLE	0	**2**	139,804		139,804
K + L + M + N = O	CURRENT LIABILITIES	362,732				502,536
P	LONG-TERM DEBT	800,000		—		800,000
Q	CAPITAL STOCK	1,550,000		—		1,550,000
R	RETAINED EARNINGS	391,687	**1B**	(139,804)		251,883
Q + R = S	SHAREHOLDERS' EQUITY	1,941,687				1,801,883
O + P + S = T	TOTAL LIABILITIES & EQUITY	$3,104,419		0		$3,104,419

Liabilities & Equity Sum

T30. Book income taxes payable.

Taxes are very simple.

For almost all corporations you just take pre-tax income and multiply it by 34% or so. Then you take out your checkbook and write a check to the government for that amount. If you fail to send in the money on time or if you fudge the books and the IRS catches you, then you go to jail.

See, I told you taxes were simple. With this transaction we will compute and then book the income taxes we owe the government. We will actually pay them later on the tax due date.

Transaction: On a pre-tax income of $391,687, AppleSeed owes 34% in federal income taxes ($133,173) and $6,631 in state income taxes for a total income tax bill of $139,804. We will not actually pay the tax for several months.

1 (1A) Book an **INCOME TAXES** expense of $139,804 in the *Income Statement.* (1B) Lower **RETAINED EARNINGS** by the same amount in the *Balance Sheet.*

2 Book $139,804 worth of **INCOME TAXES PAYABLE** in the liabilities section of the *Balance Sheet.*

Income Statement

for the period including Transactions 1 through 31		*prior*	+	*transaction*	=	*sum*
1	NET SALES	$3,055,560		—		$3,055,560
2	COST OF GOODS SOLD	2,005,830		—		2,005,830
1 - 2 = 3	GROSS MARGIN	1,049,730				1,049,730
4	SALES & MARKETING	328,523		—		328,523
5	RESEARCH & DEVELOPMENT	26,000		—		26,000
6	GENERAL & ADMINISTRATIVE	203,520		—		203,520
4 + 5 + 6 = 7	OPERATING EXPENSE	558,043				558,043
3 - 7 = 8	INCOME FROM OPERATIONS	491,687				491,687
9	NET INTEREST INCOME	(100,000)		—		(100,000)
10	INCOME TAXES	139,804		—		139,804
8 + 9 - 10 = 11	NET INCOME	$251,883		0		$251,883

IS Transaction Sum

Cash Flow Statement

for the period including Transactions 1 through 31		*prior*	+	*transaction*	=	*sum*
a	BEGINNING CASH BALANCE	$0				$0
b	CASH RECEIPTS	2,584,900		—		2,584,900
c	CASH DISBURSEMENTS	2,721,438	**1A**	75,000		2,796,438
b - c = d	CASH FLOW FROM OPERATIONS	(136,538)				(211,538)
e	PP&E PURCHASE	1,750,000		—		1,750,000
f	NET BORROWINGS	900,000		—		900,000
g	INCOME TAXES PAID	0		—		0
h	SALE OF CAPITAL STOCK	1,550,000		—		1,550,000
a + d - e + f - g + h = i	ENDING CASH BALANCES	$563,462		(75,000)		$488,462

CF Transaction Sum

Balance Sheet

as of this Transaction 31		*prior*	+	*transaction*	=	*sum*
A	CASH	$563,462	**1B**	(75,000)		$488,462
B	ACCOUNTS RECEIVABLE	454,760		—		454,760
C	INVENTORIES	414,770		—		414,770
D	PREPAID EXPENSES	0		—		0
A + B + C + D = E	CURRENT ASSETS	1,432,992				1,357,992
F	OTHER ASSETS	0		—		0
G	FIXED ASSETS @ COST	1,750,000		—		1,750,000
H	ACCUMULATED DEPRECIATION	78,573		—		78,573
G - H = I	NET FIXED ASSETS	1,671,427				1,671,427
E + F + I = J	TOTAL ASSETS	$3,104,419		(75,000)		$3,029,419
				Assets Sum		
K	ACCOUNTS PAYABLE	$236,297		—		$236,297
L	ACCRUED EXPENSES	26,435		—		26,435
M	CURRENT PORTION OF DEBT	100,000		—		100,000
N	INCOME TAXES PAYABLE	139,804		—		139,804
K + L + M + N = O	CURRENT LIABILITIES	502,536				502,536
P	LONG-TERM DEBT	800,000		—		800,000
Q	CAPITAL STOCK	1,550,000		—		1,550,000
R	RETAINED EARNINGS	251,883	**2**	(75,000)		176,883
Q + R = S	SHAREHOLDERS' EQUITY	1,801,883				1,726,883
O + P + S = T	TOTAL LIABILITIES & EQUITY	$3,104,419		(75,000)		$3,029,419

Liabilities & Equity Sum

T31. Declare a $0.375 per share dividend and pay to the common shareholders.

This transaction will be our last for AppleSeed Enterprises this year, just before we close the books. The company has done well in its first year of operation and the board of directors decides to vote a dividend for common shareholders. The question is, how big a dividend?

Dividends are paid out of retained earnings, of which we have more than $250,000 as of the end of the year. We also have a very strong cash position, so we can afford to pay the dividend.

After much discussion, a $0.375 per share dividend is voted. With 200,000 shares outstanding, this dividend will cost the company $75,000; $56,250 to the investor group and $18,750 to you, the entrepreneur.

You go out and buy a small boat.

Transaction: Declare and pay a $0.375 per share dividend to Apple-Seed's shareholders.

1 (1A) Book a CASH DISBURSEMENT (see note below) on the *Cash Flow Statement* for the $75,000 dividend payment. (1B) Reduce CASH on the *Balance Sheet* by the same amount.

2 Reduce RETAINED EARNINGS on the *Balance Sheet* by the dividend payment of $75,000.

Note: The *Cash Flow Statements* on these transaction spreads are abbreviated. That is, they do not have all the line items that a complete statement would have. The dividend payment should really be placed on a special line titled DIVIDENDS PAID rather than in CASH DISBURSEMENTS. Paying a dividend is not an operating expense and the cash disbursements line should be reserved for operating expenses.

See the next two pages for a description of the structure of a more complete *Cash Flow Statement*.

~

Cash Flow Statement vs. Changes in Financial Position

The *Cash Flow Statement* format that we've been using for AppleSeed Enterprises's financial statements is a very simple-to-understand representation of cash movement. We have likened it to a check register, with the "sources of cash" being deposits and the "uses of cash" being checks.

However, most accountants would prefer to use another format for cash flow. This format (shown on the next page), dubbed *Statement of Changes in Financial Position* is better likened to a "bridge" between the *Balance Sheet* at the start of a period and the *Balance Sheet* at the end of a period. This bridging format specifically shows the asset, liability and equity accounts that change to provide cash, and the accounts that change using cash.

Most of the time when you look at financial statements you will see a statement like the one on the facing page (except the statement will only show the "Cash Flow for the Period" column, not the computational columns we have included as a tutorial).

Both formats allow you to get to the same answer, *Ending Cash Balance,* but in different ways. The format introduced here focuses on cash movements divided into three major categories of interest to anyone reviewing the cash performance of a business:

1. **Cash Flows from Operations.**
   Cash sources (uses) from activities such as making and selling products.

2. **Cash Flows from Investing.**
   Cash uses (sources) from increases (decreases) in the productive assets of the company such as property, plant and equipment.

3. **Cash Flows from Financing.**
   Cash sources (uses) from selling stock to investors, borrowing money from a bank and paying dividends.

The *Statement of Changes in Financial Position* shown on the facing page summarizes the movements of cash for AppleSeed Enterprises between **Transaction 19** and **Transaction 31.** We have selected the period between these two trans-actions because it provides an informative example; we could have used the period between any two transactions.

If we look on page 146 at AppleSeed's *Cash Flow Statement* for **Transaction 19,** we see $588,220 as an ending cash balance. Looking at AppleSeed's *Cash Flow Statement* for **Transaction 31** on page 178, we see $488,462 as an ending cash balance. Subtracting the earlier from the later cash balance, we see that in the time between these two transactions, cash has dropped by $99,758.

Refer to the statement on the facing page and review the following notes to see how this "bridging" cash flow description is constructed.

~

Statement of Changes in Financial Position

AppleSeed Enterprises, Inc. *—for Transactions 19 through 31—*	Balance Sheet Element as of T19	Balance Sheet Element as of T31	Cash Flow for the Period T19 thru T31
Cash flows from operating activities:			
Net income (see Note 1)	$(135,780)	$251,883	$387,663
Adjustments to reconcile net income to net cash used in operations:			
Depreciation (see Note 2)	14,286	78,573	64,287
Changes in working capital:			
Accounts receivable (see Note 3)	0	454,760	(454,760)
Inventories (see Note 3)	577,970	414,770	163,200
Prepaid expenses (see Note 3)	0	0	0
Accounts payable (see Note 4)	469,204	236,297	(232,907)
Accrued expenses (see Note 4)	18,480	26,435	7,955
Income taxes payable (see Note 4)	0	139,804	139,804
Net cash used in operating activities			$75,242
Cash flows from investing activities:			
PP&E purchase (see Note 5)	1,750,000	1,750,000	0
Net cash used in investing activities			0
Cash flow from financing activities:			
Sale of stock (see Note 6)	1,550,000	1,550,000	0
Change in debt (see Note 7)	1,000,000	900,000	(100,000)
Dividends paid (see Note 8)			(75.000)
Net cash from financing activities			$(175,000)
Net increase (decrease) in cash: (Transaction 19 through Transaction 31)			$(99,758)
Beginning cash: (as of Transaction 19)			$588,220
Ending cash: (as of Transaction 31)			$488,462

Note 1. Income for the period is computed from Income Statements by subtracting Net Income as of **Transaction 19** (loss of $135,780) from Net Income as of Transaction **31** (profit of $251,883).

Note 2. Computed as change in Accumulated Depreciation. Depreciation does not affect cash flow, but because it has been subtracted from the Net Income for the period, it must be added back here to get a true picture of cash movements.

Note 3. Computed as the change in these asset accounts. Note that an increase in an asset account means the company has more working capital and a positive cash flow in that account.

Note 4. Computed as the change in these liability accounts. Note that an increase in a liability account means the company has less working capital and a negative cash flow in that account.

Note 5. Computed as the change in the PP&E Asset. An increase in PP&E takes cash.

Note 6. Computed as the change in the Capital Stock account of Shareholders' Equity.

Note 7. Computed as the change in the Current Portion and Long-term Debt accounts. Lowering of overall debt decreases cash. Increasing overall debt increases cash.

Note 8. Dividends paid to shareholders lowers cash.

Income Statement

for the period including Transactions 1 through 31

NET SALES	$3,055,560
COST OF GOODS SOLD	2,005,830
GROSS MARGIN	1,049,730
SALES & MARKETING	328,523
RESEARCH & DEVELOPMENT	26,000
GENERAL & ADMINISTRATIVE	203,520
OPERATING EXPENSE	558,043
INCOME FROM OPERATIONS	491,687
NET INTEREST INCOME	(100,000)
INCOME TAXES	139,804
NET INCOME	$251,883

Cash Flow Statement

for the period including Transactions 1 through 31

BEGINNING CASH BALANCE	$0
CASH RECEIPTS	2,584,900
CASH DISBURSEMENTS	2,796,438
CASH FLOW FROM OPERATIONS	(211,538)
PP&E PURCHASE	1,750,000
NET BORROWINGS	900,000
INCOME TAXES PAID	0
SALE OF CAPITAL STOCK	1,550,000
ENDING CASH BALANCES	$488,462

Balance Sheet

as of this Transaction 31

CASH	$488,462
ACCOUNTS RECEIVABLE	454,760
INVENTORIES	414,770
PREPAID EXPENSES	0
CURRENT ASSETS	1,357,992
OTHER ASSETS	0
FIXED ASSETS @ COST	1,750,000
ACCUMULATED DEPRECIATION	78,573
NET FIXED ASSETS	1,671,427
TOTAL ASSETS	$3,029,419
ACCOUNTS PAYABLE	$236,297
ACCRUED EXPENSES	26,435
CURRENT PORTION OF DEBT	100,000
INCOME TAXES PAYABLE	139,804
CURRENT LIABILITIES	502,536
LONG-TERM DEBT	800,000
CAPITAL STOCK	1,550,000
RETAINED EARNINGS	176,883
SHAREHOLDERS' EQUITY	1,726,883
TOTAL LIABILITIES & EQUITY	$3,029,419

AppleSeed Enterprises, Inc.

Annual Report

To Our Shareholders:

I am happy to have this opportunity to report to you the results of AppleSeed Enterprises, Inc.'s first year of operation. Your company, in a very short time, has achieved its initial goal of becoming a recognized supplier of very high-quality applesauce.

Important Events

At the beginning of the year, AppleSeed raised $1 million through a successful offering of its common stock. This capitalization has allowed us to purchase high-volume production machinery and to maintain sufficient inventory to break into the highly competitive applesauce industry.

Our production continues at over 20 thousand cases per month. As demand increases, we project that the current manufacturing facility can be operated at over twice these levels. Depending, however, on the weather conditions in the Northeast, raw material supply may limit our ability to reach increased levels of production.

Financial Results

In AppleSeed's first year of operation, revenues exceeded $3 million. AppleSeed's net income for the year was over $250,000, or $1.26 per share with 200,000 shares outstanding.

Our return on sales of 8% exceeds industry averages, as does our 15% return on shareholders' equity. Return on assets was 8%. Our Balance Sheet remains strong. We end the year with $488,000 in cash and cash equivalents.

∼

AppleSeed continues to spend heavily in marketing and sales. We believe these investments will pay off handsomely in the future in significantly improved market position, especially in specialty segments of the applesauce industry.

AppleSeed's New Factory

During the coming year, we plan to introduce several new jar sizes and packaging configurations into the gift market. Product testing continues on specialty flavored and colored versions of our basic applesauce. A bright green sauce packaged in a shamrock-shaped jar will be introduced prior to St. Patrick's Day this year. We expect our new products to be well-received in the marketplace.

∼

I thank our customers for their continuing confidence in our products and in our ability to serve their applesauce needs. I thank our shareholders for their continuing support and our employees for their productive efforts throughout AppleSeed's first year of operation.

Sincerely,

I. M. Rich

President and CEO

What's the Business Worth?

We've done a super job starting up an applesauce company. What do you think the business is worth now? A good question, one of particular interest to AppleSeed's shareholders. Let's look at several methods of company valuation.

Book Value. Book value represents the value at which assets are carried on the "books" of the company. The book value of a company is defined as its total assets less its current liabilities and less any long-term debt. For AppleSeed Enterprises, Inc., book value is computed as $1,726,883 (that is, $3,029,419 in total assets less a total of $502,536 in current liabilities less some $800,000 in long-term debt outstanding).

Liquidation Value. The liquidation value is what the company's assets would bring at a forced sale. Normally the liquidation value of a going concern has little relevance since the value of an operating business is much greater than its liquidation value.

For fun (?!) let's compute AppleSeed's liquidation value. Start with the company's book value and then subtract what would lower that amount if, for example, we could only get 10 cents on the dollar for inventory and 50 cents on the dollar for machinery. Using these assumptions, AppleSeed's liquidation value would be less than $500,000.

Price-Earnings Multiple. The company has 200,000 shares outstanding and earned a net income of $251,883 last year. Dividing net income by the number of outstanding shares gives a net income of $1.26 per share.

If we assume that companies similar to AppleSeed are currently selling at, let's say, 12 times earnings, then our company is worth $1.26 times this 12 multiple times 200,000 shares outstanding that equals a value of slightly over $3 million.

Market Value. There is no market for AppleSeed's stock. Thus, there is no real "market value" for the company. Selling an untraded company is like selling a house. The business is worth what you can get for it.

Discounted Cash Flow. The discounted cash flow method of valuation is the most sophisticated (and the most difficult) method to use in valuing the business. With this method you must estimate all the cash influxes to investors over time (dividends and ultimate stock sales) and then compute a "net present value" using an assumed discount rate (implied interest rate). There are just too many assumptions in this method to make it very useful in valuing AppleSeed. However, review the discussion in **Chapter 21 Net Present Value** for a more details.

Alternative AppleSeed Enterprises Valuations

VALUATION METHOD	COMPANY VALUE
Book Value	$1,726,883
Liquidation Value	$467,877
Price-Earnings Multiple	$3,024,000
Market Value	sell to whom?
Discounted Cash Flow	too complex!

Section C. Financial Statements: Construction & Analysis

About This Section

Congratulations! You have accurately kept the books of AppleSeed Enterprises, Inc., for the year. And a good year is was. What follows in this section are some techniques and details.

Journals and Ledgers. We'll learn about journals and ledgers, the books that accountants use to make transaction entries. Well, accountants did use paper entry books and did sit atop high chairs. Now entries are made in computer memory. Some say that computers have made it easier to commit fraud. (When ledgers were paper books and entries were made with India ink, things were more difficult to fudge.)

Ratio Analysis. Next we will review the common ways of analyzing financial statements to test the financial strength of the enterprise. We will review the liquidity of the company, how efficiently it uses its assets, how profitable it is and how effectively it is using "other people's money," that is, debt.

Accounting Policies. We will review the different, but acceptable, ways to keep the company's books and why companies would want to use them. Note that some of these "creative accounting" techniques can be used to mask problems in the enterprise.

Cooking the books. Finally, we will discuss the ways of financial fraud and how to detect it. Some "tried and true" fraudulent techniques are important to understand whether you are an employee or an investor in the company.

Chapter 12. Keeping Track with Journals and Ledgers

Financial accounting means recording each and every event (transaction) that has a financial impact on the enterprise. By keeping track of these activities just as they happen, the accountant can easily summarize the firm's financial position and issue financial statements. *Journals* and *ledgers* are "the books" in which accountants scribble transaction entries.

A *journal* is a book (or computer memory) in which all of a company's financial events are recorded in chronological order. Everything is there, there is nothing missing. Journal entries can (and must) be made if:

1. We know with reasonable certainty the amount of money involved.

2. We know the timing of the event.

3. An actual exchange between the parties of cash, goods or some formal representation of value (such as stock) has occurred.

A *ledger* is a book of accounts. An account is simply any grouping of similar items that we want to keep track of. You can think of a ledger as a book with many pages. Each page of the ledger book represents one account.

The main benefit of a ledger system is that it allows us to determine how much we have of any item (account) at any point in time. Immediately after making a chronological journal entry, we update our ledger for each account that has changed as a result of that entry.

Note that every time we make a journal entry, we will be changing the amount that we have in at least two accounts (ledger pages) in order to keep the Balance Sheet and the basic equation of accounting in balance: *Assets equals liabilities plus equity.*

Any event having a financial impact on the firm affects this basic equation. The equation summarizes the entire financial

---

A *journal* is a book (or computer memory) in which all of a company's financial events are recorded in chronological order. Everything is there, nothing is missing.

A *ledger* is a book of accounts. An account is any grouping of items that we want to keep track of. You can think of a ledger as a book with many pages. Each page of the ledger book represents one account.

position of the firm. Furthermore, the equation must always stay in balance. To keep this equation in balance, a change in any one number in the equation must change at least one other number. *Accountants call this system of making ledger changes in pairs the double-entry bookkeeping system.*

Following are several of the account ledgers for AppleSeed Enterprises. Each ledger shows how our transactions have affected a single account. Note that at all times the ledgers present a current picture of AppleSeed's account balances.

The Cash Ledger shown below lists all transactions that affect the amount of cash in AppleSeed Enterprises's checking account. The *ending cash balance* on the Cash Ledger is the same amount as shown for the **CASH** account on the *Balance Sheet* for the date of the last transaction.

Shown on the following pages are additional AppleSeed Enterprises, Inc., ledgers.

AppleSeed Enterprises, Inc.

Cash Ledger

	TRANSACTION NUMBER & DESCRIPTION	INCOMING CASH (+)	OUTGOING CASH (-)	ENDING CASH BALANCE (=)
	Beginning of period balance			$50,000
T1.	Sell 150,000 shares at $10 each	$1,500,000		$1,550,000
T2.	G&A payroll checks		$3,370	$1,546,630
T3.	Borrowing to purchase building	$1,000,000		$2,546,630
T4.	Purchase building for $1.5 million		$1,500,000	$1,046,630
T5.	SG&A payroll		$7,960	$1,038,670
T6.	Pay payroll taxes to government		$9,690	$1,028,980
T7.	Make partial payment for machinery		$125,000	$903,980
T8.	Make final payment for machinery		$125,000	$778,980
T9.	Supervisor's payroll		$2,720	$776,260
T12.	Pay manufacturing payroll		$9,020	$767,240
T14.	Pay for jar labels		$20,000	$747,240
T17.	Partial payment to raw material suppliers		$150,000	$597,240
T18.	Pay manufacturing payroll		$9,020	$588,220
T23.	Receipts from customer, commission payment	$234,900	$4,698	$818,422
T25.	Pay insurance premiums		$26,000	$792,422
T26.	Pay mortgage principal and interest		$50,000	$742,422
T27.	Pay payroll taxes and benefit premiums		$18,480	$723,942
T28.	Pay hungry suppliers		$150,000	$573,942
T29.	Nine months' summary transactions (net)		$10,480	$563,462
T31.	Dividend payment		$75,000	$488,462

Note that for each of AppleSeed's ledgers shown here, the right-most column shows the account value as of the completion of the transaction listed. Ledgers should always be kept current. Then, when statements need to be prepared, the ledgers will always provide correct account values.

AppleSeed Enterprises, Inc.
Accounts Payable Ledger

	TRANSACTION NUMBER & DESCRIPTION	TRANSACTION AMOUNT	ACCOUNTS PAYABLE
	Opening balance		$0
T10.	Receive labels	$20,000	$20,000
T11.	Receive two months' raw materials	$332,400	$352,400
T13.	Book a month's "all other" mfg. expense	$8,677	$361,077
T14.	Pay for labels received in **T10**	$(20,000)	$341,077
T17.	Partial payment to raw material suppliers	$(150,000)	$191,077
T18l.	Receive additional month's raw materials	$166,200	$357,277
T18p.	Book another month's "all other" mfg. expense	$8,677	$365,954
T19.	Book advertising flier and T-shirt expense	$103,250	$469,204
T28.	Pay hungry suppliers	$(150,000)	$319,204
T29.	Nine months' summary transactions (net)	$(82,907)	$236,297

AppleSeed Enterprises, Inc.
Inventory Ledger

	TRANSACTION NUMBER & DESCRIPTION	BEGINNING INVENTORY	TRANSACTION	ENDING INVENTORY
	Opening balance			0
T10.	Receive applesauce jar labels	$0	$20,000	$20,000
T11.	Receive two months' inventory	$20,000	$332,400	$352,400
T12.	Pay manufacturing salaries	$352,400	$17,180	$369,580
T13.	Book depreciation and other mfg. overhead	$369,580	$15,820	$385,400
T16.	Scrap the value of 500 cases of applesauce	$385,400	$(5,100)	$380,300
T18.	Mfg another month's worth of applesauce	$380,300	$197,670	$577,970
T20.	Ship 1,000 cases of applesauce	$577,970	$(10,200)	$567,770
T22.	Ship 15,000 cases of applesauce	$567,770	$(153,000)	$414,770

AppleSeed Enterprises, Inc.
Accrued Expenses Ledger

	TRANSACTION NUMBER & DESCRIPTION	TRANSACTION AMOUNT	ACCRUED EXPENSES
	Opening balance		0
T2.	Payroll-associated taxes and benefits	$2,860	$2,860
T5.	Payroll-associated taxes and benefits	$6,830	$9,690
T6.	Pay payroll taxes and associated premiums	$(9,690)	$0
T9.	Payroll-associated taxes and benefits	$2,160	$2,160
T12.	Payroll-associated taxes and benefits	$8,160	$10,320
T18.	Payroll-associated taxes and benefits	$8,160	$18,480
T20.	Sales commission due	$318	$18,798
T22.	Sales commission due	$4,698	$23,496
T23.	Payment of sales commission	$(4,698)	$18,798
T24.	Reversal of sales commission due from **T20.**	$(318)	$18,480
T27.	Pay payroll taxes, fringe benefit, premiums	$(18,480)	$0
T29.	Nine months' summary transactions (net)	$26,435	$26,435

AppleSeed Enterprises, Inc.
Accounts Receivable Ledger

	TRANSACTION NUMBER & DESCRIPTION	TRANSACTION AMOUNT	ACCOUNTS RECEIVABLE
	Opening balance		$0
T20.	Applesauce sale - 1,000 cases @ $15.90	$15,900	$15,900
T22.	Applesauce sale - 15,000 cases @ $15.66	$234,900	$250,800
T23.	Payment received for **T22**	$(234,900)	$15,900
T24.	Bad debt from **T20** - write off receivable	$(15,900)	$0
T29.	Nine months' summary transactions (net)	$454,760	$454,760

Chapter 13. Ratio Analysis

It is not so much the absolute numbers of sales, costs, expenses and assets that are important in judging the financial condition of an enterprise, but rather, the relationships between them.

For example:

- Cash available relative to the level of payables is a good indicator of how easily the company will be able to pay its bills in the future.

- Asset levels relative to sales volume indicates just how efficiently the company's investments in productive assets (machinery and inventory) generate revenue.

- Gross margin as a percentage of sales determines how much the company is able to spend on various selling development and administrative activities and still make a profit.

Ratio analysis (that is, comparing one number on a company's financial statement with another number) is most useful when you wish to: (1) compare year-to-year performance to determine if things are getting better or getting worse for the enterprise, or (2) compare companies in an industry to see which is performing best given common constraints.

~

In this section, we will review Apple-Seed Enterprises's first-year financial performance by analyzing the company's financial statements and the common ratio indicators of:

- Liquidity
- Asset management
- Profitability
- Leverage

Finally, we will compare ratios across industries. Some businesses are naturally more profitable than others. Some require more capital; some require less.

The ratios computed on the following pages use AppleSeed Enterprises, Inc.'s *Income Statement* and *Balance Sheet* for the period from **Transaction 1** through **Transaction 31** shown in AppleSeed's Annual Report on page 182.

Common Size Statements—

Both the *Income Statement* and the *Balance Sheet* can be converted into "common size" statements for analysis. Common size statements present each item as a percentage of the statement's largest item.

Common Size Income Statement. Normally, the largest item in the *Income Statement* is sales. Thus, when the *Income Statement* is converted into a common size statement, all items are presented as a percentage of sales. Reviewing the common size income statement focuses on the proportion of sales dollar absorbed by various cost and expense items.

AppleSeed's cost of goods sold is 34% of sales, our company's operating expense is 18%, net income is 8% and so forth. Not bad percentages for a company such as our little enterprise. See AppleSeed's Common Size Income Statement shown on the facing page.

Common Size Balance Sheet. To convert the *Balance Sheet* into a common size statement, all components are expressed as a percentage of total assets. For example, AppleSeed's current assets are 45% of total assets, long-term debt is 26% of total liabilities and equity and so forth.

Common size balance sheets help focus analysis on the internal structure and allocation of the company's financial resources. Common size statements are especially useful for the side-by-side analyses of several years of a company's performance, or when two companies of different size are being compared.

∼

Appropriate year-to-year questions to ask are: "Why did we do better last year in this area than we did this year?" and "How well are we doing when we are compared to other companies in the industry?"

Common Size Income Statement
for the period including Transactions 1 through 31

NET SALES	$3,055,560	100%	◀— *100%*
COST OF GOODS SOLD	2,005,830	66%	
GROSS MARGIN	1,049,730	34%	
SALES & MARKETING	328,523	11%	
RESEARCH & DEVELOPMENT	26,000	1%	
GENERAL & ADMINISTRATIVE	203,520	7%	
OPERATING EXPENSE	558,043	18%	
INCOME FROM OPERATIONS	491,687	16%	
NET INTEREST INCOME	(100,000)	(3%)	
INCOME TAXES	139,804	5%	
NET INCOME	$251,883	8%	

Common Size Balance Sheet
as of this Transaction 31

CASH	$488,462	16%	
ACCOUNTS RECEIVABLE	454,760	15%	
INVENTORIES	414,770	14%	
PREPAID EXPENSES	0	0%	
CURRENT ASSETS	1,357,992	45%	
OTHER ASSETS	0	0%	
FIXED ASSETS @ COST	1,750,000	58%	
ACCUMULATED DEPRECIATION	78,573	3%	
NET FIXED ASSETS	1,671,427	55%	
TOTAL ASSETS	$3,029,419	100%	◀— *100%*
ACCOUNTS PAYABLE	$236,297	8%	
ACCRUED EXPENSES	26,435	1%	
CURRENT PORTION OF DEBT	100,000	3%	
INCOME TAXES PAYABLE	139,804	5%	
CURRENT LIABILITIES	502,536	17%	
LONG-TERM DEBT	800,000	26%	
CAPITAL STOCK	1,550,000	51%	
RETAINED EARNINGS	176,883	6%	
SHAREHOLDERS' EQUITY	1,726,883	57%	
TOTAL LIABILITIES & EQUITY	$3,029,419	100%	◀— *100%*

Liquidity Ratios—

The so-called liquidity ratios measure the ease with which a company can pay its bills when due. This ability is determined by whether the enterprise has cash in the bank or expects to generate cash (by sale of goods and by the collection of accounts receivable) in sufficient amount to pay its bills as they become due.

There are periods of illiquidity in almost every company's life—when the company is unable to pay bills on time. Most often this situation is infrequent or only temporary and is usually no major problem. It's happened to all of us at one time or another.

However, if a company is illiquid on a regular basis, or for a long period of time, it is likely to find itself *busted, tapped-out, bankrupt.*

Everyone is interested in AppleSeed's ability to pay short-term debts, including its employees, suppliers and the bank that lent us money for our building. Even our customers care. They need a reliable supply of product.

> *Liquidity* and *profitability* are different. It's possible—and indeed not all that uncommon—for a company to be profitable and illiquid at the same time. A company can show a profit on the *Income Statement* and still have very little cash on hand to pay its bills.

Balance Sheet
as of this Transaction 31

CASH	$488,462	**A**
ACCOUNTS RECEIVABLE	454,760	**B**
INVENTORIES	414,770	
PREPAID EXPENSES	0	
CURRENT ASSETS	1,357,992	**C**
OTHER ASSETS	0	
FIXED ASSETS @ COST	1,750,000	
ACCUMULATED DEPRECIATION	78,573	
NET FIXED ASSETS	1,671,427	
TOTAL ASSETS	$3,029,419	
ACCOUNTS PAYABLE	$236,297	
ACCRUED EXPENSES	26,435	
CURRENT PORTION OF DEBT	100,000	
INCOME TAXES PAYABLE	139,804	
CURRENT LIABILITIES	502,536	**D**
LONG-TERM DEBT	800,000	
CAPITAL STOCK	1,550,000	
RETAINED EARNINGS	176,883	
SHAREHOLDERS' EQUITY	1,726,883	
TOTAL LIABILITIES & EQUITY	$3,029,419	

Profitability coupled with illiquidity can often occur in companies experiencing unexpected high growth. These companies need increased working capital to finance inventories and accounts receivable. Cash can be very tight. Happily, in these conditions, bankers love to lend money to those companies experiencing illiquidity due to rapid profitable growth.

Current Ratio. The current ratio is one of the oldest and best-known measures of short-term financial strength. The ratio determines whether current assets (cash or assets that are expected to be converted into cash within a year) are sufficient to pay current liabilities (those obligations that must be paid within one year).

A current ratio for a general manufacturing company above 2.0 is considered good. It means that the company has twice the amount of current assets as it has current liabilities. A 1:1 ratio means that a company can *just* meet its upcoming bills. With a 2:0 ratio or better, there is a big financial cushion.

Quick Ratio. The quick ratio is an even more conservative measure of liquidity than the current ratio. It is sometimes called the "acid test." The quick ratio is the company's "quick assets" (cash and accounts receivable) divided by current liabilities. Inventories are left out.

As shown in the computations here, AppleSeed Enterprises is quite liquid.

AppleSeed's Liquidity Ratios

$$\textbf{Current Ratio} = \frac{Current\ Assets}{Current\ Liabilities} = \frac{C}{D} = \frac{\$1,357,992}{\$502,536} = 2.7$$

$$\textbf{Quick Ratio} = \frac{Cash + Receivables}{Current\ Liabilities} = \frac{A+B}{D} = \frac{\$488,462 + \$454,760}{\$502,536} = 1.9$$

Asset Management Ratios—

Assets are the financial engine of the enterprise. But how do we know that our assets are being used efficiently? Are we getting the biggest bang for our asset buck? Asset management ratios provide a tool to investigate how effective in generating profits the company's investment in accounts receivables, inventory and fixed assets is.

Inventory Turn. The inventory turn measures the volume of business that can be conducted with a given investment in inventory. AppleSeed "turns" its inventory four times each year. That is, AppleSeed needs to maintain an inventory value level of one-quarter of the total cost of its products sold (COGS) in a year.

Different types of businesses have dramatically different inventory turns. For example, a supermarket may turn its inventory 12 or more times a year while a typical manufacturing company turns its inventory twice.

Because inventory is built in anticipation of sales, inventory turn is especially sensitive to changes in business activity. If sales slow down, inventory can balloon and the inventory turn will decrease, a sign of pending trouble.

Asset Turn Ratio. The asset turn ratio is a more general measure of efficient asset use. It shows the sales volume that a company can support with a given level of assets. Companies with low asset turns will require a large amount of capital to generate more sales. Conversely, a high asset turn means that the company can expand sales with a low capital investment.

Receivable Days. Receivables shown as days outstanding is the average length of time the company's accounts receivable are outstanding—that is, how long between when the goods are shipped (on credit) and when the customer pays.

Credit sales create accounts receivable, shown as current assets on the *Balance Sheet*. These accounts receivable represent future cash in-flows into the business. The receivable days ratio (also known as the *average collection period*) just measures how fast, on average, the company gets this cash.

Income Statement

for the period including Transactions 1 through 31

NET SALES	$3,055,560	**A**
COST OF GOODS SOLD	2,005,830	**B**
GROSS MARGIN	1,049,730	
SALES & MARKETING	328,523	
RESEARCH & DEVELOPMENT	26,000	
GENERAL & ADMINISTRATIVE	203,520	
OPERATING EXPENSE	558,043	
INCOME FROM OPERATIONS	491,687	
NET INTEREST INCOME	(100,000)	
INCOME TAXES	139,804	
NET INCOME	$251,883	

AppleSeed's sales terms state *"net 30."* This means that we expect to receive payment within 30 days after we ship our applesauce. As shown below, AppleSeed has a receivable days ratio of 54 days. Generally, companies average between 45 and 65 days receivables.

Note that if AppleSeed could get its customers to pay faster—let's say in 35 days on average—and/or if it could get by on less inventory in stock (a higher turn), then a lot of cash would be "freed up" for other uses.

Balance Sheet
as of this Transaction 31

CASH	$488,462	
ACCOUNTS RECEIVABLE	454,760	**C**
INVENTORIES	414,770	**D**
PREPAID EXPENSES	0	
CURRENT ASSETS	1,357,992	
OTHER ASSETS	0	
FIXED ASSETS @ COST	1,750,000	
ACCUMULATED DEPRECIATION	78,573	
NET FIXED ASSETS	1,671,427	
TOTAL ASSETS	$3,029,419	**E**
ACCOUNTS PAYABLE	$236,297	
ACCRUED EXPENSES	26,435	
CURRENT PORTION OF DEBT	100,000	
INCOME TAXES PAYABLE	139,804	
CURRENT LIABILITIES	502,536	
LONG-TERM DEBT	800,000	
CAPITAL STOCK	1,550,000	
RETAINED EARNINGS	176,883	
SHAREHOLDERS' EQUITY	1,726,883	
TOTAL LIABILITIES & EQUITY	$3,029,419	

AppleSeed's Asset Management Ratios

$$\text{Inventory Turn} = \frac{Cost\ of\ Goods\ Sold}{Inventory} = \frac{B}{D} = \frac{\$2,005,830}{\$414,770} = 4.8\ \text{turn}$$

$$\text{Asset Turn Ratio} = \frac{Annual\ Sales}{Assets} = \frac{A}{E} = \frac{\$3,055,560}{\$3,029,419} = 1.0\ \text{turn}$$

$$\text{Receivable Days} = \frac{Receivables \times 365}{Annual\ Sales} = \frac{C \times 365}{A} = \frac{\$454,760 \times 365}{\$3,055,560} = 54\ \text{days}$$

Profitability Ratios—

Profitability ratios are common *"return on"* ratios: *"return on sales," "return on assets"* and so forth. Profitability ratios relate profits to some other piece of financial information such as sales, equity or assets. These ratios measure some aspects of management's operating efficiency; that is, management's ability to turn a profit given a level of resources.

> **Although the liquidity measures are most important indicators of short-term corporate health, profitability measures are most important in the long term.**

In the long term, a business must consistently show a profit to remain viable and to provide its owners with a satisfactory return on their original investment.

~

Return on Assets. The return on assets (ROA) ratio measures management's success in employing the company's assets to generate a profit.

Return on Equity. The return on equity (ROE) ratio measures management's success in maximizing return on the owner's investment. In fact, this ratio is often called "return on investment," or ROI.

Return on Sales. A company's return on sales (also called "profit margin") compares what is left over after all expenses and costs are subtracted from sales.

Gross Margin. A company's gross margin (also called "gross profit") measures how much it costs to make a company's products and, consequently, how much the company can afford to spend in SG&A and still make a profit.

Gross margin varies greatly between industries. For example, retail businesses generally have a gross profit of around 25%. Computer software businesses can have a gross profit as high as 80% to 90% of sales. That means that for every dollar in sales, the computer software company spends only 10¢ to 20¢ to produce its product.

Income Statement
for the period including Transactions 1 through 31

NET SALES	$3,055,560	**A**
COST OF GOODS SOLD	2,005,830	**B**
GROSS MARGIN	1,049,730	
SALES & MARKETING	328,523	
RESEARCH & DEVELOPMENT	26,000	
GENERAL & ADMINISTRATIVE	203,520	
OPERATING EXPENSE	558,043	
INCOME FROM OPERATIONS	491,687	
NET INTEREST INCOME	(100,000)	
INCOME TAXES	139,804	
NET INCOME	$251,883	**C**

AppleSeed is doing rather well. An 8% return on sales (profit margin) is good for the industry. A 15% return on equity is fine too. The 8% return on assets is rather low, but not all that bad for AppleSeed's first year.

Balance Sheet
as of this Transaction 31

CASH	$488,462
ACCOUNTS RECEIVABLE	454,760
INVENTORIES	414,770
PREPAID EXPENSES	0
CURRENT ASSETS	1,357,992
OTHER ASSETS	0
FIXED ASSETS @ COST	1,750,000
ACCUMULATED DEPRECIATION	78,573
NET FIXED ASSETS	1,671,427
TOTAL ASSETS	$3,029,419 **D**
ACCOUNTS PAYABLE	$236,297
ACCRUED EXPENSES	26,435
CURRENT PORTION OF DEBT	100,000
INCOME TAXES PAYABLE	139,804
CURRENT LIABILITIES	502,536
LONG-TERM DEBT	800,000
CAPITAL STOCK	1,550,000
RETAINED EARNINGS	176,883
SHAREHOLDERS' EQUITY	1,726,883 **E**
TOTAL LIABILITIES & EQUITY	$3,029,419

AppleSeed's Profitability Ratios

$$\text{Return on Assets} = \frac{Net\ Income}{Total\ Assets} = \frac{C}{D} = \frac{\$251,883}{\$3,029,419} = 8\%$$

$$\text{Return on Equity} = \frac{Net\ Income}{Shareholders'\ Equity} = \frac{C}{E} = \frac{\$251,883}{\$1,726,883} = 15\%$$

$$\text{Return on Sales} = \frac{Net\ Income}{Net\ Sales} = \frac{C}{A} = \frac{\$251,883}{\$3,055,560} = 8\%$$

$$\text{Gross Margin} = \frac{Net\ Sales - COSG}{Net\ Sales} = \frac{A-B}{A} = \frac{\$3,055,560 - \$2,005,830}{\$3,055,560} = 34\%$$

Leverage Ratios—

Leverage ratios (also called "safety" ratios) measure how much of the company's assets are financed with debt. These ratios (1) reveal the extent of a company's "equity cushion" available to absorb losses, and (2) measure the company's ability to meet its short-term and long-term debt obligations.

Leverage is the use of other people's money to generate profits for yourself. By substituting debt (other people's money) for equity dollars (your own money), you hope to make more profit per dollar that you invest than if you had provided all the financing yourself.

Thus debt "leverages" your investment. The leverage ratios measure the extent of this leverage. The reason leverage ratios are also called safety ratios is that too much leverage in a business can be risky...unsafe to lenders. A lender may think of these ratios as safety ratios, while a business owner may think of them as leverage ratios.

Use too little financial leverage and the firm is not reaching its maximum profit potential for its investors. On the other hand, too much debt and the firm may be taking on a high risk of being unable to pay interest and principal if business conditions worsen. Using just the right amount of debt is a management call.

Debt-to-Equity Ratio. This ratio shows how much debt the company has relative to its investor equity. Lenders want a low level of debt relative to the company's equity.

Balance Sheet
as of this Transaction 31

CASH	$488,462	
ACCOUNTS RECEIVABLE	454,760	
INVENTORIES	414,770	
PREPAID EXPENSES	0	
CURRENT ASSETS	1,357,992	
OTHER ASSETS	0	
FIXED ASSETS @ COST	1,750,000	
ACCUMULATED DEPRECIATION	78,573	
NET FIXED ASSETS	1,671,427	
TOTAL ASSETS	$3,029,419	**A**
ACCOUNTS PAYABLE	$236,297	
ACCRUED EXPENSES	26,435	
CURRENT PORTION OF DEBT	100,000	**B**
INCOME TAXES PAYABLE	139,804	
CURRENT LIABILITIES	502,536	
LONG-TERM DEBT	800,000	**C**
CAPITAL STOCK	1,550,000	
RETAINED EARNINGS	176,883	
SHAREHOLDERS' EQUITY	1,726,883	**D**
TOTAL LIABILITIES & EQUITY	$3,029,419	

It gives them comfort that the loan can be repaid (even out of equity) if things go bad for the company.

Debt Ratio. This ratio measures the amount of debt relative to the total assets of the corporation. The debt ratio is a measure of operating leverage.

AppleSeed's debt-to-equity and its debt ratio are relatively conservative for its type of business.

AppleSeed's Leverage Ratios

$$\textbf{Debt-to-Equity} = \frac{Current + Long\text{-}Term\ Debt}{Shareholders'\ Equity} = \frac{B+C}{D} = \frac{\$100,000 + \$800,000}{\$1,726,883} = 0.5$$

$$\textbf{Debt Ratio} = \frac{Current + Long\text{-}Term\ Debt}{Total\ Assets} = \frac{B+C}{A} = \frac{\$100,000 + \$800,000}{\$3,029,419} = 0.3$$

Industry and Company Comparisons—

Just looking at a single ratio does not really tell you much about a company. You also need a standard of comparison, a benchmark. There are three principal benchmarks used in ratio analysis.

Financial ratios can be compared to the (1) ratios of the company in prior years, (2) ratios of another company in the same industry, and (3) industry average ratios. We'll discuss each.

History. The first useful benchmark is history. How has the ratio changed over time? Are things getting better or worse for the company? Is gross margin going down, indicating that costs are rising faster than prices can be increased? Are receivable days lengthening, indicating there are payment problems?

Competition. The second useful ratio benchmark is comparing a specific company ratio with that of a competitor. For example, if a company has a significantly higher return on assets than a competitor, it strongly suggests that the company manages its resources better.

Industry. The third type of benchmark is an industry-wide comparison. Industry-wide average ratios are published and can give an analyst a good starting point in assessing a particular company's financial performance. The chart on the facing page shows various ratios for a variety of companies in different industries. Note that there can be large differences in ratio values between industries and companies.

～

Review the chart on the facing page. What do the ratios tell us about companies and industries?

Microsoft shows the very high *return on assets* and *return on equity* characteristic of good companies in the computer software industry. In contrast, Boston Edison and ConEd show a lower *return on assets*

and *return on equity* that is characteristic of the utility industry.

The *inventory turn* for companies in the pharmaceutical industry is relatively low, meaning a high inventory level in relation to cost of goods sold. On the other end of the spectrum is McDonald's with an *inventory turn* of almost 90. Such a high turn is characteristic of the restaurant industry where inventory is made up of perishable food "raw materials." McDonald's high *inventory turn* means that the uncooked hamburger waiting to be made into Big Macs is on average only several days old.

Note that grocery stores and restaurants have very low accounts receivables as measured in *receivable days*. Not surprising, since both industries are so-called "cash businesses" with little credit given to customers.

The high *debt to equity* ratios for automobile companies and to a lesser extent retail stores indicates use of leverage. By carrying a large amount of debt, these companies can achieve a high *return on equity* in a business that offers only a low *return on assets*.

Note there is not much room for mistakes in businesses with a very low *profit margin*. In grocery stores, only 1¢ on a dollar of sales turns into profit. In contrast, Microsoft earns a quarter for every dollar of sales.

Also note that the high *gross profit* in the software and pharmaceutical industries allows companies to have a high SG&A spending level and still make a healthy profit. Some companies are just inherently more profitable than others, often because of proprietary technology.

Also note, these ratios can flop around depending on the business cycle but do provide guidance within and among company and industry groups.

Comparative Industry Financial Ratios *(as of Q4 1999)*

	LIQUIDITY RATIO	ASSET RATIOS			PROFITABILITY RATIOS				LEVERAGE RATIO
	CURRENT RATIO	INVENTORY TURN	RECEIVABLE DAYS	ASSET TURNS	GROSS MARGIN	PROFIT MARGIN	RETURN ON ASSETS	RETURN ON EQUITY	DEBT TO EQUITY
AppleSeed	**2.7**	**4.8 turn**	**54 days**	**1.0 turn**	**34%**	**8%**	**8%**	**15%**	**0.5**
Automobile									
General Motors	6.9	11 turn	143 days	0.7 turn	21%	3%	3%	21%	7.7
Ford	1.0	17 turn	9 days	0.6 turn	19%	3%	3%	17%	7.5
Grocery									
Amer. Stores	1.2	7.9 turn	6 days	2.4 turn	27%	2%	2%	11%	1.0
Kroger	0.9	11 turn	5 days	4.3 turn	24%	1%	1%	N/A	N/A
Computer									
IBM	1.2	7.7 turn	79 days	0.9 turn	40%	7%	7%	25%	0.5
Intel	2.8	7.1 turn	65 days	0.9 turn	56%	25%	25%	31%	0.0
Software									
Symantec	2.4	9.6 turn	69 days	1.4 turn	79%	8%	8%	18%	0.0
Microsoft	3.2	4.6 turn	27 days	0.9 turn	86%	25%	25%	29%	0.0
Electric Utility									
Boston Edison	0.6	10 turn	59 days	0.4 turn	65%	8%	8%	11%	0.8
ConEd	0.2	8.7 turn	29 days	0.5 turn	61%	10%	10%	11%	0.7
Food Process									
Campbell Soup	0.7	5.9 turn	29 days	1.2 turn	43%	10%	10%	29%	0.3
General Mills	0.8	5.7 turn	23 days	1.6 turn	59%	9%	9%	N/A	N/A
Retail Store									
Sears	1.9	5.4 turn	206 days	1.1 turn	35%	3%	3%	26%	3.0
Federated	1.8	2.8 turn	68 days	1.1 turn	39%	2%	2%	6%	1.0
Restaurant									
McDonald's	0.5	88 turn	16 days	0.6 turn	42%	15%	15%	18%	0.6
Wendy's	1.6	43 turn	10 days	1.1 turn	26%	8%	8%	12%	0.2
Petroleum									
Exxon	0.9	11 turn	27 days	1.3 turn	49%	5%	5%	16%	0.2
Mobil	0.8	15 turn	37 days	1.7 turn	41%	4%	4%	16%	0.4
Big Pharma									
Lilly	0.9	2.4 turn	73 days	0.5 turn	71%	21%	21%	25%	0.4
Merck	1.6	4.3 turn	49 days	0.8 turn	53%	20%	20%	32%	0.1

Chapter 14. Alternative Accounting Policies and Procedures

Various alternative accounting policies and procedures are completely legal and widely used, but may result in significant differences in the values reported on a company's financial statements. Some people would call this chapter's topic "creative accounting."

All financial statements are prepared in accordance with Generally Accepted Accounting Principles (GAAP). But within these accepted principles are a variety of alternative policies and procedures that may be used.

Selection of one policy over another can depend upon management's judgment and upon circumstance. The financial books can look quite different depending upon which policy is chosen. These alternative accounting policies can be used creatively by management as the "cosmetics" of financial reporting.

The table below shows major alternative accounting policies in use today. Management, with assistance from their auditors, will select from this list of acceptable accounting principles those that best suit their particular enterprise and management philosophy. Generally, the alternative policies can be grouped into two main categories: those that are financially "aggressive" and those that are financially "conservative."

Conservative Policies. So-called conservative accounting policies tend to understate profits and lower inventory and other asset values. Many accountants think these actions take on a "conservative" posture for the business. Few expenses are capitalized, that is, placing asset value on the *Balance Sheet* and amortizing it over time rather than classifying it as an expense immediately. Thus, expenses are higher and profits are lower in the short term, but more "solid" or conservative in the long term.

Aggressive Policies. The so-called aggressive accounting policies tend to inflate earnings and raise asset values, taking an "aggressive" financial posture. Reserves and allowances are low, which keeps profits high. This selection of policy can lead to negative surprises, such as if returns or repairs were seriously underestimated.

Alternative Accounting Policies and Procedures

ACCOUNTING POLICY	AGGRESSIVE APPLICATION	CONSERVATIVE APPLICATION
Revenue Recognition	At Sale *(Some risk remains)*	After Sale *(Buyer carries all Risk)*
Cost of Goods & Inventory Valuation Method	FIFO *(First-in, first-out)*	LIFO *(Last-in, first-out)*
Depreciation Method	Accelerated *(Faster)*	Straight-Line *(Slower)*
Reserves & Allowances *(Warranty, Bad Debt, Returns)*	Low Estimates *(Higher profit now)*	High Estimates *(Higher profit later)*
Contingent Liabilities	Footnote only *(Postpone bad news)*	Accrue When Known *(Take losses now)*
Advertising & Marketing Expenditures	Capitalize *(Write-off later)*	Expense *(Write-off now)*

Neither conservative nor aggressive policies are "right" or "wrong." They are just different ways of viewing the same financial information. However, it is important when reviewing financial statements with the purpose of determining a company's financial condition to understand the aggressive or conservative posture the company takes in compiling its books.

With conservative accounting policies, you can take comfort that the profits are real. With aggressive policies, profits may be overstated. *If however, you see a company change its accounting policies from conservative to aggressive, watch out. This change may be a sign of big trouble ahead.*

GAAP does give management latitude to select certain accounting policies and procedures. However, these policies, once selected, must be used consistently and the year-to-year distortions are usually small. However, in periods of inflation, the difference between common inventory valuation methods can be large.

Inventory Valuation & Costing Methods

No, FIFO is not the name of a dog. It's one of the three methods that accountants may use to compute (1) cost of goods sold for the *Income Statement* and (2) inventory value for the *Balance Sheet.*

Cost of goods sold is most often the single biggest deduction from sales revenue on the way to net profit. How best to value the inventory that makes up this large cost? GAAP offers three basic choices. In an inflationary period, or when costs of raw materials fluctuate, these three methods of inventory valuation will yield considerably different values. The three alternative valuation methods are:

1. Average Cost Method. Under the average cost method, the separate purchases of goods placed into inventory are summed to give the total inventory value and are averaged to give a cost of goods sold value. The average cost method is seldom used, offering no real convenience or added accuracy.

Balance Sheet and Income Statements Effects of Inventory Valuation Method Choice on Inventory Value and COGS

	UNITS	PURCHASE PRICE	AVERAGE COST METHOD	LAST-IN, FIRST-OUT (LIFO)	FIRST-IN, FIRST-OUT (FIFO)
FIRST INVENTORY PURCHASE	1,000	$1,000 ●			
SECOND INVENTORY PURCHASE	1,000	1,050			
THIRD INVENTORY PURCHASE	1,000	1,100			
FOURTH INVENTORY PURCHASE	1,000	1,150 ●			
TOTAL INVENTORY	4,000	$4,300			
AVERAGE COST PER 1,000 UNITS		$1,075 ●			
SALES REVENUE *(1,000 units @ $1.50)*			$1,500	$1,500	$1,500
COST OF GOODS SOLD			↳1,075	↳1,150	↳1,000
GROSS PROFIT			$ 425	$ 350	$ 500
STARTING INVENTORY VALUE			$4,300	$4,300	$4,300
LESS COST OF GOODS SOLD VALUE			1,075	1,150	1,000
ENDING INVENTORY VALUE			$3,225	$3,150	$3,300

Summary of FIFO vs. LIFO Financial Statements Effects

	LIFO	FIFO
COST OF GOODS	↑	↓
INVENTORY VALUE	↓	↑
PROFITS	↓	↑

2. FIFO Method. Under FIFO (first-in, first-out) methods of valuation, the costs of the earliest materials purchased are assigned to cost of goods sold and the costs of the more recent purchases are summed and allocated to yield ending inventory values.

This method conforms to the actual flow of goods in a factory with the most recent purchases placed at the back of the fridge, and the oldest purchases placed in front to use before they spoil.

3. LIFO Method. Under LIFO (last-in, first-out) method, costs of the latest purchases become cost of goods sold and the costs of the oldest purchases are assigned to inventory. When inventory costs are rising as in a period of inflation, using the FIFO method means higher profits (and higher taxes) than if the LIFO method were used.

The table on the previous page shows *Income Statement* and *Balance Sheet* effects of the three alternative inventory valuation and product costing methods in an inflationary period. Depending on the method used, gross profit can vary from a low of $350 with the LIFO method to a high of $500 with the FIFO method. The average cost method is in the middle of the muddle at $425 in gross profit.

All are "correct" values; they just result from applying different acceptable procedures. The table above summarizes the effects of FIFO and LIFO valuation.

Note: While financial statements most often provide accurate, essential information, they do have limitations:

1. Some important corporate "assets" that are difficult to quantify (valued employees and loyal customers) are disregarded.

2. Only the historic values of tangible assets are presented, not current values.

3. Fallible estimates are made for many important items such as receivables collection, depreciation and the salability of inventory.

4. Profits shown on the Income Sheet and inventory values shown on the Balance Sheet can be significantly affected by accounting method choices.

Chapter 15. Cooking the Books

The vast majority of audited financial statements are prepared fairly. They are assembled in accordance with GAAP and evidence sound fiscal controls and integrity of management. However, sometimes this is not the case and financial fraud is committed: illegal payments made, assets misused, losses concealed, expenses under-reported, revenue over-recorded and so forth.

The New Shorter Oxford English Dictionary has two definitions for the noun "cook." The first describes a person in the white hat behind the counter. The second definition is more appropriate to our discussion: "A person who falsifies or concocts something." So, the first cook *cooks* your lunch; the second cook *eats* your lunch.

"Cooking the books" means intentionally hiding or distorting the real financial performance or actual financial condition of a company.

～

This chapter will give you recipes for book-cooking. The goal here is *not* to make you able to prepare fraudulent financial statements yourself. Leave this task to trained professionals. Rather, this discussion should make you better able to see the clues of fraud and remind you to be vigilant.

Managers most often cook the books for personal financial gain—to justify a bonus, to keep stock prices high and options valuable or to hide a business's poor performance. Companies most likely to cook their books have weak internal controls and have a management of questionable character facing extreme pressure to perform.

Cooking is most often accomplished by moving items that should be on the *Income Statement* onto the *Balance Sheet* and sometimes vice versa. A variety of specific techniques can be used to raise or lower income, raise or lower revenue, raise or lower assets and liabilities, and thereby reach whatever felonious objective the businessperson desires. A simple method is outright lying by making fictitious transactions or ignoring required ones.

Cooking the books is very different from "creative accounting." It is creative to use accounting rules to best present your company in a favorable financial light. It is legal and accepted. Cooking the books is done for a deceptive purpose and is meant to defraud.

Income Statement. Puffing up the *Income Statement* most often involves reporting some form of bogus sales revenue that results in increased profits. See Box A in the chart on the next page.

"Cooking the books" means intentionally hiding or distorting the real financial performance and/or financial condition of a company. Whether baked or pan-fried, this cooking is most often performed with a felonious purpose such as to defraud.

Techniques to Puff Up the Income Statement

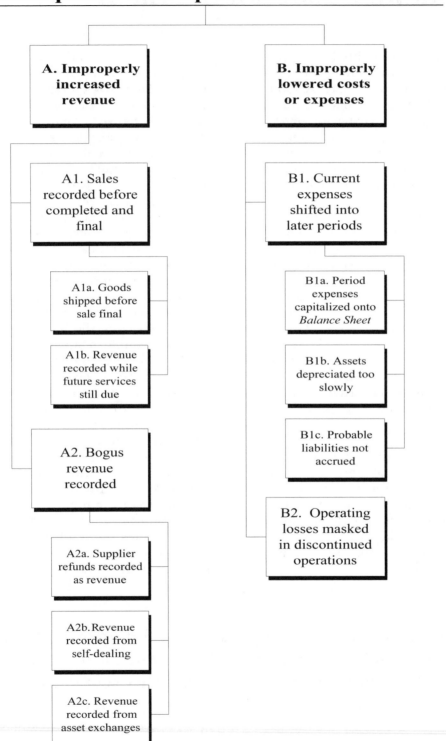

A. Improperly increased revenue

A1. Sales recorded before completed and final

A1a. Goods shipped before sale final

A1b. Revenue recorded while future services still due

A2. Bogus revenue recorded

A2a. Supplier refunds recorded as revenue

A2b. Revenue recorded from self-dealing

A2c. Revenue recorded from asset exchanges

B. Improperly lowered costs or expenses

B1. Current expenses shifted into later periods

B1a. Period expenses capitalized onto *Balance Sheet*

B1b. Assets depreciated too slowly

B1c. Probable liabilities not accrued

B2. Operating losses masked in discontinued operations

One of the simplest methods of cooking the books is padding the revenue; that is, recording sales before all the conditions required to complete a sale have occurred. The purpose of this action is to inflate sales and associated profits. A particularly creative technique is self-dealings such as increasing revenue by selling something to yourself *(Box A2b)*.

Revenue is appropriately recorded *only* after all these conditions are met:

1. An order has been received.
2. The actual product has been shipped.
3. There is little risk the customer will not accept the product.
4. No significant additional actions are required by the company.
5. Title has transferred and the purchaser recognizes his responsibility to pay.

The other common route to illegal reporting of increased profit is to lower expenses or to fiddle with costs. *(Box B)* A simple method to accomplish this deception involves shifting expenses from one period into another with the objective of reporting increased profits in the earlier period and hoping for the best in the later period.

Balance Sheet. Most often both the *Balance Sheet* and the *Income Statement* are involved in cooking the books. A convenient cooking is exchanging assets with the purpose of inflating the *Balance Sheet* and showing a profit on the *Income Statement* as well! *(Box D1a* on page 214.)

For example, a company owns an old warehouse, valued on the company books at $500,000, its original cost minus years of accumulated depreciation. In fact, the present value of the warehouse if sold would be 10 times its book value, or $5 million. The company sells the warehouse, books a $4.5 million profit and then buys a similar warehouse next door for $5 million.

Nothing has really changed. The company still has a warehouse, but the new one is valued on the books at its purchase price of $5 million instead of the lower depreciated cost of the original warehouse. The company has booked a $4.5 million gain, yet it has less cash on hand than it had before this sell-buy transaction.

Question: How many sets of books should a company have?

Answer: Generally, companies keep three different sets of books, each serving a separate and legitimate purpose:

1. One complete set of books for financial reporting to the outside world and to the owners of the business.

2. One modified set of financial statements focusing on determining and defending tax liability.

3. Other special presentation formats of financial information for management to use to control the business operations.

Techniques to Sweeten the Balance Sheet

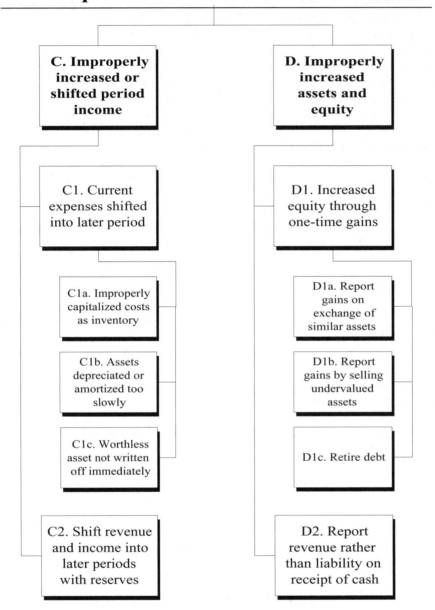

Why would a company exchange one asset for a very similar one...especially if it cost them cash and an unnecessary tax payment? The only "real" effect of this transaction is the sale of an under-valued asset and booking of a one-time gain. If the company reports this gain as part of "operating income," the books have been cooked—income has been deceptively inflated. If the company purports that this one-time capital gain is reoccurring operating income, it has misrepresented the earning capacity of the enterprise.

～

Just as some people cheat on their tax returns, thinking they will not be caught, some companies "cook the books" hoping auditors and regulators will not catch them either.

Like "borrowing" $20 from the till until payday, and then not being able to repay the "loan," small illegalities can snowball into major fraud.

Remember, an auditor's job is only to review systematically the company's accounting and control procedures and then sample its business transaction to see whether appropriate policies and procedures are being followed in practice. But it is quite possible for a dedicated and corrupt management to mask transactions and deceive these auditors.

All fast-growing companies must eventually slow down. Managers may be tempted to use accounting gimmicks to give the appearance of continued growth. Managers at weak companies may want to mask how bad things really are. Managers may want that last bonus before bailing out. Maybe there are unpleasant loan covenants that would be triggered but can be avoided by cooking the books. A company can just be sloppy and have poor internal controls.

One key to watch for is management changing from a conservative accounting policy to a less-conservative one, for example changing from LIFO to FIFO methods of inventory valuation or from expensing to capitalizing certain marketing expenses, easing of revenue recognition rules, lengthening amortization or depreciation periods.

Changes like these should be a red flag. There may be valid reasons for these accounting policy changes, but not many. Be warned.

Section D. Business Expansion: Strategy, Risk & Capital

About This Section

Our startup enterprise has done well. The investors are happy with our progress and we can feel change jingle in our pockets. "AppleSeed" has become a well-recognized brand name and the demand for our products is strong.

It was not easy to raise the initial capital for our risky startup venture. Nevertheless, Great Aunt Lillian saw our potential, placed a bet and financed us. Now even Great Uncle Fred, skeptical before, is happy with their investment. In fact, at the company picnic he asked me to see him first if we needed money to expand!

Yes, we have come to that happy time in the history of a business—time to ask the questions: "Should we expand?" And if so, "How?" The rest of this book will deal with AppleSeed Enterprises's growth.

Historical vs. Proforma Financials

Previous chapters show how to report a company's *historical* financial performance. Now we are going to look forward and predict the future. We will learn how to analyze alternative investment choices and make plans that will shape our company's future success.

In our analysis of future investment alternatives, we will be preparing so-called *proforma* financial statements. Proforma means "for form."

Proforma financial statements are in the exact same format as regular historical statements but are used to model the expected future performance of the company. Proforma financials (especially proforma cash flow statements) are useful tools to evaluate the impact of major capital investment by the company. They answer the question, "How might our financial future look if we make this investment?"

Qualitative and Quantitative Methods

The essence of business is to mobilize capital (money) to generate profit (more money). How successful we are often depends on making good capital investment decisions.

In this section, we discuss *qualitative* tools useful in analyzing business decisions: building decision trees, using strategic planning methods and understanding risk and uncertainty in any decision.

But it takes money to make money, and in the last chapter in this section, AppleSeed Enterprises will sell additional equity and take on more debt to finance an aggressive expansion.

Then **Section E** will focus on important *quantitative* tools (net present value, internal rate of return and others) useful in selecting between alternative capital investments.

"The chief determinant of what a company will become is the investments it makes today. The generation and evaluation of creative investment proposals is far too important to be left to financial specialists; instead it is the ongoing responsibility of all managers throughout the organization."

Prof. Robert C. Higgins
University of Washington
in *Analysis for Financial Management*

Financial Statements

Finally, in **Chapter 22**, we will take all that we have learned and apply it to AppleSeed Enterprises's business expansion.

~

Let's go! We will refocus and reconfirm our mission and vision of the future. We will discuss decision tree analysis, a structured way to assess the alternative pathways for AppleSeed's growth. Then we will select the best path to follow.

We will explore the strategic choices a business faces when investing for growth.

We will learn how to plan the actions and tactics that will make our strategies real.

However, no matter how good the proforma financial statements may look, a flawed strategy will lead to failure. We will look at the difference between risk and uncertainty, and how companies can deal with the potential negative consequences of their actions.

Finally, confident in our plans and in our future, we will raise capital by adding debt and additional equity to AppleSeed Enterprises's Balance Sheet.

Chapter 16. Mission, Vision, Goals, Strategies, Actions and Tactics

Business strategy is the highest level planning and command in the organization directed at reaching specific commercial and financial goals.

We at AppleSeed Enterprises are going to make some important decisions. Sometimes deciding what to do is easy. Not much planning, analysis, or consultation is required to pick up a box of cornflakes on the way home from work. And we were running out of 1% milk anyway.

However, when a lot is riding on getting a business decision right, it is a good idea to be thoughtful and strategic. But what does strategy mean? How do we develop it?

Developing good strategy is a process. We ask some questions, test some assumptions, gather some information, look inward at our strengths and weaknesses, and look outward at our customers and the economic environment.

The process is "strategic" because we seek the best way to respond to our competitive environment given the resources available to us. The process is "planning" because we set goals and develop structured approaches to reach those goals. Strategic planning is a disciplined effort to produce fundamental decisions and actions that will shape and guide our organization toward our agreed-upon company goals.

- Strategy is systematically thinking things through and coming up with creative ways to reach business goals.

- Strategy is of the very highest importance to the success of the business and is thus the responsibility of top-level management.

- Strategy is always actionable. We plan and execute actions to implement strategy. Strategy is measurable and thus we will know if it works or not.

- Strategy is forward thinking. It is not about past actions but rather about shaping the future. However, strategy must also be in the moment and reflect the current environment facing the business.

- Strategy is systematic, realistic and inclusive. Strategy that is creative and unique will be more powerful.

- Strategy is constrained by the limited resources a company has available, but will optimally use all those available resources. Strategy capitalizes on a company's strengths but also will support its weaknesses.

Okay, got that! Now let's apply strategic thinking, strategic planning and strategic management to map a happy future for AppleSeed Enterprises. Ultimately, we'll answer the all-important question, "Are we doing the right things to reach our goals?" See the helpful planning pyramid on the following page.

"Our plans miscarry because they have no aim. When a man does not know what harbor he is making for, no wind is the right wind."

Seneca the Younger
Roman philosopher and playwright, tutor and advisor of Nero

Strategic Planning Hierarchy

- Think of **Mission, Vision** and **Goals** as a hierarchy of company "destinations."

- Think of **Strategies**, **Actions** and **Tactics** as the hierarchy of "ways to get there."

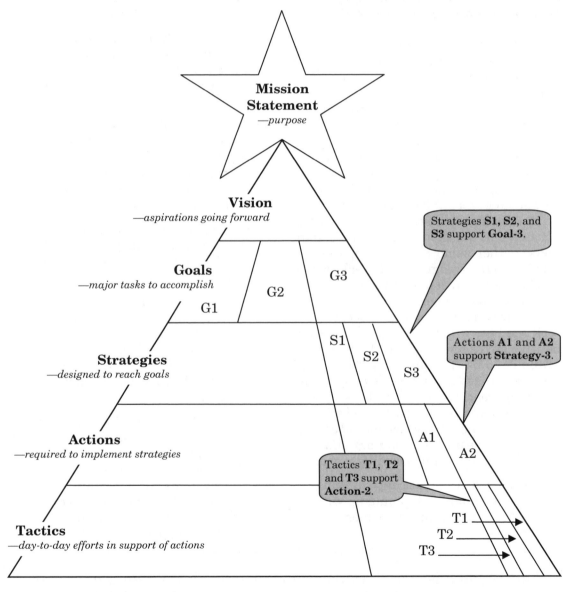

- The planning pyramid is populated with goals, strategies, actions and tactics, all designed and integrated to meet the company's mission and vision.

Strategic Planning Terms

- ***Mission*** Mission comes from the Latin word *missio,* meaning "sending away" a group to a foreign country and the business with which such a group is charged.

  A company's mission (or mission statement) describes the fundamental purpose of the organization—why we exist.

- ***Vision*** Vision comes from the Old English word *witan,* meaning "to know," as in the power of anticipating that which will or may come to be.

  A company's vision is an expression of the business's aspirations going forward—what we desire to become.

- ***Goals*** Goal comes from the Middle English word *gal,* meaning boundary; limit; end point of a race.

  A company's goals are the three or four broad objectives the company sets for itself...the key results to achieve.

- ***Strategies*** Strategy comes from the Ancient Greek word *strategia,* meaning "office of general, command, general-ship; to lead to conduct."

  A company's strategies are high-level, long-term plans designed to accomplish specific goals. Each individual company goal may have several strategies required for implementation.

- ***Actions*** Action comes from the Latin word *acto,* meaning "doing."

  Multiple coordinated actions are often required to best implement a strategy.

- ***Tactics*** Tactic comes from the Greek word *taktikós,* meaning "fit for arranging or ordering."

  Tactics are day-to-day tasks that people in the company perform to accomplish an action in support of a strategy.

Let's apply these strategic planning terms and definitions to AppleSeed Enterprises. Then we can show our strategic plan to the Board of Directors to get their comments and sign off on our plans for the future.

~

After a few meetings of the staff and some market research and then brainstorming sessions, this is what we have:

Mission Statement AppleSeed Enterprises's mission is to be a leading regional supplier of high-end specialty food products and provide a superior financial return to our shareholders.

Vision AppleSeed Enterprises's vision is to be recognized for its delicious and wholesome food products manufactured and marketed in an environmentally friendly manner.

Goal 1 Remain the premier supplier of gourmet applesauce in the region.

Goal 2 Become a premier supplier of other gourmet food products in the region.

Now, both of our goals will need separate strategies to make them real. Each of our strategies will need actions and actions will need tactics to implement them. At each stage of the pyramid, we will assign responsibility, allocate resources, and measure results as we go forward.

> There are all sorts of cute techniques to assist managers in understanding their business environment and thinking strategically. Try a **SWOT** *analysis* (Strengths, Weaknesses, Opportunities and Threats), a **PEST** *analysis* (Political, Economic, Social and Technological) or a **STEER** analysis (Sociocultural, Technological, Economic, Ecological and Regulatory). Though don't get too carried away.

Strategic planning is about predicting the future, and predicting the future is an inherently risky business, fraught with uncertainty. We will discuss business risk and uncertainty in the next chapter.

Chapter 17. Risk and Uncertainty

AppleSeed Enterprises is planning a major expansion. We will be making a significant investment with hope for a good return. However, things may go wrong. Ideally, we want a high return, but with a manageable and understood risk—that is what we call a "businesswoman's risk."

Risk

What is risk? Can we understand risk and take actions to lower it? A simple definition of risk is a business event that would generate a "negative surprise." Risk is something that we would regret if it occurred. In financial terms, risk is the probability of an investment's actual return being lower than expected.

We now have the two elements necessary to start us on a path of business risk management. How can we lower the potential financial downside of risk and/or lower the probability of occurrence?

Risk can be both intrinsic (within ourselves) and extrinsic (from outside). Having to scrap a lot of product because of a quality problem is an intrinsic risk that could lead to very large business losses. A rival company unexpectedly introducing a competitive product that results in our lower sales revenue is an extrinsic risk.

If risk is the potential for a business loss, a business project may be deemed a high risk because either: (1) there is a high likelihood of a loss of any size, or (2) there is even a very small likelihood of a large loss. Almost every business action carries some degree of risk. High-risk actions require careful management because of their potential large negative consequences to the business.

Uncertainty

"Uncertainty" is different from risk. Uncertainty is not knowing what the future will bring. However, under the cloak of uncertainty, high risk can lurk. Thus, lowering uncertainty can lower risk too.

Uncertainty can be more dangerous than risk. Because we can often know the elements of risk, we can plan for risk and take measures to mitigate the negative consequences of risk. However, with uncertainty we are often flying blind. It is hard to lower uncertainty if you do not know what it is and thus what to do to lower it.

"The consequences of our actions are so complicated, so diverse, that predicting the future is a very difficult business indeed."

J.K. Rowling
British fantasy author in *Harry Potter and the Prisoner of Azkaban*

"The best way to predict the future is to invent it."

Alan Kay
American computer scientist known for his pioneering work on object-oriented programming and windowing graphical interface design

"It's tough making predictions, especially about the future."

attributed to **Yogi Berra**
American baseball player; actually first said by **Niels Bohr**, Danish Nobel laureate

Threat

A threat is a potential event with a very low probability but a high negative impact. People buy insurance to protect themselves against threats such as their house burning down. Businesses can buy fire insurance too, but they cannot insure against an uncollectable debt caused by the business failure of their largest customer.

Note that specialized insurance instruments called "credit default swaps" were developed by the financial services industry in an attempt to offer protection against such unlikely, negative financial events as failure of a creditor. But as we now know, things have not gone well with this type of insurance.

Bet Your Company Risk

Avoid taking a *"bet-your-company risk."* The potential negative consequences of such a risk are just too, too large. For example, a bet-your-company risk would be spending all your available resources on developing a risky new product. The company could fail if development were to be delayed or if sales were much lower than projected.

However, entrepreneurial companies usually must face *bet-your-company risks* as they start up and grow. Understanding and managing risk and uncertainty is especially important in these fledgling enterprises. Startups must be focused, innovative, responsive and also very lucky to survive. Most often, they are not.

∼

When planning AppleSeed's expansion we recognize that the future is uncertain and that financial projections are just that—projections. Our estimates of what may happen in the future are based on assumptions and on our ability to execute. Assumptions may prove not to be valid and future performance may not go according to plan.

Chapter 18. Making Decisions About AppleSeed's Future

AppleSeed Enterprises's Board of Directors thinks that we can successfully expand our business and that now is a good time to do it. The Board has asked management—that's us—to prepare several alternative expansion plans for Board review.

The most astute member of the Board reminds us to think strategically. She recommends writing a strategic plan for the business and she counsels a judicious look at capital requirements and sources. First, however, we need to make some decisions.

Where do we want our company to be in five or 10 years? How will we get there from here? What level of risk are we comfortable with? How much money will we need to expand and where will we get it? What is our plan?

Let's generate ideas; let's brainstorm. Adding a new and complementary product line could be just the thing. Our trucks regularly deliver AppleSeed's gourmet applesauce to supermarkets and specialty stores around town. Adding more products to the truck would be easy and economical. Gourmet potato chips could be a nice fit to increase our sales. We could buy that floundering, low-end potato chip company across town, Chips-R-Us, Inc., and then rebrand. Alternatively, we could just build a new factory from scratch.

Decisions, decisions! The question is how to expand our business. What follows are several useful methods to analyze AppleSeed's business expansion opportunities.

Decision Tree Analysis

Building a "decision tree" is a thoughtful and structured approach to making business decisions. A decision tree is an easy-to-understand graphic made up of a series of ordered forks (called nodes) that visualize a decision pathway. Drawing a

AppleSeed Expansion Decision Tree

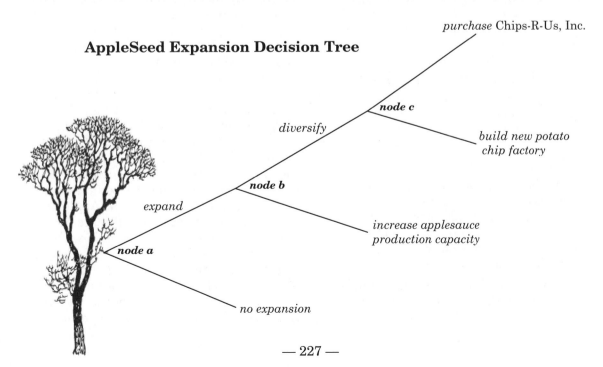

purchase Chips-R-Us, Inc.

node c

diversify

build new potato chip factory

node b

expand

increase applesauce production capacity

node a

no expansion

decision tree is useful in arraying all the key alternatives in a business decision. Then, just follow the decision tree to a decision!

Start at the lower-left base of the tree and follow through to each decision node. First, should AppleSeed expand, or not (**node a**)? Second, if we do expand, then should we diversify our product line beyond applesauce (**node b**)? Last, if we were to diversify into potato chips, should we buy an existing company or build a new plant from scratch (**node c**)?

Each fork on the decision tree carries its own benefits and risks, costs, expenses and revenues. The decision tree structure helps us systematically review pros and cons at each key stage of our decision.

Strategic Alternatives

Another way to analyze AppleSeed's expansion decision is to prepare a strategic alternatives table as shown here. AppleSeed could expand by selling new products or by entering new markets or both. These choices result in four strategic options:

PRODUCT LINE EXPANSION?

	NO	YES
NO	**Option I.** *Same product into the same market.*	**Option II.** *New product into the same market.*
YES	**Option III.** *Same product into a new market.*	**Option IV.** *New product into a new market.*

(Left axis label: **MARKET EXPANSION?**)

Let's look at each option in detail:

Option I. Same product into the same market. This option is the *status quo*. All growth would come from selling more of our applesauce into our existing markets. Because we want to expand rapidly, this option is not for us.

Option II. New product into the same market. Expanding AppleSeed's product line to include gourmet potato chips and selling them through our existing retailers is an attractive and low-risk strategy. We are experts at manufacturing food products and we understand the needs of our existing customers. Plus, they like us and would be happy to buy more products with our brand name.

Option III. Same product into a new market. Selling into a new market could require costly new distribution methods. In addition, penetration could be time consuming. New markets can be risky. We lack experience with these customers.

Option IV. New product into a new market. Simultaneously entering a new market with a new product is perhaps the most risky of our four potential strategies, carrying the uncertainties of both the risks of product development and sales.

Overall, **Option II** seems to make the most sense for AppleSeed Enterprises, Inc. Potato chips it is!

Make vs. Buy Decision

Now, by expanding into a new product line, we will face a standard "make versus buy" strategic choice. See **node c** on the decision tree. Should we build our gourmet potato chip factory from scratch or should we buy an existing concern? We hear that a low-end potato chip company across town, Chips-R-Us, Inc., is not doing well and may be for sale cheap.

Purchase Alternative If we were to buy an existing company, we would have to refurbish their equipment to make our high-end product, but the cost would be less than starting from scratch. Chips-R-Us's capacity is not what we would want in the long term but would be adequate for a couple of years, and then we could expand.

"Greenfield" Alternative AppleSeed could start from scratch and build a new plant (on an empty "greenfield") with all new machinery. It will take a little longer to get going than if we bought Chips-R-Us, but the new plant would be perfect.

How should we decide whether to build from scratch or make the acquisition?

Well, let's prepare some proforma cash flow statements that will allow us to compare the financial returns of the two alternatives under consideration. We will need to consider the dollar amounts and timing of a series of cash investments and the ultimate returns on these investments.

～

In **Sections E,** we will review quantitative tools to help us and the Board of Directors compare the *purchase option* versus the *greenfield* option for AppleSeed's expansion into potato chip manufacture. Regardless of the option we choose, AppleSeed will need more capital to proceed. So, in the next chapter we will look at sources and costs of new capital.

"You will either step forward into growth or you step back into safety."

Abraham Maslow
American psychologist noted for his concept of the "hierarchy of human needs"

Chapter 19. Sources and Costs of Capital

We've decided on an expansion strategy. However, AppleSeed does not have enough cash on hand to finance either an acquisition or major expansion of its business. However, we do have a very solid Balance Sheet with a 0.5 debt-to-equity ratio. Total debt is only one-half of our equity. (See the discussion of liquidity ratios on page 203.)

Our preliminary analysis of cash flows shows that AppleSeed will need $2 million for additional property, plant and equipment, plus more working capital to finance the expansion. We'll discuss how we prepared these projections in **Chapter 22**.

We are on good terms with the local bank. We could take on additional debt. Also, our venture capital investors have offered to purchase more stock in Apple-Seed, that is, if the price is right.

More Debt for AppleSeed?

Banks will not lend unless they are almost positive that we will be able to repay what we owe. The amount of equity capital (stock) in the business acts as a safety cushion for the bank. The stockholders will lose everything before the bank would lose a penny. In general, debt is a cheap form of financing—if you can get it.

So what will debt financing actually cost AppleSeed? Banks set their interest rate on loans with two components. They add the current "risk free" lending return from government bonds to a "risk premium" based on how risky they judge the company to be. For example, if government bonds are yielding 4% and our friendly loan officer sees us as a moderate risk justifying an additional 4% as a risk premium, then our total interest rate will be 8% for a loan.

More Equity for AppleSeed?

On page 184, we asked the question "What's the Business Worth?" The answer was only of academic importance for Apple-Seed back then. Now things are different and valuation is important. We want to sell more stock to help finance Apple-Seed's expansion. But how much stock and at what price? The money raised will be added to AppleSeed's Balance Sheet and new shares will be issued.

We meet with our friendly venture capitalist and she says:

"We like what you have done and we support your expansion plans. We're prepared to buy more stock, investing an additional $800,000 at a pre-money valuation of $2.5 million (and thus a post-money valuation of $3.3 million)."

Say what? Pre-money? Post-money? We say thanks and we'll get back to you. The next step is to crack an entrepreneurial finance textbook to figure out what our friendly VC is talking about.

Pre-Money Valuation

It all turns out to be rather simple. AppleSeed currently has 200,000 shares outstanding. (See **Transaction 1** on page 97.) We own 50,000 founders' shares that we got for cheap at $1.00 per share. Our venture investors own 150,000 shares for which they paid $10.00 per share.

Currently, a conservative valuation for the company (based on a 12 times earnings multiple) would be about $3 million, or about $15.00 per share (computed as a $3 million value divided by 200,000 shares outstanding). This $3 million total value and $15.00 per share is what is meant as the "pre-money" valuation of the company, —the company's total estimated value before the sale of additional stock.

Post-Money Valuation

We're looking to raise $800,000 in new equity capital. Right after we raise this amount and place it into the company's coffers (in our bank account and on the Balance Sheet), the so-called "post-money" value of the company will be:

$3,000,000 *pre-money company value*
+ 800,000 *new investment*
_____
$3,800,000 *post-money company value*

Total pre-money and post-money valuations are intuitive. The post-money value of the company is just the pre-money value plus the amount of new money raised.

Now we come to the real point of negotiation with our friendly venture capitalist. How many new shares of stock does she get for investing $800,000 in AppleSeed stock? And then, importantly, how much of the company will we still own after the financing?

Dilution

Remember: Ms. Venture Capitalist has offered us $800,000 in new equity at a pre-money valuation of $2.5 million. We think that her valuation is on the low side and counter with an offer to issue stock with a $3.5 million pre-money valuation. Now we need to compute how many new shares we would issue to close this deal. We can determine how "dilutive" this offering will be to our ownership percentage. *Dilution means how much less as a percentage of the total company will we own after we issue more shares.*

Of the current 200,000 shares of stock outstanding for AppleSeed, we own 50,000 shares and the venture capitalists own 150,000 shares. Thus, we own 25% of the company and they own 75%. After the company issues more shares to the venture capitalists, we will still own our original 50,000 shares, but they will own 150,000 shares *plus* however many new shares the company needs to issue to induce the venture capitalists to trade the new stock for $800,000 in capital.

The negotiation we are having with our venture capitalist is over what pre-market valuation of the company to be used in computing the share price of the new offering. Look at the following table to see how pre-market valuation and the offering share price will affect both our and the venture capitalist's percentage ownership. (Note that the pre-money share price and the post-money share price are always the same. It is just how the math works.)

∼

After much to-and-fro, we split the value difference and agree on a share price of $15.00 with a $3 million pre-money value of the company. See the details of the **DEAL B** in the table.

To summarize, AppleSeed's plan is to raise $800,000 of new equity by issuing 53,333 shares of common stock and selling

Equity Ownership & Dilution at Several Pre-Money Valuations

	PRE-OFFERING	DEAL A	DEAL B	DEAL C	DEAL D
INITIAL SHARES	200,000	200,000	200,000	200,000	200,000
PROPOSED PRE-MONEY VALUATION		$2,500,000	$3,000,000	$3,500,000	$4,000,000
SHARE PRICE (PRE & POST-MONEY)		$12.50	$15.00	$17.50	$20.00
EQUITY $ TO BE RAISED		$800,000	$800,000	$800,000	$800,000
NEW SHARES TO BE ISSUED		64,000	53,333	45,714	40,000
+ OUR SHARES (INITIAL)	50,000	50,000	50,000	50,000	50,000
+ INVESTORS' SHARES (INITIAL)	150,000	150,000	150,000	150,000	150,000
+ NEW INVESTOR SHARES		64,000	53,333	45,714	40,000
= TOTAL SHARES		264,000	253,333	245,714	240,000
OUR % OWNERSHIP	25.0%	18.9%	19.7%	20.3%	20.8%

them to our friendly venture capitalists for $15.00 per share. In addition, our friendly banker has offered to lend us another $800,000 at an interest rate of 8% per year. This additional $1.6 million in capital is probably enough to finance our planned expansion.

In **Transaction 32** on the following pages, we will issue stock and negotiate a line of credit.

Cost of Equity Capital

We know that the additional debt will cost AppleSeed interest at an 8% annual rate. But what does selling more equity cost? Well, there is no explicit "interest" rate attached to common stock, but venture investors do expect a very good return on their investment.

Before we closed the deal for the additional expansion equity, we did ask our venture capitalist what return she was expecting. She said she would be happy with a similar return to that received in the original investment. Investors paid $10.00 per share originally and we have estimated that the share price has increased to about $15.00 in two years. Therefore, this increase in value represents about a 22.5% annual return.

A 22.5% annual return is a lot higher than the 8% interest that the bank requires. But then, equity investors are taking a much higher risk. Note also that the bank would not have lent us money if we had not raised enough additional equity to keep our debt-to-equity ratio low and lower the risk that the bank would lose capital if we were to default.

Weighted Average Cost of Capital

Most companies have several types and sources of capital. AppleSeed has both equity and debt in its capital structure, each costing a different amount. When making capital investment decisions it is useful to compute the "weighted average cost of capital" considering all the capital sources that the company employs.

See the capital structure table on this page. After the financing, 60% of AppleSeed's capital is equity with an estimated cost of capital of 22.5%. Further, 40% of AppleSeed's capital comes from debt, with half at an interest rate of 10% (mortgage rate from **Transaction 3** on page 101) and the other half at 8% for the proposed new line of credit. Note that because interest is tax deductible as a business expense, the effective cost of debt capital is lower by the 34% expected tax savings (the 10% rate becomes a 6.6% cost; the 8% rate becomes a 5.3% cost).

AppleSeed's weighted average cost of capital (WACC) is calculated by "weighting" the individual capital source costs by their percentage in the company's total capital structure.

Thus,

60%	x	22.5%	= 13.5%	cost of equity
21%	x	6.6%	= 1.3%	mortgage cost
19%	x	5.3%	= 1.0%	credit line cost
100%			15.8%	WACC

We will see in the next section that this 15.8% return should be a minimum target for our expansion investments. Much more later.

AppleSeed Enterprises Capital Structure Pre- & Post-Financing

	CAPITAL AS OF TRANSACTION 31 *(page 179)*	PROPOSED NEW FINANCING	TOTAL AFTER NEW FINANCING	% OF TOTAL CAPITAL
+ SHAREHOLDERS' EQUITY	$1,726,883	$800,000	$2,526,883	60%
+ MORTGAGE OUTSTANDING	$900,000		$900,000	21%
+ NEW CREDIT LINE		$800,000	$800,000	19%
= TOTAL CAPITAL	$2,626,883	$1,600,000	$4,226,883	100%
DEBT-TO-EQUITY RATIO	0.5		0.7	

Income Statement

for the period including Transactions 1 through 32

			prior	+	transaction	=	sum
	1	NET SALES	$3,055,560		—		$3,055,560
	2	COST OF GOODS SOLD	2,005,830		—		2,005,830
1 - 2 = 3		GROSS MARGIN	1,049,730				1,049,730
	4	SALES & MARKETING	328,523		—		328,523
	5	RESEARCH & DEVELOPMENT	26,000		—		26,000
	6	GENERAL & ADMINISTRATIVE	203,520		—		203,520
4 + 5 + 6 = 7		OPERATING EXPENSE	558,043				558,043
3 - 7 = 8		INCOME FROM OPERATIONS	491,687				491,687
	9	NET INTEREST INCOME	(100,000)		—		(100,000)
	10	INCOME TAXES	139,804		—		139,804
8 + 9 - 10 = 11		NET INCOME	$251,883		0		$251,883

IS Transaction Sum

Cash Flow Statement

for the period including Transactions 1 through 32

			prior	+	transaction	=	sum
	a	BEGINNING CASH BALANCE	$0				$0
	b	CASH RECEIPTS	2,584,900		—		2,584,900
	c	CASH DISBURSEMENTS	2,796,438		—		2,796,438
b - c = d		CASH FLOW FROM OPERATIONS	(211,538)				(211,538)
	e	PP&E PURCHASE	1,750,000		—		1,750,000
	f	NET BORROWINGS	900,000	**2B**	100,000		1,000,000
	g	INCOME TAXES PAID	0		—		0
	h	SALE OF CAPITAL STOCK	1,550,000	**1B**	800,000		2,350,000
a + d - e + f - g + h = i		ENDING CASH BALANCES	$488,462		900,000		$1,388,462

CF Transaction Sum

Balance Sheet

as of this Transaction 32

			prior	+	transaction	=	sum
	A	CASH	$488,462	**3**	900,000		$1,388,462
	B	ACCOUNTS RECEIVABLE	454,760		—		454,760
	C	INVENTORIES	414,770		—		414,770
	D	PREPAID EXPENSES	0		—		0
A + B + C + D = E		CURRENT ASSETS	1,357,992				2,257,992
	F	OTHER ASSETS	0		—		0
	G	FIXED ASSETS @ COST	1,750,000		—		1,750,000
	H	ACCUMULATED DEPRECIATION	78,573		—		78,573
G - H = I		NET FIXED ASSETS	1,671,427				1,671,427
E + F + I = J		TOTAL ASSETS	$3,029,419		900,000		$3,929,419

Assets Sum

			prior	+	transaction	=	sum
	K	ACCOUNTS PAYABLE	$236,297		—		$236,297
	L	ACCRUED EXPENSES	26,435		—		26,435
	M	CURRENT PORTION OF DEBT	100,000	**2A**	100,000		200,000
	N	INCOME TAXES PAYABLE	139,804		—		139,804
K + L + M + N = O		CURRENT LIABILITIES	502,536				602,536
	P	LONG-TERM DEBT	800,000		—		800,000
	Q	CAPITAL STOCK	1,550,000	**1A**	800,000		2,350,000
	R	RETAINED EARNINGS	176,883		—		176,883
Q + R = S		SHAREHOLDERS' EQUITY	1,726,883				2,526,883
O + P + S = T		TOTAL LIABILITIES & EQUITY	$3,029,419		900,000		$3,929,419

Liabilities & Equity Sum

T32. Finance expansion! Sell 53,333 shares of AppleSeed's common stock ($1 par value) for $15 per share and draw down $100,000 from a new line of credit.

This stock sale transaction is similar to that shown in **Transaction 1.** We have exchanged a percentage ownership in the company for capital.

In that transaction the stock price was only $10.00 per share, and thus for every $100,000 we raised we exchanged 10,000 shares of stock worth almost 5% of the company.

Because the stock price is higher now at $15.00 per share, we will only transfer 6,666 shares (2.6% of the company) to raise that same $100,000.

Flush with this new equity and to add some borrowing flexibility, we negotiated a *line of credit* with the local bank.

A **line of credit** is a flexible, short-term business loan in which the bank agrees that AppleSeed can borrow ("draw down") up to a prearranged maximum loan balance, but only if and when the money is needed. Interest is not charged on the part of the line of credit that is unused, and money is available without having to re-apply every time we draw down money from the line.

Transaction: Our friendly venture capitalist has happily agreed to finance our expansion into gourmet potato chip manufacture. She purchases 53,333 shares of common stock at $15.00 per share for a total of $799,995 and throws in a $5 bill to make our accounting easier.

Our friendly banker is impressed that we were able to sell more stock and offers us a *line of credit* that matches the $800,000 additional equity we raised. The interest rate 0.666% per month (8% per year) on the outstanding balance only. We draw down $100,000 to seal the deal.

1 (1A) Issuing stock creates a liability for the company. AppleSeed "owes" the new stockholders a portion of its assets, so increase **CAPITAL STOCK** on the *Balance Sheet* by $800,000. (1B) In the *Cash Flow Statement* add the $800,000 from this stock sale to **SALE OF CAPITAL STOCK.**

2 (2A) We have established an $800,000 line of credit, but have only taken down $100,000 to-date. Thus add this amount to **CURRENT PORTION OF DEBT** in the liabilities section of the *Balance Sheet.* (2B) Add in the *Cash Flow Statement* this $100,000 as **NET BORROWINGS.**

3 The total of $900,000 in cash received from the stock sales plus new borrowings is added to assets as **CASH** on the *Balance Sheet.*

Section E. Making Good Capital Investment Decisions

About This Section

Capital investment decisions are among the most important that management can make. Often capital is a company's scarcest resource, and using capital wisely is essential for success. Capital investments are long-term bets to build a better future. More than any other business action, capital investment decisions will define the company and its ultimate value.

Faced with limited capital resources, management must carefully decide which capital projects are economically feasible. Management must select projects that will contribute the most to increasing the company's value. This process of evaluating, comparing and selecting projects is called "capital budgeting."

> **Budget**, from the French *bougette*, or purse, refers to a list of all planned expenses and revenues. It is a plan for saving and spending.

Capital budgeting is a systematic approach to determining whether a company's planned major capital investments are worth pursuing. Capital budgeting is concerned with the justification of capital expenditures. Capital budgeting analysis can provide a rationale to select between alternative projects by answering the question "Which proposed project will most increase the company's value over time?"

~

This section will introduce you to the quantitative tools necessary to make good capital investment decisions. Then in the last chapter, **Chapter 22**, we will apply all this new knowledge evaluating our own expansion plans and capital budgeting for AppleSeed Enterprises.

Long-term projects usually spend cash (i.e., negative cash flow) early in the project's lifetime and harvest rewards (i.e., positive cash flow) later. Different projects can have very different cash flows both in dollar amounts and in timing. To compare project values, we will use numeric techniques that take into account the "time value of money."

First, the analysis requires estimating the size and timing of all incremental cash flows from the project. These future cash flows are then "discounted" to estimate their *present value (PV)*. These present values (both investments and returns) are then summed to get the so-called *net present value (NPV)* of the project in today's dollars. NPV is the estimated value added to the company by executing the project. Generally, the project with the highest NPV is selected to go forward.

A *discount rate* is used in NPV calculations. This rate is similar to an interest rate, but in reverse. A commonly used discount rate for capital budgeting is the company's *weighted average cost of capital (WACC)*, which takes into account the company's financing mix. An additional rate increment is added if the project carries a higher risk than that of the company as a whole. This discount rate is sometimes called the "hurdle rate," the company's minimum acceptable return.

> ### But Beware!
>
> Having a quantitative basis for evaluating business decisions can provide objectivity. However, the rigid methodologies used can force potentially flawed assumptions and projections that will compromise the analysis. Just because resultant numbers look precise and accurate does not mean they are meaningful. Don't forget the maxim "garbage in; garbage out."

Financial Statements

It is best to look at quantitative project evaluation tools as just one of several useful decision-making resources. Careful strategy selection, management intuition, and study of historic precedent go well with quantitative measures such as NPV in making capital budget decisions.

Just "eyeballing" a set of numbers provides as much guidance as an overly precise computation, especially when the required input variables are not predictable with much accuracy. Some practitioners have gone so far as to say that most detailed quantitative analysis is not as important as good management judgment and thoughtful strategy.

Using *both* quantitative and qualitative measures is important in making business decisions about the future of the company. However, no matter how good the "numbers" may look, sound strategies are absolutely essential. No matter how high the computed NPV for a capital project, if the company's basic strategies are defective, the capital project will fail to reach its goals.

Chapter 20. The Time Value of Money

Capital budgeting decisions require analyzing business cash flows often spanning years. Accounting for the *time value of money* is essential in these analyses.

~

"*A bird in the hand (today) is worth two in the bush (tomorrow).*" Now you know most of what you need to know about the time value of money. It is intuitive.

Everybody would rather have a dollar in his or her pocket today than to receive a dollar far into the future. Finance types say that today's dollar is worth more—that it has more value—than a dollar received tomorrow. The rest of this chapter will answer the questions "Why so?" and "How much?"

The three main reasons for this difference in value are:

1. **Inflation** Inflation does reduce purchasing power (value) over time. With a 5% per year inflation, a dollar received a year from today will only buy 95¢ worth of goods.

2. **Risk** There is always the chance that the promise of a dollar in the future will not be met and you will be out of luck. The risk could be low with a CD at an FDIC insured bank; or the risk could be high if it is your brother-in-law who is promising to repay a personal loan.

3. **Opportunity Cost** If you loan your dollar to someone else, you have lost the opportunity to use it yourself. That opportunity has a value to you today that makes today's dollar worth more than tomorrow's.

These three concepts—inflation, risk and opportunity cost—are the drivers of *present value* (PV) and *future value* (FV) calculations used in capital budgeting.

> ***Present Value (PV)*** Present value calculations are used in business to compare cash flows (cash spent and received) at different times in the future. Converting cash flows into present values puts these different investments and returns onto a common basis and makes capital budgeting analysis more meaningful and useful in decision-making.

The mathematics of present value and future value calculation are a bit more difficult than the addition and subtraction we have used in the Balance Sheet, Income Statement and Cash Flow Statement. However, if you only understand the concepts—but not all the math—you will still get 95% of the way.

There is a special vocabulary used to discuss capital budgeting and the time value of money. Just as with the three major financial statements, there are new words to learn (or perhaps, old words with new specific meanings). It is a necessary short ride and not all that complex.

All will become clear. Trust me.

Values, Rates and Time

Values are measured in currency. We will use U.S. dollars. Other places use different currency. Some interesting values are *present value, future value, discounted value, terminal value, net present value* and so forth.

But note that in financial calculations spanning time, currency value can be looked at from two different perspectives: as so-called "nominal" dollars or as so-called "real" dollars.

Nominal dollars are just the actual amount spent in dollars taken out of your wallet. *Real dollars,* on the other hand, are adjusted for inflation.

Why bother calculating both? Well, when you take out inflation (i.e., convert from "nominal dollars" into "real dollars") the price difference becomes much more comparable and easy to explain.

See **Appendix A** on page 277 for more details.

~

Rates are measured in percentages and with an associated time period (for example, 5% per year). The period could be a month or a day or even continuous. Some interesting rates are *inflation rate, interest rate, discount rate,* and *hurdle rate.* Specialized rates include *internal rate of return, risk premium* and *return on investment.* Details follow.

Capital Budgeting

In capital budgeting, different projects require different investment and will have different returns over time. In order to compare projects "apples to apples" and "oranges to oranges" on a financial basis, we will need to convert their cash flows into a common and comparable form. That common form is *present value.*

Simply put, a little bit of cash that is invested today followed by lots of cash returned in the near future would be a *really good* financial investment. However, lots of cash invested today followed by a little bit of cash returned in a long time would be a *really bad* investment.

Capital budgeting analysis is as simple as that. All the complex net present value (NPV) and internal rate of return (IRR) calculations are just details. Nevertheless, details can be important, so let's continue.

Equations?! The equations on the facing page (and the ones on following pages) are really not all that daunting. But if you are having trouble, just read the words and try to understand the concepts.

Present Value (PV) & Future Value (FV)

- The most commonly applied model of the "time value of money" is compound interest. *Compounding* is the process of computing the future value of money you have today given a certain interest rate.

  Use this formula to determine how much money **FV** *(future value)* you will have in your savings account after **y years** if you deposit an amount **PV** *(present value)* now and receive interest at a rate of **i per year.**

$$FV = PV \times (1+i)^y$$

  So if the amount you deposit **PV** is $100.00 and the interest rate **i** is 4% per year and you leave the money in the bank for **y** years = 7, you will be able to withdraw a total of $131.59 in seven years as **FV**. See following.

$$FV = \$100.00 \times (1+0.04)^7 = \$131.59$$

  Note: The interest rate is placed in the above equation as 0.04 *(4% = 4/100 = 0.04)*. Also, the expression $(1+0.04)^7$ with the "exponent" 7 means to multply the expression by itself 7 times, thus: $(1+0.04) \times (1+0.04) \times (1+0.04) \times (1+0.04) \times (1+0.04) \times (1+0.04) \times (1+0.04) = 1.3159$.

- Now, if you want to compute the present value **PV** of a future value **FV** to be received in **y years** using the discount rate of **d per year**, then you would rearrange the equation above as:

$$PV = \frac{FV}{(1+d)^y}$$

- Note, *discounting* is the process of computing the present value of money to be received in the future. Discounting future project cash flows *(future values)* into *present values* will be important when we financially evaluate alternative capital projects. More later.

Interest and Interest Rates

- Think of **interest** as the "rent" you must pay to borrow and use someone else's money.

- **Interest rates** are analogous to miles-per-hour speed measures. Both interest and speed measures have a numeric rate applied in a unit of time.

  "Sixty miles per hour" means that if you are traveling at that rate, in an hour you will go sixty miles. An interest rate of 4% per year means that if you deposit $100 in a bank account you will be able to withdraw $104 in a year.

- **Interest** is a financial operation used to compute from a starting amount of money today, the larger amount of money to be received in the future. Both amounts are in "nominal" dollars, the currency of the day. The chart following shows how $100 deposited in a bank today grows to $132 in seven years at 4% annual interest.

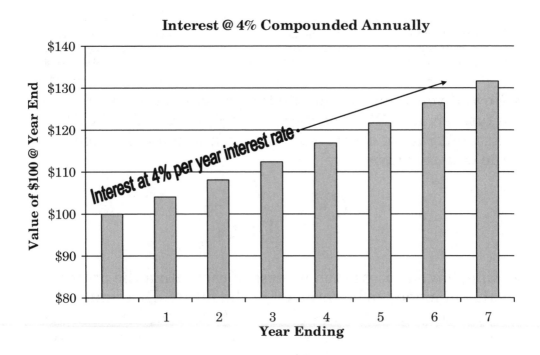

Interest @ 4% Compounded Annually

Discounting and Discount Rates

- **Discounting** is the process of finding the *present value* today of cash projected to be received at some future date. The projected amount of cash in the future is reduced using a discount rate for each unit of time between now and the future. Got that?

  Think of *discounting* as computing interest but going backwards. In discounting (going backward), you use a *discount rate* instead of using an *interest rate* (going forward). Discounting future returns is very important in capital budgeting. More later when we discuss NPV.

- The following chart shows how $132 projected to be received seven years in the future would be discounted back to $100 using a 4% annual discount rate. Both amounts are in "nominal" dollars, currency of the day.

  These charts on pages 244 and 245 are identical except that the "interest arrow" is going up into the future while the "discount arrow" is going down, back to the past.

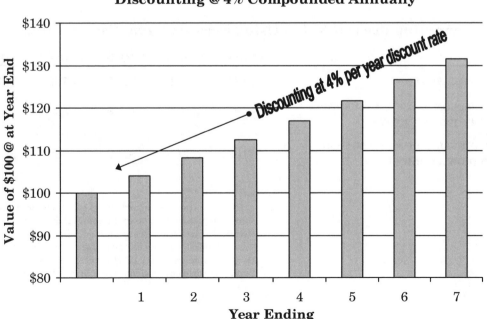

Discounting @ 4% Compounded Annually

Financial Statements

Computing Discounted Values

A shortcut to actually computing discounted values of future cash flows is to use a *present value–future value* table such as the one on the facing page. All the computation work has been done for you.

For example, look in the table for the fractional value seven years out at a 12% discount rate. The value shown is 0.452.

This number means that the present value of $1 to be received seven years *(y)* from now discounted *(d)* at 12% per year is 45.2¢.

Another way to describe this relationship between value now and value later is that having 45.2¢ in your pocket today is financially equivalent to $1.00 in your pocket in seven years (discounted at 12%).

To see how this present value table was constructed, solve the present value equation on page 249:

$$PV = \frac{FV}{(1+d)^y}$$

then,

$$PV = \frac{\$1.00}{(1+0.12)^7}$$

solved,

$$PV = \$0.452$$

Now let's use the present value table to compute the present value of an actual cash flow projection. See following table.

~

In the next chapter we will take what we have learned and apply it to understanding net present value (NPV) analysis, the most powerful and widely used analytic technique in capital budgeting.

Computing Present Value Using Present Value Factor Table.

		YEAR 1	YEAR 2	YEAR 3	YEAR 4	SUM
A.	NOMINAL CASH FLOW	($124)	$88	$225	$135	$324
B.	FACTOR FROM PRESENT VALUE TABLE AT A 14% DISCOUNT RATE	0.877	0.769	0.675	0.592	
C	PRESENT VALUE OF NOMINAL CASH FLOW (ROW A × ROW B)	($109)	$68	$152	$80	$191

Row A in the table above shows cash flow projections for a project for four years in nominal dollars (actual). **Row B** shows the discount factor using a discount rate of 14% for each year as shown in the Present Value Table on page 247. **Row C** shows the *present value* of the cash flow computed by multiplying these values.

Present Value (PV) of $1.00 Received at the End of Year y Discounted at an Annual Discount Rate d

Year End (y)										Annual Discount Rate (d)									
	2%	4%	6%	8%	10%	12%	14%	16%	18%	20%	22%	24%	26%	28%	30%	35%	40%	45%	50%
1	0.980	0.962	0.943	0.926	0.909	0.893	0.877	0.862	0.847	0.833	0.820	0.806	0.794	0.781	0.769	0.741	0.714	0.690	0.667
2	0.961	0.925	0.890	0.857	0.826	0.797	0.769	0.743	0.718	0.694	0.672	0.650	0.630	0.610	0.592	0.549	0.510	0.476	0.444
3	0.942	0.889	0.840	0.794	0.751	0.712	0.675	0.641	0.609	0.579	0.551	0.524	0.500	0.477	0.455	0.406	0.364	0.328	0.296
4	0.924	0.855	0.792	0.735	0.683	0.636	0.592	0.552	0.516	0.482	0.451	0.423	0.397	0.373	0.350	0.301	0.260	0.226	0.198
5	0.906	0.822	0.747	0.681	0.621	0.567	0.519	0.476	0.437	0.402	0.370	0.341	0.315	0.291	0.269	0.223	0.186	0.156	0.132
6	0.888	0.790	0.705	0.630	0.564	0.507	0.456	0.410	0.370	0.335	0.303	0.275	0.250	0.227	0.207	0.165	0.133	0.108	0.088
7	0.871	0.760	0.665	0.583	0.513	0.452	0.400	0.354	0.314	0.279	0.249	0.222	0.198	0.178	0.159	0.122	0.095	0.074	0.059
8	0.853	0.731	0.627	0.540	0.467	0.404	0.351	0.305	0.266	0.233	0.204	0.179	0.157	0.139	0.123	0.091	0.068	0.051	0.039
9	0.837	0.703	0.592	0.500	0.424	0.361	0.308	0.263	0.225	0.194	0.167	0.144	0.125	0.108	0.094	0.067	0.048	0.035	0.026
10	0.820	0.676	0.558	0.463	0.386	0.322	0.270	0.227	0.191	0.162	0.137	0.116	0.099	0.085	0.073	0.050	0.035	0.024	0.017
11	0.804	0.650	0.527	0.429	0.350	0.287	0.237	0.195	0.162	0.135	0.112	0.094	0.079	0.066	0.056	0.037	0.025	0.017	0.012
12	0.788	0.625	0.497	0.397	0.319	0.257	0.208	0.168	0.137	0.112	0.092	0.076	0.062	0.052	0.043	0.027	0.018	0.012	0.008
13	0.773	0.601	0.469	0.368	0.290	0.229	0.182	0.145	0.116	0.093	0.075	0.061	0.050	0.040	0.033	0.020	0.013	0.008	0.005
14	0.758	0.577	0.442	0.340	0.263	0.205	0.160	0.125	0.099	0.078	0.062	0.049	0.039	0.032	0.025	0.015	0.009	0.006	0.003
15	0.743	0.555	0.417	0.315	0.239	0.183	0.140	0.108	0.084	0.065	0.051	0.040	0.031	0.025	0.020	0.011	0.006	0.004	0.002
16	0.728	0.534	0.394	0.292	0.218	0.163	0.123	0.093	0.071	0.054	0.042	0.032	0.025	0.019	0.015	0.008	0.005	0.003	0.002
17	0.714	0.513	0.371	0.270	0.198	0.146	0.108	0.080	0.060	0.045	0.034	0.026	0.020	0.015	0.012	0.006	0.003	0.002	0.001
18	0.700	0.494	0.350	0.250	0.180	0.130	0.095	0.069	0.051	0.038	0.028	0.021	0.016	0.012	0.009	0.005	0.002	0.001	0.001
19	0.686	0.475	0.331	0.232	0.164	0.116	0.083	0.060	0.043	0.031	0.023	0.017	0.012	0.009	0.007	0.003	0.002	0.001	0.000
20	0.673	0.456	0.312	0.215	0.149	0.104	0.073	0.051	0.037	0.026	0.019	0.014	0.010	0.007	0.005	0.002	0.001	0.001	0.000
21	0.660	0.439	0.294	0.199	0.135	0.093	0.064	0.044	0.031	0.022	0.015	0.011	0.008	0.006	0.004	0.002	0.001	0.000	0.000
22	0.647	0.422	0.278	0.184	0.123	0.083	0.056	0.038	0.026	0.018	0.013	0.009	0.006	0.004	0.003	0.001	0.001	0.000	0.000
23	0.634	0.406	0.262	0.170	0.112	0.074	0.049	0.033	0.022	0.015	0.010	0.007	0.005	0.003	0.002	0.001	0.000	0.000	0.000
24	0.622	0.390	0.247	0.158	0.102	0.066	0.043	0.028	0.019	0.013	0.008	0.006	0.004	0.003	0.002	0.001	0.000	0.000	0.000
25	0.610	0.375	0.233	0.146	0.092	0.059	0.038	0.024	0.016	0.010	0.007	0.005	0.003	0.002	0.001	0.001	0.000	0.000	0.000
26	0.598	0.361	0.220	0.135	0.084	0.053	0.033	0.021	0.014	0.009	0.006	0.004	0.002	0.002	0.001	0.000	0.000	0.000	0.000
27	0.586	0.347	0.207	0.125	0.076	0.047	0.029	0.018	0.011	0.007	0.005	0.003	0.002	0.001	0.001	0.000	0.000	0.000	0.000
28	0.574	0.333	0.196	0.116	0.069	0.042	0.026	0.016	0.010	0.006	0.004	0.002	0.002	0.001	0.001	0.000	0.000	0.000	0.000
29	0.563	0.321	0.185	0.107	0.063	0.037	0.022	0.014	0.008	0.005	0.003	0.002	0.001	0.001	0.000	0.000	0.000	0.000	0.000
30	0.552	0.308	0.174	0.099	0.057	0.033	0.020	0.012	0.007	0.004	0.003	0.002	0.001	0.001	0.000	0.000	0.000	0.000	0.000

Chapter 21. Net Present Value (NPV)

We're going to invest cash now with high hopes of a large future return. But will the anticipated payback be enough to cover our initial investment given the project's high risk? Further, would any of our alternative projects provide us with a better financial return? *Answering these questions is the essence of capital budgeting, and **net present value (NPV)** analysis provides "gold standard" answers.*

~

The NPV of a proposed project is the value of future cash benefits minus costs, all restated in terms of today's money. In NPV analysis, relevant cash inflows and outflows are discounted to compute the present value for each and then added. The resultant NPV is an estimate of how much the project will increase the wealth of the company.

If NPV is positive, the project will add that value. A project with a negative NPV should never be pursued. If we must choose between several project alternatives, the project with the highest NPV will provide the highest value to the company. The higher the NPV, the better.

As you will see in the next few pages, actually computing NPV is a piece of cake. All the heavy lifting is done by computer spreadsheets. The hardest part of an NPV analysis is estimating the right cash flows to use in the formulas.

The very foundation of NPV analysis is the accurate forecasting of cash flows associated with a capital project. These *proforma* cash flow projections answer the questions "What initial investment will be required for this project?" and then "How will this project impact the company's future total cash flows?"

But beware: Application of these concepts and formulas without understanding their limits will often lead to erroneous and misleading results. Also, the mistaken impression of accuracy given by computation of overly precise variables can give a false confidence in proforma projections. And don't forget strategy. No matter how high an NPV, if a company's strategies are defective, its capital investment projects will most likely fail.

~

Later in the chapter, we'll discuss other analysis techniques used in capital budgeting, including IRR, ROI and payback period. But most often, all you will need is NPV. In the next chapter, we will apply NPV analysis to our planned business expansion at Appleseed Enterprises!

Different capital projects have different cash flows in both dollar amounts and time. **Net Present Value (NPV)** capital budgeting analysis attempts to answer the question "What is the 'lump-sum' worth of this project in today's dollars?"

NPV analysis makes comparing the financial worth of alternative projects possible in a standardized way. NPV accounts for the time value of money by calculating the present value of future project cash flows. NPV is a direct measure of expected value-added to the company from executing the capital project.

Net Present Value (NPV) Formula

- The "net present value" (NPV) of a proposed project is the sum of all the project's projected cash flows over time discounted by an appropriate rate to bring them to a present value. If the NPV of a project is positive, the project is projected to increase the value of the business by that amount.

- Shown here is an annotated version of the standard **Net Present Value (NPV)** equation. It is not very daunting once you get the hang of the concepts and work through some examples. Anyway, spreadsheets will do all the heavy lifting.

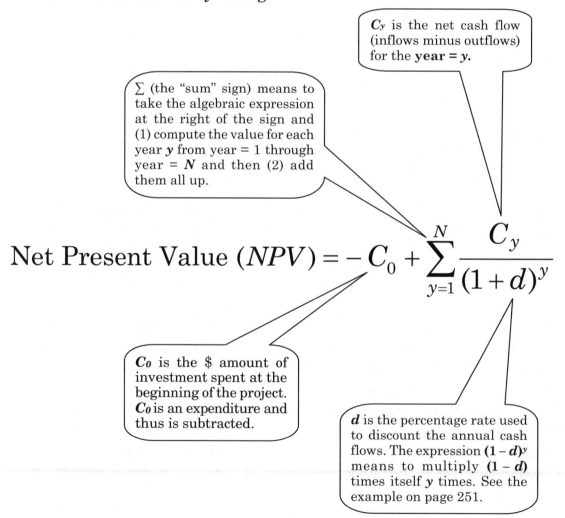

C_y is the net cash flow (inflows minus outflows) for the **year = y.**

Σ (the "sum" sign) means to take the algebraic expression at the right of the sign and (1) compute the value for each year y from year = 1 through year = N and then (2) add them all up.

$$\text{Net Present Value } (NPV) = -C_0 + \sum_{y=1}^{N} \frac{C_y}{(1+d)^y}$$

C_0 is the \$ amount of investment spent at the beginning of the project. C_0 is an expenditure and thus is subtracted.

d is the percentage rate used to discount the annual cash flows. The expression $(1-d)^y$ means to multiply $(1-d)$ times itself y times. See the example on page 251.

Net Present Value (NPV) Example

- Using the sample capital project cash flows in this table, we will calculate the NPV for the project.

CASH FLOWS	START	YEAREND YEAR 1	YEAREND YEAR 2	YEAREND YEAR 3
– Initial Investment (C_0)	$C_0 = \$725$			
+ Cash Inflow in Year		$500	$800	$950
– Cash Outflow in Year		$200	$350	$450
= Net Cash Flow for Year	($725)	$C_1 = \$300$	$C_2 = \$450$	$C_3 = \$500$

Take the standard NPV equation:

$$NPV = -C_0 + \sum_{y=1}^{N} \frac{C_y}{(1+d)^y}$$

Then array the equation for three years including the initial investment (C_0):

$$NPV = -C_0 + \frac{C_1}{(1+d)^1} + \frac{C_2}{(1+d)^2} + \frac{C_3}{(1+d)^3}$$

Then substitute variables for cash flow amounts and use a discount rate of, say, 12%:

$$NPV = -\$725 + \frac{\$300}{(1+0.12)} + \frac{\$450}{(1+0.12)(1+0.12)} + \frac{\$500}{(1+0.12)(1+0.12)(1+0.12)}$$

Solving...

$$NPV = -\$725 + \frac{\$300}{1.120} + \frac{\$450}{1.254} + \frac{\$500}{1.405}$$

$$NPV = -\$725 + \$268 + \$359 + \$356$$

$$NPV = \$258$$

- The graph on the next page shows NPV computed for this cash flow example but using different discount rates ranging from 5% to 35%.

Internal Rate of Return (IRR)

- The **internal rate of return (IRR)** of a project is the discount rate that makes the present value of future cash flows equal to the initial investment. Thus the IRR is that point where NPV = $0.

- A project's NPV is *higher* when using a low discount rate because the computed value of future cash flows is higher if discounted less. A project's NPV is *lower* when using a high discount rate because the computed value of future cash flows is lower if discounted more.

  See the following graph. Using a discount rate of 12%, we computed NPV = $258 for our sample project. With a 5% discount rate, the NPV would be over $400. With a 35% discount rate, the NPV would be negative—the project would cost us more than it would bring in. The IRR in this example is 30% (where NPV = $0).

- IRR is often misunderstood as the annual profitability of the project investment, but this level of return is only the case if cash flows out from the project can be invested at the same rate as the IRR—which is seldom the case.

Net Present Values at Different Discount Rates

The *discount rate* when NPV = $0 is the project's **internal rate of return (IRR)**.

NPV vs. IRR?

- NPV and IRR measure two different, but complementary, aspects of capital use. The two methods of evaluating capital investments each have inherent advantages and disadvantages. See the table below.

Net Present Value vs. Internal Rate of Return

	NPV	IRR
ADVANTAGES	—**NPV** is a direct measure of expected value-added to the company from executing the project. —Comparing the value of alternative projects is easy with **NPV** analysis: just pick the project with the highest **NPV.**	—**IRR** is a popular capital budgeting tool because it shows the efficiency of capital use in an easy-to-understand percent return format. —Computing **IRR** is valid without having to estimate a discount rate.
DISADVANTAGES	—**NPV** requires an assumed input discount rate (capital cost plus risk premium), which may be difficult to estimate.	—**IRR** computes only a percent return, not a value, and thus disregards project scale and is not a measure of ultimate worth to the company. —**IRR** can make a small project appear more attractive than a large project. In fact, a very small project could have a very high **IRR** but also have a low and very unattractive **NPV.** —**IRR** assumes cash flow returns are invested at an often unrealistically high rate (the **IRR**). MIRR (modified internal rate of return) analysis solves this problem.

Cash Flow Forecasting

Accurately estimating the amounts and timing of all the project cash inflows and outflows can be tricky. Forecasting cash flows requires a detailed understanding of the business and the project being analyzed, its input variables and expected outcomes.

We must estimate the amount and timing of original investments, changes in working capital and in ongoing costs and expenses. We must understand customers' needs, wants, and market conditions to properly forecast revenues. In addition, the current and future financial environment, expected rates of inflation, project risk and tax considerations each play a part in NPV computations. Moreover, each of these elements of cash flow must be sequenced so that the NPV analysis will properly account for the time value of money. It is a lot to ask. See the box on this page for more on cash flow forecasting.

Selecting a Discount Rate

Selecting the appropriate discount rate is also difficult. The minimum discount rate would be equal to the company's weighted average cost of capital. Any project must return that amount or it will dilute the value of the company. Then a "risk

---

Cash Flow Forecasting The total cash flows used in an NPV analysis should come from well-prepared proforma financial statements developed for the project. Total project cash flows for a period can be computed as:

> **Income from Operations**
> **+ Depreciation**
> **− Taxes**
> **− Capital Spending**
> **− Increase in Working Capital**
> _____
> **Total Cash Flow**

Income from operations equals revenue minus costs and expenses and is the major source of cash. *(See page 53 for more details.)* However, we must make two adjustments to get to actual cash inflow: (1) Income from operations is before taxes are deducted, so we need to subtract taxes here to get a corrected cash flow. (2) Also, depreciation charges are included in income from operations but do not lower cash in the period, so we must add depreciation back to get a correct cash flow. *(See page 27 for more details.)* Finally, only changes (up or down) to the components of working capital (inventory, receivables, payables, etc.) in the period are part of computing cash flow. If working capital has increased, cash is required and we will need to subtract that amount from total cash flow. *(See page 36 for more details.)*

premium" should be added if there is increased risk in the project relative to the inherent risk associated with the company.

Venture capitalists add a risk premium of 30% or more to startup company projects. A more modest risk premium of 5% to 15% might be more appropriate for an expansion project for an established company. Developing an NPV versus discount rate graph may be helpful. See page 252.

Sensitivity Analysis

Not all of the input variables in a capital budgeting analysis are equally important. For example, sales forecasts are almost always critical variables. Costs +/- 10% for a high gross profit product may not be all that important.

Performing a "sensitivity" analysis can help identify the key variables in a capital budgeting analysis. In a sensitivity analysis, variables are systematically changed to see how the resultant NPV or IRR is affected. If changing an assumption results in a big change in the computed project value, then it is an important variable to get right. If changing an assumption results in just a small change, then it is less important.

In "scenario analysis," you might want to look at all your financial assumptions from a conservative perspective and see how cash flows are affected. For example, assume that everything will cost more and take longer to accomplish than your original projections. Often it is useful to prepare three sets of proforma statements: one with conservative (pessimistic) assumptions, one with realistic assumptions (most probable), and one with optimistic assumptions.

NPV Guidelines

Here are some operating guidelines for cash flow forecasting and NPV analysis:

1. **Count ALL incremental cash flows.** Incremental cash flows are those that arise from the project, from sales, costs, expenses, capital investment, increase in working capital or other sources.

   Opportunity costs count too. If an existing asset or employee will be part of the project, then these costs should be included in the project's cash flow.

2. **Count ONLY incremental cash flows.** Don't include sunk costs. We have already spent that money and they should not be a part of the forward-looking decision process.

   Accounting conventions used in balance sheet and income statement construction can mask the value of a project. Cash flow and profits are not the same. Being profitable does not necessarily mean the project has a positive cash flow.

3. **Use nominal dollars in cash flow projections.** A portion of the selected discount rate used in NPV calculations accounts for inflation. We must use nominal dollars in our forecasts so as not to double-count.

   See ***Appendix B.*** *Nominal vs. Real Dollars* on page 277.

4. **Account for time.** Capital budgets often show initial cash outflow (the investment) and then a future cash inflow (the return). When analyzing cash flow, take into account that a dollar spent today is worth more than a dollar received in the distant future.

   The discounted value of a future cash flow is determined by reducing its value by the appropriate discount rate for each unit of time (period) between when the cash flow is to be valued and the actual time of the cash flow in the future.

5. **Don't include costs of financing.** In capital budgeting, the costs of financing should not be in the cash flow projections. Remember: Part of the discount rate used in NPV computations includes a cost of capital estimate.

6. Account for risk. Not all projects have the same risk. A project that is riskier should generate a higher expected return. A portion of the discount rate used in the NPV computation deals with risk degree.

7. Understand assumptions. Numeric tools used to evaluate capital projects often can provide valuable insights, but misapplied, they are worthless. Understand the assumptions upon which these calculations rest.

Microsoft Excel makes the computation part of NPV and IRR analysis easy. However, estimating cash flows and NPV discount rates can still be problematic. Nevertheless, using spreadsheet functions to perform sensitivity analyses quickly on key variables can greatly add to the value of analyses.

Using Spreadsheets

To compute NPV or IRR, the cash flow inputs are entered as an array (a sequence of spreadsheet cells) and the financial functions are computed using the formulas shown here. Be sure to review all the "help" screens available for each function to understand its application.

NPV(rate,value1,value2,...) *Rate* means the selected discount rate over one period. *Value* represents the array of each cash outflow or cash inflow equally spaced at the end of each period.

IRR(values,guess) *Values* represents an array of cells that contain the numbers for which you want to calculate the IRR. *Guess* input is an estimate of the resultant IRR. The spreadsheet uses an iterative technique starting with the guess to calculate the IRR.

Other spreadsheet functions are available for modified internal rate of return (MIRR) calculations using a lower discount rate for cash inflows and also for calculations to be used with projects with irregular cash flows (XNPV and XIRR).

Other Measures

Finance types regard NPV as the all-around best measure of value-added from a capital project, but there is a place for IRR in determining how efficiently capital is employed. NPV and IRR measure two different, complementary aspects of capital use. NPV and IRR can be used together in making capital budgeting decisions.

What follows are other common capital budgeting techniques—some with flaws, others helpful but complex.

Return on Investment (ROI) There is no standard way of computing ROI. Many organizations use ROI to mean a number of different analytical techniques. Thus, ROI measurement is flexible but also subject to confusion. Use the well defined NPV and IRR instead.

Payback Period Payback period refers to the period of time required for the return on an investment to *repay* the sum of the original investment. Shorter payback periods are obviously preferable to longer payback periods (assuming all else being equal).

Payback period as a measurement is easy to compute and is intuitively understandable. However, payback period computations ignore the time value of money and ignore any cash flows occurring after the payback period ends. As a method of capital budgeting analysis though, payback period has serious limitations. Don't use it for that purpose.

"Our advice: Beware of geeks bearing formulas."

Warren Buffett
commenting on financial models and the financial collapse of 2008

Real Option Analysis Real option analysis allows for go/no-go decisions during a project. The flexibility to slow down, or to even stop a project if necessary, lowers risk to the company. This lowered risk adds initial value to the project over a project that could not be stopped. Real option analysis can be quite complex but is very useful for large capital projects.

Monte Carlo Analysis A Monte Carlo analysis is a complex multivariable NPV calculation that first assigns various probability values to capital project variables and then simulates outcomes using brute force of computing power. The Monte Carlo analysis output is a probability distribution histogram showing the volatility and sensitivity in a project's NPV. It is a very powerful technique, but requires sophistication to apply.

Summary

Different projects require different amounts and varying timing of investment, and they will generate different returns over time.

The NPV of a proposed project is the sum of all the project's projected cash flows, each discounted by an appropriate rate to bring them to a comparable present value. Generally, when comparing projects, the project with the highest NPV should be accepted.

The IRR of the project is the discount rate where the NPV equals zero and discounted costs of the project equal discounted returns. Generally, if a project's IRR is greater than the company's hurdle rate, it should be accepted.

Capital budgeting using NPV and IRR measures allows management to select rationally from alternative project proposals with very different initial costs and future cash flows.

In the last section of this book, we will apply what we have learned about capital budgeting to help AppleSeed Enterprises choose between alternative expansion plans: (1) building a factory from scratch, or (2) buying an existing business. Decisions, decisions.

Chapter 22. Making Good Capital Investment Decision

At the last board meeting, our esteemed directors approved AppleSeed's plans for a major product line expansion into gourmet potato chips. Now we are weighing two alternative capital projects designed to meet that goal: (1) building a new plant from scratch—the so-called "greenfield" option, or (2) acquiring an existing business, Chips-R-Us—the "purchase" option. In this chapter, we'll prepare a cash flow forecast for both alternatives and then perform an NPV analysis to help us select the best capital project for AppleSeed going forward.

Projecting Sales

Projecting sales is a good place to start when preparing a cash flow forecast. So here we go. See the graph following.

AppleSeed's purchase of Chips-R-Us would allow us to continue selling their low-end branded product while we start up our gourmet potato chip product line. Alternatively, if we build a potato chip plant from scratch we won't be selling anything for a year or so. The profitability of

Proforma Revenue Estimates

- ◆ Purchase Option
- ▲ Greenfield Option

the current Chips-R-Us brand is lower than what we expect to receive from our new gourmet potato chips, but at least we would be receiving some income while we launch our own branded product.

∼

Now that we have sales forecasts, let's estimate cash flows for the two alternative capital projects. See page 260 for details.

Estimating Cash Flows

Cash flow forecasts are constructed from estimates of three major "cash-using" and "cash-generating" business elements: (1) *cash from operations*, (2) *capital spending*, and (3) *increase in working capital*. The following two pages detail cash flow forecasts for AppleSeed's alternative capital projects

Here is how we arrived at these numbers.

Cash from Operations Estimating cash from operations begins with preparing proforma Income Statements for each of the years being analyzed. We start by projecting incremental sales expected from the capital project and then match those sales with the incremental costs and expenses necessary to generate the sales. These costs and expenses are then subtracted from sales. (Note: We must add back depreciation charges since these charges are included as a cost in the Income Statement but do not lower cash in the period. See pages 27 and 118 for more explanation.) Finally, we will subtract taxes paid, thus yielding an estimated *cash from operations* for each year.

Capital Spending Next we must estimate for both capital projects the amount and timing of capital to be invested in property, plant and equipment. With the

Financial Statements

Appleseed Enterprises Inc. Expansion Alternatives—Purchase Option
Cash Flow Analysis (in $ thousands)

Purchase Option	Initial	Year 1	Year 2	Year 3	Year 4	Year 5	Year 6	Year 7
1. Cash Flow from Operations (*added to cash flow*)		$120	$230	$465	$656	$788	$920	$1,035
Depreciation (*added back to cash flow*)		131	150	160	198	195	182	168
Taxes (*subtracted from cash flow*)		(24)	(58)	(140)	(223)	(268)	(313)	(352)
2. Capital Spending:								
Purchase assets of Chips-R-Us, Inc. including old factory building and equipment	(1,125)							
Repair old Chips-R-Us factory building		(275)	(150)	(50)	(50)	(10)	(10)	(10)
Refurbish old potato-chip-making machines		(200)	(75)	(5)	(5)	(5)	(5)	(5)
Purchase and install new fancy packaging machinery		(75)	0	0	0	0	0	0
Purchase and install state-of-the-art QC laboratory		(50)	0	0	0	0	0	0
Repair old delivery trucks and decorate with distinctive potato chip art		(25)	(25)	(5)	(5)	(5)	(5)	(5)
Enlarge factory to increase production capacity		0	0	(200)	(100)	0	0	0
Purchase/install additional potato-chip-making machines		0	0	0	(500)	(100)	0	0
3. Increases in Working Capital (*subtracted from cash flow*)		(300)	(88)	(138)	(156)	(131)	(138)	(125)
4. Terminal Value of Business (*estimated 8x cash flow*)		0	0	0	0	0	0	5,813
Sum of Cash Flows and Terminal Value	($1,125)	($698)	($15)	$88	($185)	$463	$631	$6,519
PV of Annual Cash Flows Discounted at 15.8%	($1,125)	($603)	($11)	$56	($103)	$223	$262	$2,335

Net present value (NPV) for purchase option @ 15.8% Discount Rate = $1,034

Cumulative Cash Flows	($1,125)	($1,823)	($1,838)	($1,750)	($1,935)	($1,472)	($841)	$5,679

Lowest Cumulative Cash Flow (in year 4) = ($1,935)

Total Capital Spending = ($3,080)

Appleseed Enterprises Inc. Expansion Alternatives—Greenfield Option
Cash Flow Analysis (in $ thousands)

Greenfield Option	Initial	Year 1	Year 2	Year 3	Year 4	Year 5	Year 6	Year 7
1. Cash Flow from Operations (*added to cash flow*)		$0	$50	$250	$400	$681	$850	$1,000
Depreciation (*added back to cash flow*)		216	238	235	219	201	185	170
Taxes (*subtracted from cash flow*)		0	(13)	(75)	(136)	(232)	(289)	(340)
2. Capital Spending:								
Build large new factory building specifically designed for potato chip processing	(2,150)	0						
Purchase and install high-capacity potato-chip-making machinery		(600)	(250)	(100)	0	0	0	0
Purchase and install new fancy packaging machinery		(75)	0	0	0	0	0	0
Purchase and install state-of-the-art QC laboratory		(50)	0	0	0	0	0	0
Purchase new delivery trucks and decorate with distinctive potato chip art		0	(50)	(75)	(25)	0	0	0
3. Increases in Working Capital (*subtracted from cash flow*)		0	(63)	(188)	(250)	(181)	(169)	(150)
4. Terminal Value of Business (*estimated 8x cash flow*)		0	0	0	0	0	0	5,439
Sum of Cash Flows and Terminal Value	($2,150)	($509)	($87)	$48	$208	$470	$577	$6,119
PV of Annual Cash Flows Discounted at 15.8%	($2,150)	($440)	($65)	$31	$116	$226	$239	$2,191

Net present value (NPV) for greenfield option @ 15.8% Discount Rate = **$148**

Cumulative Cash Flows	($2,150)	($2,659)	($2,746)	($2,699)	($2,491)	($2,021)	($1,443)	$4,676

Lowest Cumulative Cash Flow (in year 2) = ($2,746)

Total Capital Spending = ($3,375)

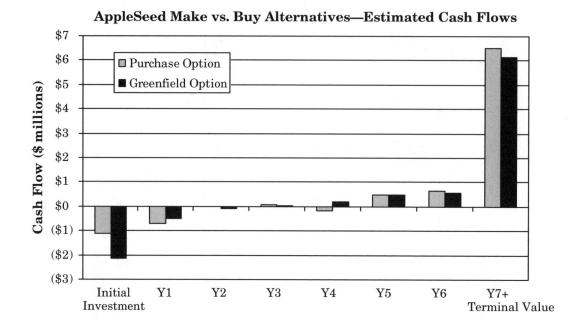

AppleSeed Make vs. Buy Alternatives—Estimated Cash Flows

greenfield option we will have large capital expenditures for land, a new building and new machinery. If we purchase Chips-R-Us, we will need capital to refurbish both the plant and old machinery to bring them up to standard. Also, we will purchase additional potato-chip-making machines to expand Chips-R-Us's production capacity.

The costs to buy land and construct a new building will be high in the greenfield option. Purchasing Chips-R-Us is less expensive, but their existing factory will need extensive refurbishment.

Increases in Working Capital Now we need to forecast the additional working capital (primarily accounts receivable and inventory) required to support our expanded business. It takes money to make money, and the more we sell the more working capital we will need.

Because purchasing Chips-R-Us will result in earlier and higher sales, we will need more early working capital with that alternative capital project.

~

There is one last, but very important projection we must make before we compute NPV: the "terminal value" of both our proposed capital projects.

Terminal Value Forecasting cash flows beyond a certain period is often too uncertain and impractical for an NPV analysis. So *terminal values* are often added to the last year's cash flow forecast to estimate and account for the long-term value of the capital project as an ongoing business.

The terminal value can be thought of as the price of the whole capital project's business if it were sold as an ongoing concern. Note that for many projects the terminal value can be a major part of the value added by the whole project, especially when starting a new business or making a major business expansion.

In our NPV comparisons, we have estimated terminal values conservatively at eight times the projected after-tax income for each expansion alternative. Note that, though the terminal values are large for both alternatives, the amount received is projected seven years out in our analysis and thus is deeply discounted.

For example, we see from the chart on page 247 that the present value of $1 received seven years from today is only 35¢ when using a discount rate of 16%. This amount is still significant, but not so overwhelming.

Financial Comparison of AppleSeed's Expansion Alternatives

Checks (✓) show the superior alternative.

	ACQUIRE CHIPS-R-US, INC.	BUILD FROM SCRATCH
NET PRESENT VALUE (NPV)	✓ $1,034,000	$148,000
INTERNAL RATE OF RETURN (IRR)	✓25%	17%
LOWEST CUMULATIVE CASH	✓ ($1,935,000)	($2,746,000)
TOTAL CAPITAL SPENDING	✓ ($3,080,000)	($3,375,000)

Computing NPV and IRR

We've carefully projected cash flows for both of AppleSeed's expansion alternatives. See the detailed projections on pages 260 and 261.

Now we must select a discount rate before we can perform NPV computations. Neither the purchase option nor the greenfield option seems more risky than the other. Also, neither would add a significantly greater risk to our business than what we already have. Thus, using AppleSeed's average weighted cost of capital (WACC) of 15.8% seems reasonable for our NPV comparison. (See page 233 for a discussion of AppleSeed's WACC.)

Purchase vs. Greenfield IRR

The next step is for us to go to the computer, feed the numbers into an Excel spreadsheet, and let the electrons fly.

～

Voila! The table at the top of this page summarizes the results of our comparative cash flow forecasts and NPV calculations. Our computed NPV of the purchase alternative capital project is significantly higher than that of the greenfield alternative. The IRR is higher for the Chips-R-Us purchase as well. Further, the amount of cash we will need at one time (lowest cumulative cash) is significantly lower for the purchase alternative than for the greenfield alternative. Capital spending is about the same, plus or minus 10% or so.

Financially, the purchase of Chips-R-Us makes most sense for AppleSeed's expansion into the potato chip market. Note that even though the greenfield alternative "only" has an NPV of $148,000, it still would have been an attractive project and would return value to AppleSeed. However, because the purchase alternative offers a higher NPV of $1,034,000, it makes good financial sense to choose that alternative.

～

We present our NPV and IRR analysis to AppleSeed's board and they agree that purchasing Chips-R-Us is the way to go. I call Chips-R-Us's owner and invite him to dinner to finalize the negotiations. We won't go to a fancy place because I don't want him to think we have a lot of money to spend.

Over dinner, we settle on a price of $1.25 million, just as we have projected in our NPV analysis. We will only be purchasing assets, leaving Chips-R-Us liabilities for them to liquidate. I call our lawyers and ask them to work on the purchase and sale agreement. Then I call our accountant and ask her the best way for us to book AppleSeed's acquisition. She mumbles something about new regulations that she needs to review and says she'll get back to us—FASB Rule 141(R).

Acquisition Accounting

FASB does have new regulations to account for business combinations like ours. Prior to 2001 there were two methods that combining businesses could use when they merged: the "pooling'" rules and the "purchase" rules. The books can look quite different using the two different rules, and that's the rub. FASB eliminated this confusion and in 2009 promulgated new rules—the so-called "acquisition" method of business combination. So that's what we will use to account for AppleSeed's takeover of Chips-R-Us.

Using this acquisition method, all the acquired tangible assets of Chips-R-Us will be recorded on AppleSeed's book at fair market value on the date we acquire them. Fair market value is defined by FASB as "the price that would be received to sell an asset or paid to transfer a liability in an orderly transaction between market participants at the measured date."

We are going to have an appraiser come out and value the land, factory and equipment we will be purchasing. The inventory value we can figure out ourselves. Also, there will be significant one-time legal and accounting fees associated with the acquisition. These additional acquisition expenses will be run through the Income Statement as incurred instead of being "capitalized," as was allowed in the older methods of business combination.

Most of the assets we are purchasing from Chips-R-Us are tangible "bricks and mortar" assets, which are easy to value. But we are also purchasing harder to value, "intangible" assets such as customer lists, trade names, supply contracts, trade secrets (recipes for potato chips) and such.

Any excess we pay for Chip-R-Us over and above the fair market value of net assets recorded on our Balance Sheet will be reported as "goodwill." Goodwill will just sit on our books until it is "impaired," and then we will have to write it off (amortize) through the Income Statement and take a loss for the amount.

Note amortization of intangible assets is similar to the process of depreciation for tangible assets, written off each year according to a formula.

∼

Transaction 33 on the following pages completes our acquisition of Chips-R-Us and starts AppleSeed on its great adventure as a larger business.

With the addition of potato chips to our applesauce product offering, perhaps we should change our name from AppleSeed Enterprises, Inc., to something more flashy like Amalgamated Gourmet Food Products Corporation—*AGFPC* for short. What do you think?

Financial Statements

Income Statement

for the period including Transactions 1 through 33

		prior	+	transaction	=	sum
1	NET SALES	$3,055,560		—		$3,055,560
2	COST OF GOODS SOLD	2,005,830		—		2,005,830
1 - 2 = 3	GROSS MARGIN	1,049,730				1,049,730
4	SALES & MARKETING	328,523		—		328,523
5	RESEARCH & DEVELOPMENT	26,000		—		26,000
6	GENERAL & ADMINISTRATIVE	203,520	**2A**	35,000		238,520
4 + 5 + 6 = 7	OPERATING EXPENSE	558,043				593,043
3 - 7 = 8	INCOME FROM OPERATIONS	491,687				456,687
9	NET INTEREST INCOME	(100,000)		—		(100,000)
10	INCOME TAXES	139,804		—		139,804
8 + 9 - 10 = 11	NET INCOME	$251,883		(35,000)		$216,883

IS Transaction Sum

Cash Flow Statement

for the period including Transactions 1 through 33

		prior	+	transaction	=	sum
a	BEGINNING CASH BALANCE	$0				$0
b	CASH RECEIPTS	2,584,900		—		2,584,900
c	CASH DISBURSEMENTS	2,796,438		—		2,796,438
b - c = d	CASH FLOW FROM OPERATIONS	(211,538)				(211,538)
e	PP&E PURCHASE	1,750,000	**1A**	1,250,000		3,000,000
f	NET BORROWINGS	1,000,000		—		1,000,000
g	INCOME TAXES PAID	0		—		0
h	SALE OF CAPITAL STOCK	2,350,000		—		2,350,000
a + d - e + f - g + h = i	ENDING CASH BALANCES	$1,388,462		(1,250,000)		$138,462

CF Transaction Sum

Balance Sheet

as of this Transaction 33

		prior	+	transaction	=	sum
A	CASH	$1,388,462	**1B**	(1,250,000)		$138,462
B	ACCOUNTS RECEIVABLE	454,760		—		454,760
C	INVENTORIES	414,770		—		414,770
D	PREPAID EXPENSES	0		—		0
A + B + C + D = E	CURRENT ASSETS	2,257,992				1,007,992
F	OTHER ASSETS	0	**1D**	50,000		50,000
G	FIXED ASSETS @ COST	1,750,000	**1C**	1,200,000		2,950,000
H	ACCUMULATED DEPRECIATION	78,573		—		78,573
G - H = I	NET FIXED ASSETS	1,671,427				2,871,427
E + F + I = J	TOTAL ASSETS	$3,929,419		0		$3,929,419
				Assets Sum		
K	ACCOUNTS PAYABLE	$236,297	**2B**	35,000		$271,297
L	ACCRUED EXPENSES	26,435		—		26,435
M	CURRENT PORTION OF DEBT	200,000		—		200,000
N	INCOME TAXES PAYABLE	139,804		—		139,804
K + L + M + N = O	CURRENT LIABILITIES	602,536				637,536
P	LONG-TERM DEBT	800,000		—		800,000
Q	CAPITAL STOCK	2,350,000		—		2,350,000
R	RETAINED EARNINGS	176,883	**2C**	(35,000)		141,883
Q + R = S	SHAREHOLDERS' EQUITY	2,526,883				2,491,883
O + P + S = T	TOTAL LIABILITIES & EQUITY	$3,929,419		0		$3,929,419

Liabilities & Equity Sum

T33. Buy Chips-R-Us, Inc., assets and treat this business combination as an acquisition under FASB Rule 141(R)

We've done it! Chips-R-Us is ours! But after the euphoria subsides we realize that there is a lot of work to do. As a good start, let's adjust the books to account for this momentous purchase. Then we'll drive over to our new plant and begin to learn how to make the world's best potato chips.

Transaction: Purchase certain assets of Chips-R-Us for $1.25 million and combine the business into our financial statements as an acquisition as per FASB Rule 141(R). The appraised fair market value of the purchased assets is $1.20 million, leaving a $50,000 balance as the intangible asset, goodwill.

Receive from our appraiser, lawyers and accountant bills totaling $35,000 for professional services performed on our behalf. Gasp.

1 Write a check to the owners of Chips-R-Us for $1.25 million. (1A) Book that amount in **PP&E PURCHASE** in the *Cash Flow Statement* and (1B) lower **CASH** by that amount on the *Balance Sheet*. (1C) Add the $1.2 million appraised value of the purchased assets to **FIXED ASSETS @ COST** on the *Balance Sheet*. (1D) Finally, add the remaining $50,000 spent to **OTHER ASSETS** on the *Balance Sheet* as "goodwill."

2 (2A) Charge **GENERAL & ADMINISTRATIVE** expense in the *Income Statement* for $35,000 for the professional services bills and also (2B) add that amount to **ACCOUNTS PAYABLE** in the liabilities section of the *Balance Sheet*. (2C) This expense has lowered net income, so subtract the amount from **RETAINED EARNINGS** as well.

> ᔐ
>
> **Note from the Management:** It has been a pleasure navigating the financial statements of AppleSeed Enterprises, Inc., with you. E-mail us at *financialstatements@mercurygroup.com* with comments and questions, or just to say hello. Visit us at *www.mercurygroup.com*.
>
> ᔐ

Conclusion

We've come a long way. Our fears of both accounting and financial reporting have melted away. We've learned the vocabulary; we've learned the structure. We know what FASB means and we appreciate the importance of GAAP.

We understand:

- That accrual has nothing to do with the Wicked Witch of the West. *(pages 58-59)*

- When negative cash flow is a sign of good things happening and when it is a sign of impending catastrophe. *(page 197)*

- Why discounts "drop" directly to the bottom line. *(page 157)*

- The important difference between liquidity and profitably. *(pages 194-195)*

- Those expenditures that are costs and those that are expenses. *(page 50)*

- Depreciation's differing effect on income and on cash. *(pages 118-119)*

- Why product cost always depends on volume. *(pages 148-151)*

- Three common—and different—definitions of what a business is worth. *(page 184)*

- Why assets must always equal liabilities plus shareholders' equity (worth) on the Balance Sheet. *(page 16-17)*

- Why working capital is so important and what business actions leads to more and what actions lead to less. *(page 36)*

- The difference between cash in the bank and profit on the bottom line and how they are related. *(page 181)*

- How many sets of books a company actually keeps. *(page 213)*

- Why some qualitative business analysis tools are as important as the numbers *(pages 221-229)*

- The difference between risk and uncertainty and which is worse when you try to plan. *(pages 225-226)*

- The difference between pre-money and post-money company valuations when you sell stock. *(pages 231-232)*

- Which business financing is more expensive, equity or debt? *(page 233)*

- How to compute today's value of a dollar received tomorrow. *(page 243)*

- When to use NPV analysis and when to use IRR and why. *(page 253)*

- *and more...*

~

We have come a long way. We're able to appreciate my young accountant friend's poetic remark:

"It's so symmetrical, so logical, so beautiful and it always comes out right."

It always comes out right.

Appendix A. Short History of Business Fraud and Speculative Bubbles

The Spanish-born American philosopher George Santayana said, "Those who cannot remember the past are condemned to repeat it." To save you, the potentially poor reader, from financial ruin, what follows is a rogue's gallery of financial frauds to avoid. First, here are a few investing rules that will help you avoid such frauds:

1. Do not invest in arcane schemes with promoters who will not explain the investments clearly. Make sure you understand exactly where the investment returns will come from and at what risk.

2. Beware the "quick buck" or getting "something for nothing." Promises of "too-good-to-be-true" returns are just that.

3. Always do reference checking before investing. Charlatans spend much time, money and effort in trying to appear legitimate. Beware. Do not be fooled.

Unfortunately, just following these three rules doesn't guarantee you will never be fleeced. So do not "put all your eggs in one basket." That way, even if you are duped, not everything is lost. Diversify your investments.

Ponzi Schemes

In a Ponzi scheme, gullible investors are enticed to purchase arcane investments that promise fantastic returns. Early investors are paid off with money raised from later victims, until no more money can be raised.

Ponzi schemes are doomed to collapse because there are no underlying earnings—just recycling of money. However, not all investors lose. The first investors can gain if they manage to get out in time.

Charles Ponzi (1919) With $200 in borrowed capital, the "Ponzi scheme" namesake, Charles Ponzi, opened up his Securities Exchange Company at 27 School Street in Boston on the day after Christmas in 1919.

Ponzi claimed to invest in an arbitrage of international postage return coupons and promised a 50% return in 45 days and a 100% return in 90 days. Early investors did get these spectacular returns. Actually, Ponzi was paying off these investors by using money received from new investors.

For a time, Ponzi was the toast of the Northeast. His investment company was a great success. In 1920, Ponzi bought a grand house in Lexington, a wealthy suburb of Boston, and even a local bank, the Hanover Trust Bank.

However, Ponzi's operation collapsed in August 1920 when, based on a tip from a local newspaper, federal agents raided Ponzi's corporate headquarters and the Massachusetts Attorney General put him in jail. In a little more than eight months, Ponzi had collected $10 million from more than 10,000 investors. In bankruptcy, investors received just 37 cents on the dollar.

At trial, Ponzi pleaded guilty to federal charges of mail fraud and was sentenced to five years in federal prison, serving three years. When released from federal prison and facing state charges, Ponzi jumped bail and fled to Florida, where he set up a real estate business and began selling "prime Florida property" (i.e., swamp land) to gullible investors. Eventually, Ponzi spent nine years in a Massachusetts prison and then was deported back to Italy.

Bernie Madoff (2008) Bernard Madoff, the former chairman of the NADASQ stock exchange, was one of the most respected financiers on Wall Street when he was

> "You only find out who's swimming naked when the tide goes out."
> **Warren Buffett**
> commenting on seeing financial fraud when markets collapse

arrested and charged in December 2008 with running a giant Ponzi scheme. The U.S. Attorney's criminal complaint against Madoff described him admitting "it's all just one big lie, basically a giant Ponzi scheme...paid investors with money that wasn't there." Estimated investor losses exceed $50 billion, making this financial scandal by far the largest in history. Madoff pleaded guilty in March 2009.

In addition to running a closely held and well-respected market-making firm, Madoff ran on the side a large hedge fund catering to wealthy investors. Madoff's hedge fund offered unnaturally steady returns, had a vague investment strategy and was audited by an obscure three-person accounting firm with only a store-front office in a strip mall. Nobody seemed to care because "returns" appeared solid.

The fraud was unmasked early in the 2008 financial crisis when Madoff received a wave of redemption notices from investors looking to preserve cash in the financial downturn. These investors sought to pull out billions of dollars from Madoff's fund, money Bernie did not have. In the end, most Ponzi schemes collapse when too many investors seek to withdraw their money at the same time and the operator does not have cash on hand to pay them.

Charles Ponzi bilked common folk in Boston; Bernie Madoff bilked rich and supposedly sophisticated New Yorkers. Both groups wanted to make an easy buck and got taken in by a schemer and sustained large losses.

～

A pyramid scheme works like a peer-to-peer version of a Ponzi scheme. Instead of payments going to a single central promoter, the investors exchange money within the group. Each participant must recruit several other investors to perpetuate the scheme. Eventually the pyramid collapses because it becomes harder and harder to find new suckers.

Pyramid schemes should not be confused with (semi) legitimate "multilevel marketing" operations practiced by companies such as Amway Corporation, Avon Products, Mary Kay Cosmetics, Primerica Financial Services and others. In legitimate multilevel marketing models, commissions are earned only on sales of the company's products or services not from recruiting alone.

Bubbles

Bubbles are fueled by speculators who are willing to pay even greater prices for already overvalued assets sold to them by the speculators who bought them in the preceding round.

Each financial bubble in history has been different, but they all involve a mix of fundamental business and psychological forces. In the beginning stages, an attractive return on a stock or commodity drives prices higher and higher. People make questionable investments with the assumption that they will be able to sell later at a higher price to a "greater fool." Unrealistic investor expectations take hold and become self-fulfilling until the bubble "pops" and prices fall back to a more reasonable underlying value.

Why do bubbles sometimes last so long? One reason is that nobody likes to be a "party pooper" and people *are* getting rich. In addition, there is nothing inherently illegal about profiting during a bubble. The only problem is getting out before the collapse. Whoever owns the overpriced asset when the bubble pops is the loser, just as the last person standing in a game of musical chairs.

Tulip Bulbs (1630s) One of the most famous market bubbles took place in the 17th century in Holland where tulip bulbs were traded for small fortunes. Flowers and bulbs became coveted luxury items and status symbols.

The most spectacular and highly sought tulip bulbs would grow flowers with vivid colors, lines and flames on the petals, especially those infected with a rare type of mosaic virus causing a variegated pattern. Spectacular single bulbs went for as much as 5,000 Dutch gilders, a truly remarkable sum given that Rembrandt received only about one-third that amount for painting *The Night Watch* in 1642.

Good bulbs were scarce. It took seven years to grow a tulip bulb from seed and there was no guarantee that the resulting flower would be as good as the parent. If divided, bulbs would breed true, but dividing bulbs could occur only every two years.

Tulips bloom in April and May for only about a week, and bulbs can be uprooted and moved safely only from June to September. Thus "spot market" purchases for actual bulb delivery occurred only during these months.

"Flame" Tulip

In early 1636, Dutch traders, meeting in local taverns, created a type of formal "futures market" where contracts to buy bulbs at the end of the season were bought and sold. Contract price of rare bulbs continued to rise all throughout the year. However, in February 1637, prices for tulip bulb contracts collapsed abruptly and the trade of tulip contracts and of bulbs ground to a halt. Bulbs then fetched less than a penny on the dollar.

In fact, no actual deliveries of bulbs were ever required to satisfy these futures contracts. The Dutch Parliament passed a decree that contracts could be voided for a small fee—perhaps the first government "bailout" of a speculative bubble!

Technology Stocks (1995–2001) The "dot-com" bubble was a speculative stock market bubble of the late 1990s, collapsing in 2001. The period was marked by the emergence of new Internet-based companies commonly referred to as "dot-coms."

A combination of rapidly increasing stock prices, individual speculation in stocks and widely available venture capital created an over-exuberant environment. Many start-up dot-com businesses dismissed standard business models and focused on increasing market share at the expense of the bottom line. Many companies become grossly overvalued.

In March 2000, the NASDAQ Composite index peaked at 5,048, more than double its value of just a year before. In the next two years the market crashed to less than 1,500, and almost $5 trillion in market value evaporated. See the graph of NASDAQ prices on the next page.

U.S. Housing Crisis (2008–2010) The U.S. housing price bubble burst in 2007, with house prices dropping everywhere. On average, house prices across the United States had increased by an unsustainable 143% in the prior decade, driven by easy loans and speculative feelings of buyers and bankers that prices would rise forever. Who knew?

NASDAQ Composite Index

Investing in bubbles can be quite profitable if you can get out before the bubble bursts. Many people did not get out in this crisis, and many lost their homes to foreclosure.

Bubbles are not caused by fraudulent activity. However, swindles and accounting fraud often come to light just after bubbles pop. Nobody is looking and few care while the good times role. Highly leveraged frauds often run out of cash and collapse when bubbles pop.

Garden-Variety Fraud

Most large business frauds are deceptively simple. Some people with power and high positions lie, cheat and steal. Often accountants and regulators do not catch the crooks until real damage has been done. Some of the more amazing recent frauds are discussed here.

Salad Oil Scandal (1963) Anthony "Tino" De Angelis was a Bayonne, New Jersey–based commodities trader who bought and sold vegetable oil for his company, Allied Crude Vegetable Oil Refining Corporation. Tino masterminded a scam where ships apparently full of salad oil (but mostly filled with water with a only a few feet of salad oil on top) would arrive at the New Jersey company docks. Inspectors would confirm that the ships were full of oil (but only by looking at the top of the tanks), and would release to Tino's company millions of dollars in loans on the supposed delivery of this new inventory.

The swindle collapsed when Tino got greedy and tried to corner the world's salad oil market by buying futures contracts using this fraudulently borrowed money. More than 50 banks including Bank of America, American Express and many international trading companies lost $1 billion in today's dollars. Tino ended up with a seven-year jail sentence.

Enron (2001) A Houston-based energy trading company, Enron Corporation was the seventh largest company (revenues of over $100 billion) in the United States in 2000. Then the bottom fell out and Enron filed for bankruptcy protection in 2001.

What happened? Willful corporate fraud through "institutionalized, systematic and creatively planned" accounting fraud said the federal indictments. Senior Enron corporate officials, including the company's chief financial officer, set up "limited partnership" shell companies to

> "...there must be a vast fund of stupidity in human nature, or else men would not be caught as they are, a thousand times over, by the same snares...while they yet remember their past misfortunes, they go on to court and encourage the causes to what they are owing, and will again produce them."
>
> **Cato the Younger** *(95–46 BC)*
> Roman Orator

mask debt liabilities. Then Enron, the parent company, would sell assets between the shell companies, book revenue and then report sham profits.

The company's stock price hit $90 per share in the summer of 2000, and insiders started to sell. The stock eventually dropped to less than 20 cents per share. More than $60 billion in company stock value and more than $2 billion in employee pension plan funds were lost.

Enron founder and chairman, Ken Lay, was convicted of fraud, but died of a heart attack before being sentenced. Former Enron CEO Jeffrey Skilling is currently serving a 24-year sentence for fraud. Andrew Fastow, the former chief financial officer and some say mastermind behind the company's complicated financial schemes, got off easy with only a six-year prison sentence; his wife went to prison for a year as an accomplice to tax fraud. Watch out when your spouse asks you to sign that joint federal tax return!

Arthur Anderson LLP, the once-large worldwide accounting firm, was Enron's accountant. In 2002, the firm was convicted of obstruction of justice for shredding documents related to its audit of Enron. Then, as a convicted felon, Anderson could no longer provide CPA services to public companies. The firm collapsed. In 2001, Arthur Anderson employed 85,000 people worldwide and 28,000 people in the United States, and had revenues exceeding $9.3 billion. Today, the firm has a single office in Chicago with 200 employees.

WorldCom (2002) Before its 2002 bankruptcy filing, WorldCom had become the second-largest long distance telephone company in the United States. (AT&T was then the largest.) The company grew primarily by buying smaller telecommunications companies, but a general business slowdown put a damper on further acquisitions and its business model faltered.

To cover up declining earnings, senior management directed underreporting of costs (interconnection expenses with other telecommunications companies) and booking bogus accounting entries to overstate revenues. By the time the scheme collapsed, WorldCom's assets were overinflated by almost $11 billion. The company's stock plummeted from over $60 per share to less than a buck.

Bernard Ebbers, WorldCom's infamous chairman and CEO, was convicted of fraud and filing false documents to regulators. He is serving a 25-year prison term at Oakdale Federal Correctional Complex in Louisiana. The earliest date that Berni (Inmate #56022054) can be released is July 2028, at which time he will be 85 years old. Five other former WorldCom executives are also serving time.

Sarbanes-Oxley

As you can see from our examples, the early 2000s were a particularly ripe time for fraud of the "garden variety." The United States Congress was outraged! Outraged by so much executive malfeasance! Something had to be done!

Financial Statements

So, Congress passed a law, the "Public Company Accounting Reform and Investor Protection Act of 2002," called "Sarbanes-Oxley" for short, named after the bill's primary sponsors Senator Paul Sarbanes (D-MD) and Representative Michael G. Oxley (R-OH). The bill passed the House 423–3 and the Senate 99–0. President George W. Bush signed it into law stating it was the "most far-reaching reforms of American business practice since the time of Franklin D. Roosevelt."

The law has 11 sections outlining new rules and regulations for the financial reporting of public companies and the behavior of their senior executives and the accounting firms that audit them.

Under the new law, making or certifying misleading financial statements exposes senior corporate officials to substantial civil and criminal penalties. Now, CEOs and CFOs must personally certify that company financial statements "do not contain any untrue statement of a material fact or omit to state a material fact necessary to make the statements made, in light of the circumstances under which such statements were made, not misleading with respect to the period covered by the report." Got that? Don't you feel safer already?

~

Sarbanes-Oxley has been criticized as just too much paperwork. Other commentators praise the law as essential to maintain the integrity of our capitalistic system. Given the effect of the financial meltdown of 2008, more laws are likely. Stay tuned.

Appendix B. Nominal vs. Real Dollars

In financial calculations spanning time, currency value can be looked at from two different perspectives. It's important when doing historical analysis or making financial projections to understand these two views of value.

One way to look at currency is as pieces of paper—you know, the ones in your wallet. A paper dollar today is the same piece of paper as a dollar tomorrow. These dollars are called *"nominal dollars,"* or *"current dollars."* Their value is in the money of the day.

In nominal dollars, a McDonald's Big Mac cost 50¢ 20 years ago and it costs $3.75 today. Nominal dollars and current prices are just the dollars that Dad took out of his wallet to buy you that Big Mac 20 years ago or the dollars that you spent today to buy one for your son.

However, prices tend to increase over time primarily due to inflation. Sometimes it is useful to look at "values" of goods in the past (or expected values in the future) rather than at their actual cost way back when in nominal dollars.

From this inflation-corrected perspective, we will use *"real dollars,"* also called *"constant dollars."* Real dollar are nominal dollars that have been adjusted to take out (or add back in) the effects of inflation.

Why bother? Well, it is very difficult to analyze financially the price of today's Big Mac at $3.75 with a 20-years-ago Big Mac at 50¢. It is basically the same burger. And thus, when you take out inflation (i.e., convert from nominal dollars into real dollars) the price difference becomes much more comparable and explainable.

Money Illusion

The term *money illusion* refers to the tendency of people (old people?) to think of currency in nominal rather than real terms. People remember and pay more attention to the numerical or face value of money (nominal dollars) than they do to its relative purchasing power (real dollars). Thus, Dad keeps talking about those 50¢ Big Macs just as Granddad kept telling us about a 10¢ breakfast of scrambled eggs, bacon and coffee. Whatever.

Nominal vs. Real Dollars

- In economic parlance, "nominal" dollars are the face value of currency, whereas "real" values have been corrected for inflation relative to some base year.

- Financial statements are reported in **nominal dollars.** If the company sold $100 in widgets in 1995 and $110 in widgets in 2006, then these numbers will be shown under the respective years in financial reports. So, sales were slightly up between the two periods. Right?

  Not really, in value terms. If we looked at sales in the two periods in **real dollars** (that is, corrected for inflation from 1995 to 2006), we would see that real sales were down in value from 1995 to 2006.

- To convert a nominal dollar amount from "year y" into real dollar purchasing power in another "year x," use the following formula. CPI is the Consumer Price Index issued by the Commerce Department. The year 1983/4 is selected as the base year equal to a CPI of 100.

$$\text{Real Dollars}_x = \text{Nominal Dollars}_y \left(\frac{CPI_x}{CPI_y} \right)$$

- Using our example and with the $CPI_{1995} = 152.4$ and the $CPI_{2006} = 201.6$, then

$$\text{Real Dollars}_{2006} = \text{Nominal Dollars}_{1995} \left(\frac{CPI_{2006}}{CPI_{1995}} \right)$$

$$\text{Real Dollars}_{2006} = \$100.00 \times \left(\frac{201.6}{152.4} \right) = \$132.28$$

  Accounting for inflation between 1995 and 2006, we would need to sell $132.28 worth of widgets in 2006 to equal the $100 value of our sales performance back in 1995. Since we only sold $110 in 2006, sales were up in nominal dollars terms, they were down in real dollar terms.

Real Dollars (Constant Dollars)

- **Real dollars** (also called *constant dollars*) are amounts that have been adjusted to account for the impact of inflation. **Nominal dollars** (also called *current dollars*) are the actual dollars paid or received at the time without any adjustments.

- The following graph shows the selling price of a pound of OREO® Cookies for each year from 1970 to 1990 in nominal dollars and also the value of the cookies in real dollars.

  The nominal price consumers paid for a pound of cookies increased from 48¢ in 1970 to $2.70 in 1990. That is an almost six-fold increase. However, much of this price rise is due to inflation during the 20-year period. See the price (nominal and real) graph below.

Price of OREO Cookies from 1970 to 1990

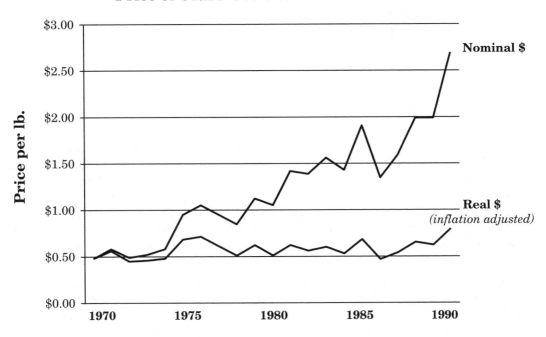

- The data table on the next page shows the relationship between nominal dollars, the CPI, and inflation-adjusted real dollars.

Price of OREO Cookies from 1970 to 1990

YEAR	A. PRICES IN NOMINAL DOLLARS	B. PRICES IN 1970 REAL DOLLARS	CONSUMER PRICE INDEX (CPI)
1970	$0.48	$0.48	37.8
1971	$0.59	$0.56	39.8
1972	$0.49	$0.45	41.1
1973	$0.52	$0.46	42.6
1974	$0.59	$0.48	46.6
1975	$0.95	$0.69	52.1
1976	$1.06	$0.72	55.6
1977	$0.95	$0.61	58.5
1978	$0.84	$0.51	62.5
1979	$1.12	$0.62	68.3
1980	$1.06	$0.51	77.8
1981	$1.42	$0.62	87.0
1982	$1.39	$0.56	94.3
1983	$1.56	$0.60	97.8
1984	$1.43	$0.53	101.9
1985	$1.91	$0.68	105.5
1986	$1.35	$0.47	109.6
1987	$1.59	$0.54	111.2
1988	$1.99	$0.65	115.7
1989	$1.99	$0.62	121.1
1990	$2.69	$0.80	127.4

Column A. *Price in Nominal Dollars* shows the actual amount consumers paid for a one-pound bag of OREO® Cookies in the year indicated.

CPI Column shows the Consumer Price Index for each year. CPI has been normalized by the Commerce Department so that 1983/84 prices are designated as 100.

Column B. *Price in Real Dollars* show the value of a one-pound bag of OREO Cookies as adjusted for inflation using the equation on the prior page and the CPI value of 1970 as a base.

For example, although consumers in 1986 would have to pay $1.35 for a pound of cookies in nominal dollars, the actual value of that amount in 1970 real dollars (that is, discounting for inflation from 1970 through 1986) would be only 47¢, a penny less than the nominal price in 1970.

∼

Inflation over time can cause dramatic differences in real and nominal dollar amounts for which analysis of present, past, or future economic and business conditions must properly account.

Index

Financial Statements

About the Author

Thomas Ittelson is a scientist, businessperson, author and teacher with over 30 years of hands-on experience in business development and marketing for technical companies. As a consultant to entrepreneurs, Mr. Ittelson has written business plans that have raised over $500 million in start-up equity capital. This book, **Financial Statements**, was born from the author's efforts to teach entrepreneurs how use financial statements in their businesses.

Ittelson's formal training—as a biochemist, not as an accountant or financial officer—contributes to the unique structure and focus in this book. He first learned accounting and financial reporting "on the job" as the strategic planner for a large multinational corporation and then as the founder, CEO and treasurer of a venture capital backed high-technology company. Currently Ittelson practices with *The Mercury Group,* a Cambridge, Massachusetts-based management consulting firm specializing in marketing, financial modeling, business strategy development and fund raising for both startup and more established technology-based businesses.

The Mercury Group's intensive, one-day management seminar, *The Architecture of Financial Statements*, is conducted for business, technical, academic and legal professionals who should know how an Income Statement, Balance Sheet and Cash Flow Statement work...but don't.

For more details please contact:

The Mercury Group
Harvard Square Station
PO Box 381350
Cambridge, MA 02238-1350

617-354-7667

financialstatements@mercurygroup.com

www.mercurygroup.com